Germans to America and *The Hamburg Passenger Lists*: Coordinated Schedules

Roger P. Minert, Ph.D., A.G.
Kathryn Boeckel
Caren Winters

HERITAGE BOOKS
2007

HERITAGE BOOKS
AN IMPRINT OF HERITAGE BOOKS, INC.

Books, CDs, and more—Worldwide

For our listing of thousands of titles see our website
at
www.HeritageBooks.com

Published 2007 by
HERITAGE BOOKS, INC.
Publishing Division
65 East Main Street
Westminster, Maryland 21157-5026

International Standard Book Number: 978-0-7884-3650-3

Other Books by Roger P. Minert, Ph.D.

Deciphering Handwriting in German Documents: Analyzing German, Latin, and French in Vital Records Written in German

Spelling Variations in German Names: Solving Family History Research Problems Through Applications of German and English Phonetics

Baden Place Name Indexes: Identifying Place Names Using Alphabetical and Reverse Alphabetical Indexes

Braunschweig, Oldenburg, Thuringia Place Name Index: Identifying Place Names Using Alphabetical and Reverse Alphabetical Indexes

Brandenburg Place Name Indexes: Identifying Place Names Using Alphabetical and Reverse Alphabetical Indexes

Hanover Place Names: Identifying Place Names Using Alphabetical and Reverse Alphabetical Indexes

Hesse Place Names Indexes: Identifying Place Names Using Alphabetical and Reverse Alphabetical Indexes

Hesse-Nassau Place Name Indexes: Identifying Place Names Using Alphabetical and Reverse Alphabetical Indexes

Kingdom of Saxony Place Name Indexes: Identifying Place Names Using Alphabetical and Reverse Alphabetical Indexes

Mecklenburg Place Name Indexes: Identifying Place Names Using Alphabetical and Reverse Alphabetical Indexes

Palatinate Place Name Indexes: Identifying Place Names Using Alphabetical and Reverse Alphabetical Indexes

Pomerania Place Name Indexes: Identifying Place Names Using Alphabetical and Reverse Alphabetical Indexes

Posen Place Name Indexes: Identifying Place Names Using Alphabetical and Reverse Alphabetical Indexes

Province of Saxony Place Name Indexes: Identifying Place Names Using Alphabetical and Reverse Alphabetical Indexes

Rhineland Place Name Indexes: Identifying Place Names Using Alphabetical and Reverse Alphabetical Indexes

Schleswig-Holstein Place Name Index: Identifying Place Names Using Alphabetical and Reverse Alphabetical Indexes

Westphalia Place Name Index: Identifying Place Names Using Alphabetical and Reverse Alphabetical Indexes

Wurttemberg Place Name Indexes: Identifying Place Names Using Alphabetical and Reverse Alphabetical Indexes

With Shirley J. Riemer:
Researching in Germany: A Handbook for Your Visit in the Homeland of Your Ancestors

with Jennifer A. Anderson
CD: Switzerland Place Name Indexes: Identifying Place Names Using Alphabetical and Reverse Alphabetical Indexes

Table of Contents

Introduction

One of the most challenging issues in German family history research in the United States is the identification of the home town of the German immigrant. Whereas there are many types of records that one can search in the United States, there are essentially none that consistently show the home town or even the native province of the immigrant who was born in Germany.

Some of the best of those records that sometimes show a home town for the new arrival are the passenger lists filed by ship captains in the respective ports of arrival since the introduction of this requirement in 1819.[1] Unfortunately, many such lists give no information on the origin of the passenger except the name of the country—at times perhaps the province. The disappointment on the part of the researcher who fails to find the name of the home town on a passenger list may be intensified by the fact that a search through the passenger lists of a single port for a single year can take literally hours to conduct (especially in New York). If one were to estimate a researcher's chance for success in finding the average immigrant's home town on a passenger list, the best guess might well lie below fifteen percent

This problem would be reason enough for researchers to jump with joy in 1988 when the first volume of the ongoing series *Germans to America* appeared. An indexed book of the names of Germans arriving in many ports in the United States was sorely needed, even if the extractors misspelled a passenger's name or a place name now and then.[2] Many researchers have been spared the difficult task of searching the passenger lists themselves.

The only comprehensive source of data on passengers departing Germany is the collection of records called *The Hamburg Passenger Lists*. Beginning with the emergence of the port of Hamburg as the point of departure for emigrants to the New World and elsewhere in 1850, lists of all passengers on ocean-going vessels were kept.[3] Those lists were to include among other important details the name of the last place of residence for each individual. From what is known about German demographics, the last place of residence was in many cases also the place of birth for the passenger. Thus *The Hamburg Passenger Lists* represent an extremely valuable source of emigrant data if one's emigrant boarded the ship there. Far fewer than one-half of German-speaking emigrants did so.

In many cases, researchers find that the lists of passengers in *Germans to America*

---

1 The legislation was passed under the title An Act Regulating Passenger Ships and Vessels (Riemer, p. 128).

2 In fact, severe criticism has been directed against *Germans to America* by such scholars as Antonius Holtmann of the University of Oldenburg. Details on several problems found in the first thirty or so volumes of the collection can be found in his article "Germans to America: 50 Volumes That Cannot be Trusted." *Palatine Immigrant* XXII:2, pp. 80-86. Despite its failings, *Germans to America* remains a very valuable source of information for researchers in Germanic family history.

3 Of course, it would be unwise to assume that a list of passengers was submitted from the captain of every ship sailing from Hamburg to the United States. Evidence suggests that vessels carrying fewer than 25 passengers did not hand in a list upon arrival. Names of crew members of ships seldom appear on the lists, while some of those crew members likely remained in the United States.

indicate that the home town of the arriving persons was not given. In many other cases, the lists show insufficient information, such as "Germany" or provinces like "Hanover" or "Hesse." In cases where the ship in question took on its passengers in Hamburg, what *Germans to America* does not provide may be available on *The Hamburg Passenger Lists*. Yet to date no coordination of the schedules has been published.

Whereas most experienced and many novice family history researchers are acquainted with the volumes of *Germans to America*, many of them have never heard of *The Hamburg Passenger Lists*. Thus many searches end prematurely in failure. On those occasions when the researcher finds the subject immigrant in *Germans to America* arriving on a ship from the port of Hamburg, he or she may know or be informed of the existence of *The Hamburg Passenger Lists* and thus initiate the process. But what does that process entail? First of all, the researcher must determine the date of the vessel's departure from Hamburg (the most recent departure before the arrival date), which may have been as little as eight days and more than three months earlier. The reference entitled *Verzeichnis der in den Jahren 1850-1914 von Hamburg ausgegangenen Auswandererschiffe* [List of Emigrant Ships Departing Hamburg 1850-1914] is known to very few researchers and available to even fewer.[4] One is left to guessing when the ship left Hamburg, or is dependent upon the indexes to find the person in question (by-passing the search for the ship).

The Hamburg Passenger Lists have two categories of departing vessels: Indirect and Direct. The terms refer to those ships that sailed from Hamburg to the destination without interruption (Direct) and those that stopped somewhere along the way (Indirect). The indexes are found on microfilms separate from the actual passenger lists. Thus the search for the correct index constitutes a search separate and distinct from the search for the name and departure date of the ship carrying the subject emigrant.

The reference work *Verzeichnis der in den Jahren 1850-1874 von Hamburg ausgegangenen Auswandererschiffe* also provides the page numbers for the lists of passengers for specific ships and specific voyages. Unfortunately, though all existing pages of *The Hamburg Passenger Lists* have been microfilmed by the Family History Library, those page numbers are not indicated in the index of microfilms that are ordered only chronologically. The process of consulting two or three records sources and self-help literature (as well written as most of it is) can be time-consuming and can result in failure.

Years ago I [RPM] found myself dreaming of an index that would take me straight from the United States passenger list to the corresponding Hamburg passenger list. I reasoned that if I could reduce the time needed for this transition from ten minutes to 30 seconds, my clients would benefit from my efficiency. What researchers will find in this book is precisely that—the only way to by-pass several methodological steps and self-help literature and go directly to the pages on which the subject emigrant will be found. We wish you success in your search and would be pleased to know if our index is of value to you.

We express our gratitude to our friends and staff members of the Family History Library for their helpful suggestions and support during our compilation of this index. Cassie Minert conducted a thorough quality assurance audit of our data. We are also grateful to have access to all volumes of *Germans to America* and all microfilms of the *Hamburg Passenger Lists* in the

---

4 The Family History Library in Salt Lake City has a photocopy of the "List of Emigrant Ships..."

collection of the Utah Valley Regional Family Center in Brigham Young University's Harold B. Lee Library.

Roger P. Minert
Kathryn Boeckel
Caren Winters

Provo, Utah
September 2004

Related Literature:

Family History Library. *The Hamburg Passenger List: Film Number, Register, and Guide* (Salt Lake City: Family History Library: unpublished, 1993)

Family History Library. *The Hamburg Passenger Lists.* Salt Lake City: Intellectual Reserve, Inc., 1999 [FHL publication no. 34047000].

Glazier, Ira A. and P. William Filby, eds. *Germans to America: Lists of Passengers Arriving at U.S. Ports.* 67 vols (1850-1897). Wilmington, DE: Scholarly Resources, Inc., 1988-2002.

Holtmann, Antonius. "Germans to America: 50 Volumes That Cannot be Trusted" in *The Palatine Immigrant* XXII:2 (1997), pp. 80-86.

Riemer, Shirley J. *German Research Companion*, 2d ed. Sacramento: Lorelei Press, 1999.

Verzeichnis der in den Jahren 1850-1874 von Hamburg ausgegangenen Auswandererschiffe [Index of the vessels leaving Hamburg carrying emigrants in the years 1850-1874] (Vol. 1). Unpublished, undated. [Family History Library book no. 943.515 H1 W3v pt. 1, microfilm no. 1732431, items 3].

Verzeichnis der in den Jahren 1875-1894 von Hamburg ausgegangenen Auswandererschiffe (Vol. 1). Unpublished, undated. [Family History Library book no. 943.515 H1 W3v pt. 2, microfilm no. 1732431, items 4].

Verzeichnis der in den Jahren 1895-1014 von Hamburg ausgegangenen Auswandererschiffe (Vol. 1). Unpublished, undated. [Family History Library book no. 943.515 H1 W3v pt. 3, microfilm no. 1732431, items 5].

How to Use the *Coordinated Schedules*

Because this index deals only with ship voyages, you will not find the names of passengers in this book. You must begin by identifying the ship on which the subject person arrived (or on which he reportedly arrived) in the United States. Search for the name of the subject immigrant(s) in a volume of *Germans to America*. If you can find him, her, or them, determine where the ship began its voyage—specifically whether it sailed from Hamburg. It is important to note that some ships leaving Hamburg are listed in *Germans to America* as coming from a Carribean port such as St. Thomas; thus a quick look in the index of this book--based on the theory that the passengers boarded the ship in Hamburg-- may yield unexpected rewards).

If the emigrant left the port of Hamburg, search for the ship name by arrival date in this index. On the same line you will find the date of the departure of that ship from Hamburg. Also listed are the pages of the lists of passengers aboard that ship (the page numbers were written on the lists when Hamburg port officials undertook the indexing of the lists). Then procure the microfilm listed by number in the far right column and proceed to search for the lowest page number shown for the passenger lists. That page should show the title page of the ship with its ownership, flag, date of departure, and intended destination.

The page numbers of the Hamburg passenger lists were often written in the far upper right or upper left corner with a grease pencil. Many are difficult to read due to the poor resolution of the microfilm. It may be necessary to move forward or backward several pages to find a highly legible page number, then to count down or up to the desired page.

Germans to America vol. and page nos.		Name of the Ship	Route and U.S. Port(s) of Arrival	Date of Arrival	Date of Departure	*HPL* Page numbers	FHL micro-film no.
1	39	Nord America	New York	17 Apr 1850	16 Mar 1850	alphabet. index only	470833
1	42-43	Romanov	New York	22 Apr 1850	2 Mar 1850	alphabet. index only	470833
1	46-47	Elbe	New York	1 May 1850	16 Mar 1850	alphabet. index only	470833
1	51-52	Leibnitz	New York	4 May 1850	16 Mar 1850	alphabet. index only	470833
1	54-55	British Queen	New York	9 May 1850	1 Apr 1850	alphabet. index only	470833
1	66-67	Rhein	New York	14 May 1850	6 Apr 1850	alphabet. index only	470833
1	90-91	Perseverance	New York	20 May 1850	2 Apr 1850	alphabet. index only	470833
1	98-99	Franklin	New York	22 May 1850	16 Apr 1850	alphabet. index only	470833
1	110-111	Elise	New York	27 May 1850	27 Apr 1850	alphabet. index only	470833
1	135-137	Herschel	New York	7 Jun 1850	30 Apr 1850	alphabet. index only	470833
1	155-157	Helena Sloman	New York	29 Jun 1850	28 May 1850	alphabet. index only	470833
1	168-170	Guttenburg	New York	5 Jul 1850	15 May 1850	alphabet. index only	470833
1	178-180	Hermann	New York	10 Jul 1850	18 May 1850	alphabet. index only	470833
1	194-195	Herman	New York	16 Jul 1850	29 Jun 1850	alphabet. index only	470833
1	201-202	Miles	New York	18 Jul 1850	31 May 1850	alphabet. index only	470833
1	223-224	Ellen	New York	8 Aug 1850	1 Jun 1850	alphabet. index only	470833
1	228-229	Nord America	New York	16 Aug 1850	29 Jun 1850	alphabet. index only	470833
1	244-245	Howard	New York	21 Aug 1850	1 Jul 1850	alphabet. index only	470833
1	252	Helena Sloman	New York	4 Sep 1850	10 Aug 1850	alphabet. index only	470833
1	254-255	Kossuth	New York	5 Sep 1850	15 Jul 1850	alphabet. index only	470833
1	280-281	Sir Isaac Newton	New York	20 Sep 1850	31 Jul 1850	alphabet. index only	470833

Germans to America vol. and page nos.		Name of the Ship	Route and U.S. Port(s) of Arrival	Date of Arrival	Date of Departure	*HPL* Page numbers	FHL micro-film no.
1	300-301	Choctaw	New York	7 Oct 1850	15 Aug 1850	alphabet. index only	470833
1	306-307	Franklin	New York	8 Oct 1850	15 Aug 1850	alphabet. index only	470833
1	312-313	Elise	New York	10 Oct 1850	31 Aug 1850	alphabet. index only	470833
1	314-316	Rhein	New York	12 Oct 1850	24 Aug 1850	alphabet. index only	470833
1	339-340	Herschel	New York	28 Oct 1850	16 Sep 1850	alphabet. index only	470833
1	349-350	Leibnitz	New Orleans	2 Nov 1850	31 Aug 1850	alphabet. index only	470833
1	383-384	Miles	New York	11 Dec 1850	16 Oct 1850	alphabet. index only	470833
1	411	Howard	New York	15 Feb 1851	27 Nov 1850	alphabet. index only	470833
1	416	Elise	New York	15 Mar 1851	missing	missing	-----
1	421	Oceanida	New York	24 Mar 1851	missing	missing	-----
1	440-441	Rhein	New York	15 Apr 1851	6 Mar 1851	alphabet. index only	470833
1	443-445	Deutschland	New York	19 Apr 1851	15 Mar 1850	alphabet. index only	470833
1	455-456	Vesta	New York	21 Apr 1851	missing	missing	-----
1	458-459	Franklin	New York	22 Apr 1851	1 Mar 1851	alphabet. index only	470833
1	465-466	Copernicus	New York	28 Apr 1851	15 Mar 1851	alphabet. index only	470833
1	489-490	Hanover	New York	7 May 1851	missing	missing	-----
1	500-502	Herschel	New York	16 May 1851	14 Apr 1851	alphabet. index only	470833
1	503-504	Enterprise	New York	19 May 1851	2 Apr 1851	alphabet. index only	470833
1	514-515	Nord America	New York	21 May 1851	15 Apr 1851	alphabet. index only	470833
1	515-516	Held	New York	22 May 1851	2 Apr 1851	alphabet. index only	470833
1	516-517	Maria Friedericke	New York	22 May 1851	21 Mar 1851	alphabet. index only	470833

Germans to America vol. and page nos.		Name of the Ship	Route and U.S. Port(s) of Arrival	Date of Arrival	Date of Departure	*HPL* Page numbers	FHL micro-film no.
2	8-9	Charlotte	New York	1 Jun 1851	12 Apr 1851	alphabet. index only	470833
2	23	Harmonica	New York	9 Jun 1851	19 Apr 1851	alphabet. index only	470833
2	30-31	Miles	New York	12 Jun 1851	30 Apr 1851	alphabet. index only	470833
2	48-49	Conrad Heinrich	New York	20 Jun 1851	6 May 1851	alphabet. index only	470833
2	49-50	Diana	New York	20 Jun 1851	3 May 1851	alphabet. index only	470833
2	54	Clara Ann	New York	22 Jun 1851	13 Nov 1850	alphabet. index only	470833
2	58	Martin Frederick	New York	24 Jun 1851	30 Apr 1851	alphabet. index only	470833
2	62-64	Oder	New York	30 Jun 1851	15 May 1851	alphabet. index only	470833
2	66-68	Gutenberg	New York	1 Jul 1851	15 May 1851	alphabet. index only	470833
2	82-83	Ann S. Lizzy	New York	7 Jul 1851	15 May 1851	alphabet. index only	470833
2	131	Jenness	New Orleans	1 Dec 1851	17 Oct 1851	alphabet. index only	470833
2	167	Deutschland	New York	28 Jan 1852	15 Nov 1852	alphabet. index only	470833
2	182	Nord America	New York	4 Feb 1852	missing	missing	-----
2	225-226	Nord Skov	New York	7 Apr 1852	1 Mar 1852	alphabet. index only	470834
2	277-279	Herschel	New York	26 Apr 1852	15 Mar 1852	alphabet. index only	470834
2	288	Rhein	New York	29 Apr 1852	1 Apr 1852	alphabet. index only	470834
2	308-309	Elize	New York	1 May 1852	15 Mar 1852	alphabet. index only	470834
2	318-320	Howard	New York	3 May 1852	2 Apr 1852	alphabet. index only	470834
2	322	Omen	New York	3 May 1852	16 Mar 1852	alphabet. index only	470834
2	344-345	Reform	New York	6 May 1852	15 Mar 1852	alphabet. index only	470834
2	345-346	Schiller	New York	6 May 1852	1 Apr 1852	alphabet. index only	470834

Germans to America vol. and page nos.		Name of the Ship	Route and U.S. Port(s) of Arrival	Date of Arrival	Date of Departure	*HPL* Page numbers	FHL micro-film no.
2	358	Sleipner	New York	7 May 1852	20 Mar 1852	alphabet. index only	470834
2	384-385	Hilding	New York	12 May 1852	1 Apr 1852	alphabet. index only	470834
2	398-399	Der Alte Peter	New York	15 May 1852	3 Apr 1852	alphabet. index only	470834
2	403	Seventeenth of May	New York	13 Jul 1852	17 May 1852	alphabet. index only	470834
2	431	Julie	New York	25 May 1852	2 Apr 1852	alphabet. index only	470834
2	437-438	Leibnitz	New Orleans	26 May 1852	16 Mar 1852	alphabet. index only	470834
2	464-466	Franciska	New York	1 Jun 1852	16 Apr 1852	alphabet. index only	470834
3	13-14	Isaac Newton	New Orleans	7 Jun 1852	10 Apr 1852	alphabet. index only	470834
3	14-15	John Hermann	New York	7 Jun 1852	15 Apr 1852	alphabet. index only	470834
3	21-22	Harriet Frances	New Orleans	8 Jun 1852	16 Apr 1852	alphabet. index only	470834
3	46-47	Nord America	New York	10 Jun 1852	3 May 1852	alphabet. index only	470834
3	47-48	Perseverance	New York	10 Jun 1852	14 Apr 1852	alphabet. index only	470834
3	48-50	Washington	New York	10 Jun 1852	15 Apr 1852	alphabet. index only	470834
3	100-102	Sir Robert Peel	New York	18 Jun 1852	1 May 1852	alphabet. index only	470834
3	106-107	Amicitia	New York	19 Jun 1852	5 May 1852	alphabet. index only	470834
3	111-113	Deutschland	New York	21 Jun 1852	1 May 1852	alphabet. index only	470834
3	123	President Christie	New York	21 Jun 1852	16 Apr 1852	alphabet. index only	470834
3	125-126	Wolff	New York	21 Jun 1852	16 Apr 1852	alphabet. index only	470834
3	145-146	Ceres	New York	23 Jun 1852	16 Apr 1852	alphabet. index only	470834
3	148-149	Eleonore	New York	23 Jun 1852	3 May 1852	alphabet. index only	470834
3	153-153	Johanna Elise	New York	23 Jun 1852	15 May 1852	alphabet. index only	470834

Germans to America vol. and page nos.		Name of the Ship	Route and U.S. Port(s) of Arrival	Date of Arrival	Date of Departure	*HPL* Page numbers	FHL micro-film no.
3	169-170	Hector	New York	26 Jun 1852	missing	missing	-----
3	180-181	Levetzon Selkendorf	New York	28 Jun 1852	1 May 1852	alphabet. index only	470834
3	182-184	Oder	New York	28 Jun 1852	15 May 1852	alphabet. index only	470834
3	192-193	August Adolph	New York	30 Jun 1852	5 May 1852	alphabet. index only	470834
3	200-203	Java	New York	1 Jul 1852	29 Apr 1852	alphabet. index only	470834
3	208-209	Ole Bull	New York	2 Jul 1852	missing	missing	-----
3	213	P.J. Behnck	New York	6 Jul 1852	20 Apr 1852	alphabet. index only	470834
3	243-244	Phoenix	New York	12 Jul 1852	15 May 1852	alphabet. index only	470834
3	252-253	P.J. Behnck	New York	13 Jul 1852	missing	missing	-----
3	253-254	Seventeenth of May	New York	13 Jul 1852	17 May 1852	alphabet. index only	470834
3	295-296	Copernicus	New York	30 Jul 1852	17 May 1852	alphabet. index only	470834
3	296-298	George Carming	New York	30 Jul 1852	27 Jun 1852	alphabet. index only	470834
3	298-300	Elbe	New York	31 Jul 1852	17 Jun 1852	alphabet. index only	470834
3	307-308	Frank Johnson	New York	3 Aug 1852	2 Jun 1852	alphabet. index only	470834
3	320-322	Irma	New York	6 Aug 1852	14 Jun 1852	alphabet. index only	470834
3	325-326	Vernon	New York	6 Aug 1852	9 Jun 1852	alphabet. index only	470834
3	327-328	Realm	New York	7 Aug 1852	5 Jun 1852	alphabet. index only	470834
3	370-371	Prince Albert	New York	17 Aug 1852	1 Jul 1852	alphabet. index only	470834
3	376-377	Rhein	New York	18 Aug 1852	1 Jul 1852	alphabet. index only	470834
3	399-401	Guttenberg	New York	26 Aug 1852	2 Jul 1852	alphabet. index only	470834
3	407-408	Elise	New York	28 Aug 1852	15 Jul 1852	alphabet. index only	470834

Germans to America vol. and page nos.		Name of the Ship	Route and U.S. Port(s) of Arrival	Date of Arrival	Date of Departure	*HPL* Page numbers	FHL micro-film no.
3	411-413	Southener	New York	2 Sep 1852	16 Jul 1852	alphabet. index only	470834
3	413	Thone	New York	2 Sep 1852	15 Jun 1852	alphabet. index only	470834
3	421-422	Thecla Josephine	New York	6 Sep 1852	missing	missing	-----
3	423-424	Nord America	New York	11 Sep 1852	31 Jul 1852	alphabet. index only	470834
3	442-444	Permgustuck	New York	16 Sep 1852	5 Aug 1852	alphabet. index only	470834
3	456-457	Gibraltar	New York	18 Sep 1852	16 Jul 1852	alphabet. index only	470834
3	461	Anna	New York	20 Sep 1852	21 Jul 1852	alphabet. index only	470834
4	5-7	Deutschland	New York	23 Sep 1852	16 Aug 1852	alphabet. index only	470834
4	13-15	John Hermann	New York	24 Sep 1852	14 Aug 1852	alphabet. index only	470834
4	41-43	Indian Queen	New York	27 Sep 1852	16 Aug 1852	alphabet. index only	470834
4	55-56	Harburg	New York	30 Sep 1852	1 Sep 1852	alphabet. index only	470834
4	56-57	Johanna Elise	New York	30 Sep 1852	1 Sep 1852	alphabet. index only	470834
4	62-63	Franklin	New York	1 Oct 1852	6 Sep 1852	alphabet. index only	470834
4	76-77	Leibnitz	New York	5 Oct 1852	1 Sep 1852	alphabet. index only	470834
4	82-83	Sir Isaac Newton	New York	6 Oct 1852	25 Sep 1852	alphabet. index only	470834
4	122	Hansa	New Orleans	27 Oct 1852	1 Sep 1852	alphabet. index only	470834
4	126-128	Sir Robert Peel	New Orleans	27 Oct 1852	1 Sep 1852	alphabet. index only	470834
4	142	Washington	New Orleans	6 Nov 1852	17 Aug 1852	alphabet. index only	470834
4	163-165	Oder	New York	12 Nov 1852	18 Sep 1852	alphabet. index only	470834
4	176-177	Copernicus	New Orleans	18 Nov 1852	15 Sep 1852	alphabet. index only	470834
4	197-200	George Caming	New York	25 Nov 1852	15 Oct 1852	alphabet. index only	470834

Germans to America vol. and page nos.		Name of the Ship	Route and U.S. Port(s) of Arrival	Date of Arrival	Date of Departure	*HPL* Page numbers	FHL micro-film no.
4	210-212	Rhein	New York	29 Nov 1852	16 Oct 1852	alphabet. index only	470834
4	214-216	Elbe	New York	30 Nov 1852	2 Oct 1852	alphabet. index only	470834
4	224-235	Elize	New York	7 Dec 1852	17 Sep 1852	alphabet. index only	470834
4	237-238	Elise	New York	8 Dec 1852	1 Nov 1852	alphabet. index only	470834
4	252-253	Quixote	New York	22 Dec 1852	15 Sep 1852	alphabet. index only	470834
4	267	Gutenberg	New York	24 Jan 1853	16 Nov 1852	alphabet. index only	470834
4	279	Alida	New York	9 Feb 1853	1 Nov 1852	alphabet. index only	470834
4	282-283	Nord America	New York	9 Feb 1853	27 Nov 1852	alphabet. index only	470834
4	288-289	Hampdon	New York	15 Feb 1853	19 Oct 1852	alphabet. index only	470834
4	303	Prince Albert	New York	3 Mar 1853	27 Nov 1852	alphabet. index only	470834
4	317-318	Herschel	New York	9 Mar 1853	12 Dec 1852	alphabet. index only	470834
4	446-447	John Hermann	New York	17 May 1853	18 Nov 1852	alphabet. index only	470834
4	461-462	Johanna Elise	New York	21 May 1853	missing	missing	-----
4	465-467	Deutschland	New York	23 May 1853	missing	missing	-----
4	467-468	Howard	New York	23 May 1853	missing	missing	-----
5	11-12	Patria	New York	30 May 1853	missing	missing	-----
5	12-14	Rhine	New York	30 May 1853	missing	missing	-----
5	16-18	Copernicus	New York	31 May 1853	missing	missing	-----
5	18-19	Hansa	New York	31 May 1853	missing	missing	-----
5	32-34	Oder	New York	1 Jun 1853	missing	missing	-----
5	49-50	Emigrant	New York	4 Jun 1853	missing	missing	-----

Germans to America vol. and page nos.		Name of the Ship	Route and U.S. Port(s) of Arrival	Date of Arrival	Date of Departure	*HPL* Page numbers	FHL micro-film no.
5	75	Seventeenth Day of May	New York	7 Jun 1853	missing	missing	-----
5	76-77	Kepler	New York	8 Jun 1853	missing	missing	-----
5	85-86	Julia	New York	11 Jun 1853	missing	missing	-----
5	87-89	Deutschland	New York	12 Jun 1853	missing	missing	-----
5	96-98	Celle	New York	13 Jun 1853	missing	missing	-----
5	106-108	Johann Smidt	New Orleans	13 Jun 1853	missing	missing	-----
5	108-110	Nord Amerika	New York	13 Jun 1853	missing	missing	-----
5	111-112	Theodore	New York	13 Jun 1853	missing	missing	-----
5	121-123	Ammerland	New York	14 Jun 1853	missing	missing	-----
5	145	Eleonore	New York	20 Jun 1853	missing	missing	-----
5	156-157	Diamant	New York	23 Jun 1853	missing	missing	-----
5	167-168	Prinz Albert	New York	24 Jun 1853	missing	missing	-----
5	172	Anna Elise	New York	27 Jun 1853	missing	missing	-----
5	178-179	Elise	New York	28 Jun 1853	missing	missing	-----
5	179-180	Franklin	New York	28 Jun 1853	missing	missing	-----
5	188-189	Hamburg	New York	5 Jul 1853	missing	missing	-----
5	201-202	Anna	New York	14 Jul 1853	missing	missing	-----
5	209	Magdalena	New York	16 Jul 1853	missing	missing	-----
5	218-219	Triton	New York	18 Jul 1853	missing	missing	-----
5	227-228	Flying Dutchman	New York	28 Jul 1853	missing	missing	-----
5	233-237	Pampero	New York	3 Aug 1853	missing	missing	-----

Germans to America vol. and page nos.		Name of the Ship	Route and U.S. Port(s) of Arrival	Date of Arrival	Date of Departure	*HPL* Page numbers	FHL micro-film no.
5	237-238	Theodore	New York	3 Aug 1853	missing	missing	-----
5	244-246	Rastede	New York	8 Aug 1853	missing	missing	-----
5	252-253	Swed	New York	9 Aug 1853	missing	missing	-----
5	256-258	Luneburg	New York	10 Aug 1853	missing	missing	-----
5	258-260	Geo Canning	New York	11 Aug 1853	missing	missing	-----
5	293-294	Hannover	New York	19 Aug 1853	missing	missing	-----
5	295-297	Herschel	New York	20 Aug 1853	missing	missing	-----
5	318-320	Donau	New York	24 Aug 1853	missing	missing	-----
5	323-324	George	New York	25 Aug 1853	missing	missing	-----
5	327-329	John Hermann	New York	26 Aug 1853	missing	missing	-----
5	340-341	Elbe	New York	29 Aug 1853	missing	missing	-----
5	350-352	Sir Robert Peel	New York	31 Aug 1853	missing	missing	-----
5	375-377	Humboldt	New York	10 Sep 1853	16 Jul 1853	alphabet. index only	470835
5	384-386	Deutschland	New York	12 Sep 1853	1 Aug 1853	alphabet. index only	470835
5	391-393	Johanna Elise	New York	12 Sep 1853	1 Aug 1853	alphabet. index only	470835
5	393	Elise	New York	13 Sep 1853	15 Jul 1853	alphabet. index only	470835
5	424-426	Oder	New York	27 Sep 1853	15 Aug 1853	alphabet. index only	470835
5	439-441	Talleyrand	New York	1 Oct 1853	4 Aug 1853	alphabet. index only	470835
5	444-445	Louisiana	New York	3 Oct 1853	17 Aug 1853	alphabet. index only	470835
5	448-449	Copernicus	New York	12 Oct 1853	16 Aug 1853	alphabet. index only	470835
5	465-467	Nord America	New York	19 Oct 1853	1 Sep 1853	alphabet. index only	470835

Germans to America vol. and page nos.		Name of the Ship	Route and U.S. Port(s) of Arrival	Date of Arrival	Date of Departure	*HPL* Page numbers	FHL micro-film no.
5	471-472	Prinz Albert	New York	20 Oct 1853	1 Sep 1853	alphabet. index only	470835
6	7-8	Leuneburg	New York	25 Oct 1853	15 Aug 1853	alphabet. index only	470835
6	23-24	Washington	New Orleans	7 Nov 1853	3 Sep 1853	alphabet. index only	470835
6	38-40	Elise	New York	12 Nov 1853	15 Sep 1853	alphabet. index only	470835
6	61-62	Caesar	New York	16 Nov 1853	24 Sep 1853	alphabet. index only	470835
6	93-94	Hampden	New York	21 Nov 1853	1 Oct 1853	alphabet. index only	470835
6	94-95	Rhein	New York	21 Nov 1853	15 Sep 1853	alphabet. index only	470835
6	97-98	Sea Lion	New York	21 Nov 1853	21 Sep 1853	alphabet. index only	470835
6	101-103	Falcon	New Orleans	22 Nov 1853	21 Sep 1853	alphabet. index only	470835
6	107-109	Esperance	New York	28 Nov 1853	1 Oct 1853	alphabet. index only	470835
6	127-129	Hudson	New York	5 Dec 1853	1 Nov 1853	alphabet. index only	470835
6	131-133	Rastede	New York	5 Dec 1853	15 Oct 1853	alphabet. index only	470835
6	144-146	Donau	New York	10 Dec 1853	2 Nov 1853	alphabet. index only	470835
6	157-158	New York Packet	New York	14 Dec 1853	25 Oct 1853	alphabet. index only	470835
6	194-195	Marion	New Orleans	22 Dec 1853	22 Oct 1853	alphabet. index only	470835
6	233-234	Elbe	New York	9 Jan 1854	16 Nov 1853	alphabet. index only	470835
6	236-238	Herschel	New York	10 Jan 1854	4 Nov 1853	alphabet. index only	470835
6	247-248	Juno	New York	12 Jan 1854	17 Nov 1853	alphabet. index only	470835
6	269-270	John Hermann	New York	16 Jan 1854	31 Oct 1853	alphabet. index only	470835
6	279-280	Deutschland	New York	19 Jan 1854	30 Nov 1853	alphabet. index only	470835
6	294-295	Sir Isaac Newton	New York	23 Jan 1854	15 Oct 1853	alphabet. index only	470835

Germans to America vol. and page nos.		Name of the Ship	Route and U.S. Port(s) of Arrival	Date of Arrival	Date of Departure	*HPL* Page numbers	FHL micro-film no.
6	299	Miles	New York	24 Jan 1854	30 Nov 1853	alphabet. index only	470835
6	414-415	Elise	New York	21 Apr 1854	15 Mar 1854	alphabet. index only	470836
6	422-423	Nord America	New York	21 Apr 1854	1 Mar 1854	alphabet. index only	470836
6	445-446	Hannover	New York	25 Apr 1854	15 Mar 1854	alphabet. index only	470836
6	462-463	Franklin	New York	1 May 1854	17 Mar 1854	alphabet. index only	470836
6	475-476	Copernicus	New Orleans	4 May 1854	14 Mar 1854	alphabet. index only	470836
7	55-57	Donau	New York	17 May 1854	1 Apr 1854	alphabet. index only	470836
7	75-77	Oldenburg	New York	18 May 1854	1 Apr 1854	alphabet. index only	470836
7	83-85	Hudson	New York	19 May 1854	1 Apr 1854	alphabet. index only	470836
7	91-92	Rhein	New York	19 May 1854	16 Mar 1854	alphabet. index only	470836
7	106-108	Elba	New York	20 May 1854	15 Apr 1854	alphabet. index only	470836
7	135-137	Elida	New York	22 May 1854	15 Apr 1854	alphabet. index only	470836
7	137-139	G Canning	New York	22 May 1854	15 Apr 1854	alphabet. index only	470836
7	151-152	Schiller	New York	22 May 1854	31 Mar 1854	alphabet. index only	470836
7	174-175	Leibnitz	New York	23 May 1854	1 Apr 1854	alphabet. index only	470836
7	176-177	Louise Ott Warbelow	New York	23 May 1854	13 Apr 1854	alphabet. index only	470836
7	184-186	Gutenberg	New York	24 May 1854	15 Mar 1854	alphabet. index only	470836
7	191	August Agnes	New York	25 May 1854	1 Apr 1854	alphabet. index only	470836
7	207-208	Annie Lizzie	New York	26 May 1854	1 Apr 1854	alphabet. index only	470836
7	214-216	Duc De Brabant	New York	29 May 1854	15 Apr 1854	alphabet. index only	470836
7	284-285	Raleigh	New York	12 Jun 1854	28 Apr 1854	alphabet. index only	470836

Germans to America vol. and page nos.		Name of the Ship	Route and U.S. Port(s) of Arrival	Date of Arrival	Date of Departure	*HPL* Page numbers	FHL micro-film no.
7	311-312	Flying Dutchman	New York	23 Jun 1854	8 May 1854	alphabet. index only	470836
7	321-324	Oregon	New York	24 Jun 1854	2 May 1854	alphabet. index only	470836
7	330	Miles	New York	27 Jun 1854	6 May 1854	alphabet. index only	470836
7	356-357	Johanna Elise	New York	29 Jun 1854	15 May 1854	alphabet. index only	470836
7	360-362	Rising Sun	New York	29 Jun 1854	4 May 1854	alphabet. index only	470836
7	363	Domingo	New York	30 Jun 1854	13 May 1854	alphabet. index only	470836
7	382-383	Europa	New York	3 Jul 1854	3 May 1854	alphabet. index only	470836
7	387-389	Nienburg	New York	3 Jul 1854	missing	missing	-----
7	389-391	Oder	New York	3 Jul 1854	22 May 1854	alphabet. index only	470836
7	405-406	Aurora	New York	8 Jul 1854	1 May 1854	alphabet. index only	470836
7	411	Mercur	New York	10 Jul 1854	21 Apr 1854	alphabet. index only	470836
7	428-430	John Bohring	New York	21 Jul 1854	22 May 1854	alphabet. index only	470836
7	436	Johanna Elisabeth	New York	24 Jul 1854	16 May 1854	alphabet. index only	470836
7	466-468	Mary Anna	New York	3 Aug 1854	8 Jun 1854	alphabet. index only	470836
7	473	Julietta	New York	4 Aug 1854	4 Jun 1854	alphabet. index only	470836
7	474-475	March of Queensbury	New York	4 Aug 1854	3 Jun 1854	alphabet. index only	470836
7	478-480	Neumuhlen	New York	4 Aug 1854	31 May 1854	alphabet. index only	470836
8	4-5	Columbia	New York	5 Aug 1854	15 Jun 1854	alphabet. index only	470836
8	28-30	Nord America	New York	10 Aug 1854	1 Jul 1854	alphabet. index only	470836
8	32-33	Parkfield	New York	10 Aug 1854	19 Jun 1854	alphabet. index only	470836
8	57-59	St. Charles	New York	14 Aug 1854	4 Jul 1854	alphabet. index only	470836

Germans to America vol. and page nos.		Name of the Ship	Route and U.S. Port(s) of Arrival	Date of Arrival	Date of Departure	*HPL* Page numbers	FHL micro-film no.
8	60-61	Star	New York	14 Aug 1854	9 Jun 1854	alphabet. index only	470836
8	65-66	Elise	New York	16 Aug 1854	1 Jul 1854	alphabet. index only	470836
8	66-68	Henschel	New York	16 Aug 1854	2 Jun 1854	alphabet. index only	470836
8	70	Hollander	New York	16 Aug 1854	12 Jun 1854	alphabet. index only	470836
8	73-74	Sir Isaac Newton	New York	16 Aug 1854	20 Jun 1854	alphabet. index only	470836
8	85-86	Skane	New York	17 Aug 1854	17 Jun 1854	alphabet. index only	470836
8	89-90	Archimedes	New York	19 Aug 1854	27 Jun 1854	alphabet. index only	470836
8	91-93	Asa Sawyer	New York	21 Aug 1854	5 Jul 1854	alphabet. index only	470836
8	116-118	Prinds Oscar	New York	26 Aug 1854	15 Jul 1854	alphabet. index only	470836
8	118-120	Humboldt	New York	28 Aug 1854	15 Jul 1854	alphabet. index only	470836
8	143-144	Donau	New York	31 Aug 1854	15 Jul 1854	alphabet. index only	470836
8	149-150	Helen Mogaw	New York	4 Sep 1854	19 Jul 1854	alphabet. index only	470836
8	161-163	Prinz Ernst August	New York	12 Sep 1854	missing	missing	-----
8	169-170	Rhein	New York	14 Sep 1854	1 Aug 1854	alphabet. index only	470836
8	182-184	Copernicus	New York	16 Sep 1854	31 Jul 1854	alphabet. index only	470836
8	227-228	Tarquin	New York	28 Sep 1854	1 Aug 1854	alphabet. index only	470836
8	235-237	Elida	New York	2 Oct 1854	15 Aug 1854	alphabet. index only	470836
8	239-241	Elbe	New York	3 Oct 1854	15 Aug 1854	alphabet. index only	470836
8	255	Franklin	New York	5 Oct 1854	19 Aug 1854	alphabet. index only	470836
8	263-265	Guttenberg	New York	9 Oct 1854	15 Aug 1854	alphabet. index only	470836
8	279-281	Isaac Allerton	New York	11 Oct 1854	1 Aug 1854	alphabet. index only	470836

Germans to America vol. and page nos.		Name of the Ship	Route and U.S. Port(s) of Arrival	Date of Arrival	Date of Departure	*HPL* Page numbers	FHL micro-film no.
8	292-294	Deutschland	New York	16 Oct 1854	1 Sep 1854	alphabet. index only	470836
8	294-296	George Canning	New York	16 Oct 1854	1 Sep 1854	alphabet. index only	470836
8	317-318	Ludwig August	New York	20 Oct 1854	5 Sep 1854	alphabet. index only	470836
8	323-324	Catharina	New York	23 Oct 1854	1 Sep 1854	alphabet. index only	470836
8	353-355	Johannes	New York	24 Oct 1854	2 Oct 1854	alphabet. index only	470836
8	374-375	Pauline	New York	30 Oct 1854	24 Aug 1854	alphabet. index only	470836
8	377-379	Luenburg	New York	31 Aug 1854	missing	missing	-----
8	384-385	Courant	New York	3 Nov 1854	16 Sep 1854	alphabet. index only	470836
8	398-400	Sir Robert Peel	New York	7 Nov 1854	15 Sep 1854	alphabet. index only	470836
8	400-402	John Hermann	New York	8 Nov 1854	15 Sep 1854	alphabet. index only	470836
8	403-405	North Carolina	Baltimore	9 Nov 1854	9 Sep 1854	alphabet. index only	470836
8	421-423	Johanna Elise	New York	13 Nov 1854	15 Sep 1854	alphabet. index only	470836
8	422-424	Oder	New York	20 Nov 1854	30 Sep 1854	alphabet. index only	470836
8	454-455	Aurora	New York	23 Nov 1854	16 Sep 1854	alphabet. index only	470836
8	465-467	Ossippee	New York	24 Nov 1854	15 Sep 1854	alphabet. index only	470836
8	469-470	Attica	New York	25 Nov 1854	30 Sep 1854	alphabet. index only	470836
8	474-475	Friederich Grosse	New York	25 Nov 1854	4 Oct 1854	alphabet. index only	470836
8	494-495	Champlain	New Orleans	5 Dec 1854	30 Sep 1854	alphabet. index only	470836
8	511-512	Nord America	New York	11 Dec 1854	16 Oct 1854	alphabet. index only	470836
9	119-120	Robert	New York	3 Jan 1855	16 Nov 1854	alphabet. index only	470836
9	159-160	Copernicus	New York	13 Feb 1855	2 Dec 1854	alphabet. index only	470836

Germans to America vol. and page nos.		Name of the Ship	Route and U.S. Port(s) of Arrival	Date of Arrival	Date of Departure	*HPL* Page numbers	FHL micro-film no.
9	237-238	Elbe	New York	8 May 1855	24 Mar 1855	5-11	470837
9	247-249	Guttenberg	New York	10 May 1855	31 Mar 1855	13-21	470837
9	253-254	Deutschland	New York	11 May 1855	2 Apr 1855	23-33	470837
9	283-285	Elise Rübcke	New York	18 June 1855	1 May 1855	133-141	470837
9	289-290	Rhein	New York	19 June 1855	1 May 1855	155-161	470837
9	299-300	Copernicus	New York	23 June 1855	15 May 1855	193-200	470837
9	311-313	Donau	New York	30 June 1855	15 May 1855	201-211	470837
9	333-335	Andrew	New York	16 Jul 1855	1 June 1855	261-267	470837
9	341-342	Panama	New York	26 Jul 1855	15 June 1855	339-345	470837
9	346-347	Herschel	New York	27 Jul 1855	1 June 1855	297-303	470837
9	351-352	Louis Napoleon	New York	30 Jul 1855	16 June 1855	321-327	470837
9	353-354	Rudolph	New York	30 Jul 1855	16 June 1855	329-337	470837
9	354-356	Howard	New York	31 Jul 1855	30 Apr 1855	117-125	470837
9	368-370	Genesee	New York	25 Aug 1855	2 Jul 1855	363-369	470837
9	384-385	Elida	New York	7 Sep 1855	14 Jul 1855	399-405	470837
9	388-390	Sir Robert Peel	New York	14 Sep 1855	16 Jul 1855	407-413	470837
9	400-401	Humboldt	New York	22 Sep 1855	3 Aug 1855	435-438	470837
9	409-410	Oder	New York	2 Oct 1855	15 Aug 1855	461-471	470837
9	413-415	Rhein	New York	9 Oct 1855	1 Sep 1855	495-501	470837
9	419-420	Copernicus	New York	15 Oct 1855	1 Sep 1855	487-493	470837
9	426-427	Elise Rübcke	New York	18 Oct 1855	15 Sep 1855	511-515	470837

Germans to America vol. and page nos.		Name of the Ship	Route and U.S. Port(s) of Arrival	Date of Arrival	Date of Departure	*HPL* Page numbers	FHL micro-film no.
9	434-435	Nord America	New York	23 Oct 1855	15 Sep 1855	503-509	470837
9	441-442	Washington	New York	29 Oct 1855	19 Sep 1855	517-523	470837
9	447-448	Donau	New York	5 Nov 1855	1 Oct 1855	545-551	470837
9	459-460	Emma Lincoln	New Orleans	13 Nov 1855	1 Sep 1855	483-486	470837
9	478-479	Havana	New York	1 Dec 1855	15 Oct 1855	587-593	470837
9	479-480	Rudolph	New York	10 Dec 1855	15 Oct 1855	579-585	470837
9	492-493	Louis Napoleon	New York	21 Dec 1855	17 Oct 1855	601-607	470837
9	494-495	Elbe	New York	22 Dec 1855	3 Nov 1855	633-635	470837
9	505-506	Howard	New York	24 Dec 1855	2 Nov 1855	625-631	470837
9	510-511	Elida	New York	31 Dec 1855	22 Nov 1855	645-646	470837
10	4	Deutschland	New York	12 Feb 1856	24 Nov 1855	653-655	470838
10	6	Sir Robert Peel	New York	25 Feb 1856	24 Nov 1855	649-650	470838
10	18-20	Snap Dragon	New York	14 Apr 1856	missing	missing	-----
10	24-26	Nord America	New York	28 Apr 1856	15 Mar 1856	13-19	470838
10	26	Raleigh	New York	28 Apr 1856	1 Mar 1856	5-7	470838
10	38-39	Gutenberg	New York	5 May 1856	15 Mar 1856	21-31	470838
10	45-46	Gellert	New York	12 May 1856	1 Apr 1856	65-71	470838
10	51-53	Insulana	New York	14 May 1856	1 Apr 1856	53-63	470838
10	54-55	Elbe	New York	21 May 1856	12 Apr 1856	79-85	470838
10	74-76	Louis Napoleon	New York	3 June 1856	19 Apr 1856	155-157-165	470838
10	78-79	Rhein	New York	5 June 1856	19 Apr 1856	131-137	470838

Germans to America vol. and page nos.		Name of the Ship	Route and U.S. Port(s) of Arrival	Date of Arrival	Date of Departure	*HPL* Page numbers	FHL micro-film no.
10	81-82	Suwa	New York	6 June 1856	22 Apr 1856	167-173	470838
10	90-92	Gerhardt	New York	9 June 1856	16 Apr 1856	123-130	470838
10	92-93	Johanna Elise	New York	10 June 1856	15 Apr 1856	107-113	470838
10	102-105	Borussia	New York	18 June 1856	31 May 1856	361-375	470838
10	109-111	Deutschland	New York	23 June 1856	3 May 1856	223-233	470838
10	111-112	Fanny Holmes	New York	23 June 1856	2 May 1856	211-221	470838
10	115-118	Rudolph	New York	23 June 1856	30 Apr 1856	187-201	470838
10	121-122	Ocilla	New York	24 June 1856	26 Apr 1856	179-185	470838
10	131-133	Elida	New York	3 Jul 1856	15 Apr 1856	95-105	470838
10	139-141	Howard	New York	9 Jul 1856	19 May 1856	321-331	470838
10	148-150	Ann Washburn	New York	12 Jul 1856	15 May 1856	293-307	470838
10	152-153	Johann	New York	14 Jul 1856	22 May 1856	333-339	470838
10	157-160	Hammonia	New York	19 Jul 1856	30 June 1856	481-493	470838
10	160-162	Humboldt	New York	21 Jul 1856	2 June 1856	417-427	470838
10	171-172	Donau	New York	2 Aug 1856	16 June 1856	449-455	470838
10	173-174	Gutenberg	New York	2 Aug 1856	15 Jul 1856	536-542	470838
10	174-175	Sir Robert Peel	New York	4 Aug 1856	16 June 1856	457-467	470838
10	180-183	Borussia	New York	16 Aug 1856	31 Jul 1856	564-579	470838
10	185-186	Nord America	New York	19 Aug 1856	3 Jul 1856	520-527	470838
10	191-192	Oder	New York	21 Aug 1856	15 Jul 1856	544-551	470838
10	194	Franklin	New York	22 Aug 1856	30 June 1856	497-499	470838

Germans to America vol. and page nos.		Name of the Ship	Route and U.S. Port(s) of Arrival	Date of Arrival	Date of Departure	*HPL* Page numbers	FHL micro-film no.
10	211-213	Hammonia	New York	16 Sep 1856	31 Aug 1856	656-675	470838
10	216-218	Louis Napoleon	New York	22 Sep 1856	4 Aug 1856	600-610	470838
10	220-222	Rhein	New York	22 Sep 1856	2 Aug 1856	588-595	470838
10	228-230	Elida	New York	29 Sep 1856	15 Aug 1856	616-623	470838
10	237-238	Elbe	New York	30 Sep 1856	16 Aug 1856	624-631	470838
10	240-241	Raleigh	New York	30 Sep 1856	16 Aug 1856	632-639	470838
10	244	Wm. B. Travis	New York	1 Oct 1856	18 Aug 1856	648-651	470838
10	254-255	Gem of the Ocean	New York	13 Oct 1856	4 Sep 1856	702-709	470838
10	263-264	Johanna Elise	New York	16 Oct 1856	1 Sep 1856	676-681	470838
10	267-268	Champion	New York	20 Oct 1856	16 Sep 1856	730-737	470838
10	271-273	Deutschland	New York	25 Oct 1856	16 Sep 1856	722-729	470838
10	276-277	Rudolph	New York	25 Oct 1856	15 Sep 1856	714-721	470838
10	287-288	Washington	New York	30 Oct 1856	1 Sep 1856	694-701	470838
10	304-306	Donau	New York	15 Nov 1856	2 Oct 1856	780-791	470838
10	306-307	Elise	New York	15 Nov 1856	1 Oct 1856	762-767	470838
10	307-309	Howard	New York	15 Nov 1856	22 Sep 1846	738-745	470838
10	309-311	Humboldt	New York	15 Nov 1856	1 Oct 1856	768-779	470838
10	313-316	Hammonia	New York	17 Nov 1856	30 Oct 1856	888-903	470838
10	320-321	James N. Cooper	New York	18 Nov 1856	7 Oct 1856	810-817	470838
10	322-324	Jenny Pitt	New York	18 Nov 1856	15 Oct 1856	844-851	470838
10	323-324	T.J. Rodger	New York	18 Nov 1856	3 Oct 1856	802-808	470838

Germans to America vol. and page nos.		Name of the Ship	Route and U.S. Port(s) of Arrival	Date of Arrival	Date of Departure	*HPL* Page numbers	FHL micro-film no.
10	342-344	Sir Robert Peel	New York	1 Dec 1856	15 Oct 1856	832-839	470838
10	347-349	William & Jane	New York	13 Dec 1856	missing	missing	-----
10	359-360	Borussia	New York	22 Dec 1856	29 Nov 1856	964-973	470838
10	366-368	Main	New York	31 Dec 1856	14 Nov 1856	936-947	470838
10	380-381	Gutenberg	New York	22 Jan 1857	18 Nov 1856	952-959	470838
10	381-382	Oder	New York	22 Jan 1857	12 Nov 1856	932-924	470838
10	393-394	John Bertram	New York	6 Feb 1857	29 Nov 1856	976	470838
10	396	Rhein	New York	12 Feb 1857	missing	missing	-----
10	398	Louis Napoleon	New York	17 Feb 1857	3 Jun 1856	503-514	470838
10	405-406	Washington	New Orleans	20 Mar 1857 [sic?]	16 Mar 1857	45-52	470839
10	408-410	Hammonia	New York	26 Mar 1857	28 Feb 1857	1-16	470839
10	418-419	Elbe	New York	14 Apr 1857	28 Feb 1857	17-20	470839
10	420-423	Borussia	New York	15 Apr 1857	31 Mar 1857	57-71	470839
10	431-432	Nord America	New York	20 Apr 1857	15 Mar 1857	37-44	470839
10	451-453	Howard	New York	23 Apr 1857	14 Mar 1857	29-36	470839
10	462	Sir Isaac Newton	New York	24 Apr 1857	28 Feb 1857	21-24	470839
11	8-10	Donau	New York	4 May 1857	1 Apr 1857	105-112	470839
11	18-20	Rudolph	New York	9 May 1857	1 Apr 1857	93-104	470839
11	25-27	Humboldt	New York	12 May 1857	1 Apr 1857	81-92	470839
11	31-34	Hammonia	New York	16 May 1857	30 Apr 1857	241-252	470839
11	52-55	Elise Rübcke	New York	21 May 1857	15 Apr 1857	137-148	470839

Germans to America vol. and page nos.		Name of the Ship	Route and U.S. Port(s) of Arrival	Date of Arrival	Date of Departure	*HPL* Page numbers	FHL micro-film no.
11	57-60	Doctor Barth	New York	22 May 1857	16 Apr 1857	181-192	470839
11	65-67	Main	New York	25 May 1857	19 Apr 1857	205-216	470839
11	89-90	Sir Robert Peel	New York	29 May 1857	16 Apr 1857	169-180	470839
11	97-99	Weser	New York	1 Jun 1857	15 Apr 1857	157-168	470839
11	112-114	John Bertram	New York	3 Jun 1857	2 May 1857	269-280	470839
11	126-127	Rhein	New York	8 Jun 1857	25 Apr 1857	233-240	470839
11	141-143	Union	New York	15 Jun 1857	2 May 1857	261-268	470839
11	145-147	Borussia	New York	17 Jun 1857	30 May 1857	465-480	470839
11	152-154	Edward Everett	New York	19 Jun 1857	5 May 1857	315-326	470839
11	156-158	Chas. C. Fowler	New York	20 Jun 1857	5 May 1857	327-336	470839
11	160-162	Johannes	New York	20 Jun 1857	1 May 1857	253-260	470839
11	168-170	Onward	New York	23 Jun 1857	5 May 1857	337-348	470839
11	215-216	Mary Hyler	New York	6 Jul 1857	29 May 1857	457-464	470839
11	222-224	Quebec	New York	10 Jul 1857	15 May 1857	417-424	470839
11	224-225	Margaretha	New York	13 Jul 1857	19 May 1857	425-432	470839
11	225-226	Flight	New York	14 Jul 1857	15 May 1857	377-384	470839
11	231-233	Hammonia	New York	16 Jul 1857	30 June 1857	591-602	470839
11	251-253	Franz McHenry	New York	1 Aug 1857	16 June 1857	551-562	470839
11	253-255	Marion	New York	1 Aug 1857	2 June 1857	495-502	470839
11	258-260	Nord America	New York	5 Aug 1857	13 June 1857	527-534	470839
11	271-272	Oder	New York	10 Aug 1857	18 June 1857	567-574	470839

Germans to America vol. and page nos.		Name of the Ship	Route and U.S. Port(s) of Arrival	Date of Arrival	Date of Departure	*HPL* Page numbers	FHL micro-film no.
11	276-279	Borussia	New York	15 Aug 1857	missing	missing	-----
11	284-285	John Hermann	New York	25 Aug 1857	1 Jul 1857	603-610	470839
11	303-304	Elida	New York	4 Sep 1857	16 Jul 1857	667-674	470839
11	305-306	Howard	New York	4 Sep 1857	7 Jul 1857	627-634	470839
11	310-312	Donau	New York	5 Sep 1857	11 Jul 1857	639-648	470839
11	314-316	Diana	New York	8 Sep 1857	27 June 1857	583-590	470839
11	318-320	Main	New York	10 Sep 1857	1 Aug 1857	691-702	470839
11	320-322	Sir Isaac Newton	New York	10 Sep 1857	16 Jul 1857	655-662	470839
11	324	Chas. Smith	New York	14 Sep 1857	16 Jul 1857	663-665	470839
11	326-328	Humboldt	New York	14 Sep 1857	1 Aug 1857	703-716	470839
11	334-336	Hammonia	New York	16 Sep 1857	31 Aug 1857	775-790	470839
11	338-340	Sir Robert Peel	New York	16 Sep 1857	15 Aug 1857	729-738	470839
11	355-356	Elise	New York	28 Sep 1857	15 Aug 1857	739-742	470839
11	362-364	Atalanta	New York	5 Oct 1857	16 Aug 1857	743-750	470839
11	377-379	Rhein	New York	6 Oct 1857	1 Sep 1857	791-798	470839
11	380-382	Doctor Barth	New York	7 Oct 1857	2 Sep 1857	807-814	470839
11	382-383	Johanna Elise	New York	7 Oct 1857	1 Sep 1857	799-806	470839
11	398-401	Borussia	New York	26 Oct 1857	30 Sep 1857	847-862	470839
11	401-403	John Bertram	New York	26 Oct 1857	30 Sep 1857	831-842	470839
11	429-431	Hammonia	New York	17 Nov 1857	31 Oct 1857	969-980	470839
11	438-441	Louis Napoleon	New York	23 Nov 1857	15 Oct 1857	921-932	470839

Germans to America vol. and page nos.		Name of the Ship	Route and U.S. Port(s) of Arrival	Date of Arrival	Date of Departure	*HPL* Page numbers	FHL micro-film no.
11	446-448	Suwa	New York	25 Nov 1857	3 Oct 1857	897-904	470839
11	448-450	Johannes	New York	27 Nov 1857	15 Oct 1857	945-952	470839
11	455-456	Elbe	New York	30 Nov 1857	9 Oct 1857	913-920	470839
12	39-41	Gutenberg	New York	12 Nov 1857	30 Sep 1857	863-874	470839
12	43-46	Elise Rübcke	New York	13 Nov 1857	1 Oct 1857	875-886	470839
12	48-50	Ocean Home	New York	2 Dec 1857	2 Oct 1857	887-896	470839
12	50-51	Oder	New York	2 Dec 1857	15 Oct 1857	937-944	470839
12	60-62	Washington	New Orleans	5 Dec 1857	15 Oct 1857	953-960	470839
12	71-72	Nord America	New York	10 Dec 1857	3 Nov 1857	997-1004	470839
12	79-80	Borussia	New York via Southampton	21 Dec 1857	30 Nov 1857	1047-1050	470839
12	81	Heinrich Von Gagern	New Orleans	22 Dec 1857	15 Oct 1857	933-935	470839
12	82-83	Donau	New York	23 Dec 1857	missing	missing	-----
12	86-87	John Herrmann	New York	26 Dec 1857	11 Nov 1857	1025-1028	470839
12	94-97	Von Berg	New York	12 Jan 1858	7 Nov 1857	1009-1020	470839
12	104-106	Howard	New York	22 Feb 1858	16 Nov 1857	1033-1041	470839
12	109-110	Sir Robert Peel	New York	25 Feb 1858	30 Nov 1857	1051-1054	470839
12	111-113	Hammonia	New York via Southampton	2 Apr 1858	15 Mar 1858	1-12	470840
12	117-120	Saxonia	New York via Southampton	20 Apr 1858	31 Mar 1858	13-32	470840
12	121-123	Borussia	New York via Southampton	1 May 1858	14 Apr 1858	83-98	470840
12	125-127	Humboldt	New York	7 May 1858	31 Mar 1858	39-50	470840
12	134-137	Austria	New York via Southampton	18 May 1858	30 Apr 1858	159-176	470840

Germans to America vol. and page nos.		Name of the Ship	Route and U.S. Port(s) of Arrival	Date of Arrival	Date of Departure	*HPL* Page numbers	FHL micro-film no.
12	141-143	Dr. Barth	New York	20 May 1858	15 Apr 1858	123-130	470840
12	148-150	John Bertram	New York	26 May 1858	1 May 1858	195-206	470840
12	150-153	Main	New York	26 May 1858	15 Apr 1858	111-122	470840
12	156-157	Johanna Elise	New York	29 May 1858	15 Apr 1858	103-110	470840
12	163-165	Hammonia	New York via Southampton	1 June 1858	14 May 1858	231-246	470840
12	166-168	Donau	New York	7 June 1858	1 May 1858	177-186	470840
12	169	Sir Isaac Newton	New Orleans	7 June 1858	9 Apr 1858	63-65	470840
12	175-177	Johannes	New York	14 June 1858	1 May 1858	187-194	470840
12	179-181	Saxonia	New York via Southampton	18 June 1858	31 May 1858	307-326	470840
12	186-187	Elise Rübcke	New York	28 June 1858	15 May 1858	255-262	470840
12	187-188	Gutenberg	New York	28 June 1858	15 May 1858	263-266	470840
12	194-195	Borussia	New York via Southampton	1 Jul 1858	14 June 1858	359-374	470840
12	201-202	Elbe	New York	6 Jul 1858	15 May 1858	247-254	470840
12	213-214	Howard	New York	14 Jul 1858	1 Jul 1858	423-426	470840
12	214-215	Austria	New York via Southampton	17 Jul 1858	30 June 1858	403-418	470840
12	218-220	Louis Napoleon	New York	23 Jul 1858	1 June 1858	335-342	470840
12	228-229	Sir Robert Peel	New York	30 Jul 1858	16 June 1858	387-390	470840
12	231-233	Hammonia	New York via Southampton	31 Jul 1858	14 Jul 1858	443-458	470840
12	235-236	Oder	New York	4 Aug 1858	16 June 1858	379-386	470840
12	239	John Hermann	New York	11 Aug 1858	1 Jul 1858	419-420	470840
12	242-243	Saxonia	New York via Southampton	18 Aug 1858	31 Jul 1858	475-484	470840

Germans to America vol. and page nos.		Name of the Ship	Route and U.S. Port(s) of Arrival	Date of Arrival	Date of Departure	*HPL* Page numbers	FHL micro-film no.
12	248-250	Borussia	New York via Southampton	31 Aug 1858	14 Aug 1858	503-516	470840
12	252	Humboldt	New York	7 Sep 1858	17 Jul 1858	459-462	470840
12	261-262	Dr. Barth	New York	14 Sep 1858	2 Aug 1858	493-496	470840
12	263	Neckar	New York	15 Sep 1858	2 Aug 1858	485-492	470840
12	269-270	John Bertram	New York	18 Sep 1858	15 Aug 1858	521-524	470840
12	276-278	Hammonia	New York via Southampton	5 Oct 1858	14 Sep 1858	579-594	470840
12	284-285	Raleigh	New York	15 Oct 1858	1 Sep 1858	559-562	470840
12	290-292	Saxonia	New York via Southampton	20 Oct 1858	30 Sep 1858	611-622	470840
12	298-300	Borussia	New York via Southampton	1 Nov 1858	14 Oct 1858	651-666	470840
12	321-322	Bavaria	New York via Southampton	25 Nov 1858	31 Oct 1858	723-730	470840
12	327-328	Donau	New York	30 Nov 1858	1 Oct 1858	627-634	470840
12	329	Hammonia	New York via Southampton	30 Nov 1858	14 Nov 1858	735-741	470840
12	329-330	Washington	New Orleans	30 Nov 1858	14 Sep 1858	595-598	470840
12	336	Oder	New Orleans	6 Dec 1858	15 Oct 1858	667-669	470840
12	338-340	Gutenberg	New York	8 Dec 1858	1 Oct 1858	635-642	470840
12	344-346	Sir Robert Peel	New York	17 Dec 1858	18 Oct 1858	699-706	470840
12	346	Saxonia	New York via Southampton	24 Dec 1858	30 Nov 1858	757-761	470840
12	351-352	Louis Napoleon	New York	6 Jan 1859	3 Nov 1858	731-734	470840
12	354	Howard	New York	24 Jan 1859	26 Nov 1858	753-754	470840
12	357	Deutschland	New Orleans	27 Jan 1859	19 Nov 1858	749-750	470840
12	364	Borussia	New York via Southampton	21 Mar 1859	28 Feb 1859	1-9	470840

Germans to America vol. and page nos.		Name of the Ship	Route and U.S. Port(s) of Arrival	Date of Arrival	Date of Departure	*HPL* Page numbers	FHL micro-film no.
12	367-368	Hammonia	New York via Southampton	31 Mar 1859	14 Mar 1859	17-28	470840
12	374-377	Saxonia	New York via Southampton	21 Apr 1859	31 Mar 1859	33-48	470840
12	377	Raleigh	New York	23 Apr 1859	1 Mar 1859	13	470840
12	378	Humboldt	New York	25 Apr 1859	missing	missing	-----
12	386-388	Bavaria	New York via Southampton	4 May 1859	14 Apr 1859	73-88	470840
12	388-389	Donau	New York	4 May 1859	1 Apr 1859	49-52	470840
12	399	Dr. Barth	New York	16 May 1859	4 Apr 1859	53-55	470840
12	399-400	Borussia	New York via Southampton	16 May 1859	30 Apr 1859	125-134	470840
12	410-411	Gutenberg	New York	27 May 1859	16 Apr 1859	97-100	470840
12	434-435	Oder	New York	15 June 1859	2 May 1859	135-142	470840
12	438-439	Sir Robert Peel	New York	16 June 1859	2 May 1859	147-154	470840
12	439-441	Saxonia	New York via Southampton	17 June 1859	31 May 1859	219-234	470840
12	446-448	Louis Napoleon	New York	24 June 1859	14 May 1859	185-196	470840
12	453-456	Hammonia	New York	30 June 1859	14 May 1859	169-184	470840
12	456-457	Bavaria	New York via Southampton	2 Jul 1859	14 June 1859	259-274	470840
12	460-461	Deutschland	New York	13 Jul 1859	1 June 1859	243-250	470840
12	461-462	Howard	New York	15 Jul 1859	31 May 1859	239-242	470840
12	466-468	Borussia	New York via Southampton	18 Jul 1859	30 June 1859	287-306	470840
12	471-472	Howard	New York	29 Jul 1859	missing	missing	-----
13	1-2	Teutonia	New York via Southampton	1 Aug 1859	14 Jul 1859	327-338	470840
13	6-7	Saxonia	New York	17 Aug 1859	30 Jul 1859	359-374	470840

Germans to America vol. and page nos.		Name of the Ship	Route and U.S. Port(s) of Arrival	Date of Arrival	Date of Departure	*HPL* Page numbers	FHL micro-film no.
13	10-11	John Bertram	New York	22 Aug 1859	4 Jul 1859	315-317	470840
13	13-14	Donau	New York	25 Aug 1859	8 Jul 1859	319-326	470840
13	15-17	Bavaria	New York via Southampton	1 Sep 1859	13 Aug 1859	395-410	470840
13	20	S. Knapp	New York	17 Sep 1859	30 Jul 1859	355-358	470840
13	21-23	Borussia	New York via Southampton	19 Sep 1859	31 Aug 1859	419-434	470840
13	24-25	Centaurion	New York	21 Sep 1859	1 Aug 1859	375-382	470840
13	31-32	Dr. Barth	New York	29 Sep 1859	16 Aug 1859	411-418	470840
13	35-38	Teutonia	New York via Southampton	4 Oct 1859	14 Sep 1859	447-466	470840
13	40-41	Humboldt	New York	17 Oct 1859	2 Sep 1859	443-445	470840
13	45-47	Hammonia	New York via Southampton	18 Oct 1859	30 Sep 1859	473-484	470840
13	47-48	Main	New York	22 Oct 1859	2 Sep 1859	435-442	470840
13	54-57	Bavaria	New York via Southampton	3 Nov 1859	14 Oct 1859	505-520	470840
13	68-69	Sir Robert Peel	New York	10 Nov 1859	17 Sep 1859	467-472	470840
13	73-74	Elbe	New York	16 Nov 1859	1 Oct 1859	489-492	470840
13	85	Louis Napoleon	New York	21 Nov 1859	4 Oct 1859	493-500	470840
13	87-88	Saxonia	New York via Southampton	22 Nov 1859	31 Oct 1859	561-576	470840
13	91-92	Gellert	New Orleans	29 Nov 1859	4 Oct 1859	501-503	470840
13	97-98	Borussia	New York	19 Dec 1859	30 Nov 1859	605-616	470840
13	98-99	Howard	New York	19 Dec 1859	15 Oct 1859	541-548	470840
13	100-101	Donau	New York	20 Dec 1859	1 Nov 1859	577-580	470840
13	101-102	Gutenberg	New York	20 Dec 1859	1 Nov 1859	581-583	470840

Germans to America vol. and page nos.		Name of the Ship	Route and U.S. Port(s) of Arrival	Date of Arrival	Date of Departure	*HPL* Page numbers	FHL micro-film no.
13	114	Oder	New Orleans	6 Jan 1860	7 Nov 1859	589-591	470840
13	119-120	John Bertram	New York	18 Jan 1860	17 Nov 1859	593-595	470840
13	124-125	Teutonia	New York via Southampton	27 Jan 1860	1 Jan 1860	1-4	470841
13	125	Raleigh	New York	31 Jan 1860	5 Dec 1859	617	470840
13	126-127	Borussia	New York via Southampton	20 Feb 1860	31 Jan 1860	9-12	470841
13	128	Dr. Barth	New York	3 Mar 1860	14 Jan 1860	5	470841
13	134-135	Teutonia	New York via Southampton	19 Mar 1860	29 Feb 1860	13-24	470841
13	136-138	Bavaria	New York via Southampton	2 Apr 1860	15 Mar 1860	29-44	470841
13	146-148	Hammonia	New York	23 Apr 1860	missing	missing	-----
13	152	Humboldt	New York	4 May 1860	2 Mar 1860	25-26	470841
13	157-160	Teutonia	New York via Southampton	8 May 1860	21 Apr 1860	109-128	470841
13	168-170	Donau	New York	11 May 1860	14 Apr 1860	81-92	470841
13	176-177	Sir Robert Peel	New York	12 May 1860	21 Mar 1860	45-52	470841
13	186-187	Louis Napoleon	New York	21 May 1860	14 Apr 1860	101-104	470841
13	190-193	Bavaria	New York via Southampton	26 May 1860	7 May 1860	153-168	470841
13	198-201	Saxonia	New York	30 May 1860	14 May 1860	169-188	470841
13	205-206	Guttenburg	New York	31 May 1860	30 Apr 1860	137-144	470841
13	225-227	Hammonia	New York	18 June 1860	31 May 1860	223-238	470841
13	227-228	John Bertram	New York	18 June 1860	14 May 1860	189-196	470841
13	230-233	Deutschland	New York	19 June 1860	16 May 1860	197-208	470841
13	250	Eleonore Jane	New Orleans	2 Jul 1860	31 Mar 1860	73-74	470841

Germans to America vol. and page nos.		Name of the Ship	Route and U.S. Port(s) of Arrival	Date of Arrival	Date of Departure	*HPL* Page numbers	FHL micro-film no.
13	252-254	Dr. Barth	New York	5 Jul 1860	1 June 1860	239-246	470841
13	259-261	Bavaria	New York	9 Jul 1860	21 June 1860	277-288	470841
13	274-276	Teutonia	New York via Southampton	20 Jul 1860	30 June 1860	297-306	470841
13	278	Ceres	New York	25 Jul 1860	missing	missing	-----
13	281-283	Saxonia	New York via Southampton	31 Jul 1860	14 Jul 1860	319-332	470841
13	286-288	Elise Rübeke	New York	4 Aug 1860	15 Jun 1860	253-264	470841
13	290-291	Regina	New York	13 Aug 1860	16 Jun 1860	269-272	470841
13	298-299	Hammonia	New York via Southampton	17 Aug 1860	31 Jul 1860	351-366	470841
13	308-311	Bavaria	New York via Southampton	3 Sep 1860	14 Aug 1860	379-394	470841
13	313-315	Donau	New York	5 Sep 1860	14 Jul 1860	333-342	470841
13	315-316	Humboldt	New York	5 Sep 1860	16 Jul 1860	343-350	470841
13	316-317	Isaac Newton	New York	6 Sep 1860	30 Jun 1860	311-318	470841
13	330-332	Teutonia	New York via Southampton	18 Sep 1860	1 Sep 1860	419-434	470841
13	335-336	Sir Robert Peel	New York	21 Sep 1860	1 Aug 1860	367-374	470841
13	340-341	Elbe	New York	1 Oct 1860	16 Aug 1860	395-402	470841
13	345-347	Saxonia	New York	3 Oct 1860	14 Sep 1860	443-458	470841
13	347-348	Louis Napoleon	New York	4 Oct 1860	16 Aug 1860	403-410	470841
13	355-356	Borussia	New York via Southampton	18 Oct 1860	1 Oct 1860	475-488	470841
13	361-362	Gutenberg	New York	19 Oct 1860	1 Sep 1860	435-442	470841
13	367-368	John Bertram	New York	22 Oct 1860	15 Sep 1860	467-470	470841
13	381-383	Deutschland	New York	27 Oct 1860	15 Sep 1860	459-466	470841

Germans to America vol. and page nos.		Name of the Ship	Route and U.S. Port(s) of Arrival	Date of Arrival	Date of Departure	*HPL* Page numbers	FHL micro-film no.
13	402-403	Hammonia	New York via Southampton	2 Nov 1860	14 Oct 1860	517-532	470841
13	409-411	Teutonia	New York via Southampton	17 Nov 1860	1 Nov 1860	545-564	470841
13	411-412	Dr. Barth	New York	19 Nov 1860	1 Oct 1860	497-504	470841
13	423	Washington	New Orleans	26 Nov 1860	15 Sep 1860	471-474	470841
13	428-430	Oder	New York	30 Nov 1860	1 Oct 1860	489-496	470841
13	433-434	Gibraltar	New York	5 Dec 1860	15 Oct 1860	533-540	470841
13	435-438	Saxonia	New York via Southampton	7 Dec 1860	14 Nov 1860	581-592	470841
13	448-449	Borussia	New York via Southampton	20 Dec 1860	1 Dec 1860	601-611	470841
13	454-455	Donau	New York	24 Dec 1860	7 Nov 1860	573-580	470841
13	456	Gellert	New York	24 Dec 1860	2 Nov 1860	569-572	470841
14	2	Elise	New York	5 Jan 1861	4 Dec 1860	613	470841
14	6	Teutonia	New York via Southampton	21 Jan 1861	1 Jan 1861	1-8	470841
14	8	Isaac Newton	New York	29 Jan 1861	19 Nov 1860	597-598	470841
14	9-10	Humboldt	New York	4 Feb 1861	8 Dec 1860	615	470841
14	22-24	Borussia	New York via Southampton	2 Apr 1861	15 Mar 1861	33-48	470841
14	28	John Bertram	New York	9 Apr 1861	2 Mar 1861	29-31	470841
14	28	Louis Napoleon	New York	10 Apr 1861	11 Feb 1861	17	470841
14	28-29	Dr. Barth	New York	15 Apr 1861	16 Mar 1861	49-52	470841
14	32-34	Bavaria	New York via Southampton	19 April 1861	31 Mar 1861	53-68	470841
14	42-45	Hammonia	New York via Southampton	30 Apr 1861	14 Apr 1861	77-92	470841
14	52-53	Robert Peel	New York	8 May 1861	2 Apr 1861	69-76	470841

Germans to America vol. and page nos.		Name of the Ship	Route and U.S. Port(s) of Arrival	Date of Arrival	Date of Departure	*HPL* Page numbers	FHL micro-film no.
14	55-58	Saxonia	New York	10 May 1861	1 May 1861	149-168	470841
14	84-86	Humboldt	New York	29 May 1861	18 Apr 1861	125-136	470841
14	87-89	Polynesia	New York	29 May 1861	15 Apr 1861	105-116	470841
14	93-96	Borussia	New York	5 Jun 1861	18 May 1861	243-262	470841
14	109-110	Bavaria	New York via Southampton	18 Jun 1861	1 Jun 1861	267-278	470841
14	116-118	Electric	New York	21 Jun 1861	4 May 1861	193-204	470841
14	128-130	Hammonia	New York via Southampton	2 Jul 1861	15 Jun 1861	307-326	470841
14	130-132	Donau	New York	12 Jun 1861	15 May 1861	219-226	470841
14	135-137	Arcole	New York	13 Jul 1861	17 May 1861	235-242	470841
14	137-139	Mary Hyler	New York	13 Jul 1861	17 May 1861	227-234	470841
14	150	Saxonia	New York via Southampton	16 Jul 1861	29 Jun 1861	343-350	470841
14	160-161	Borussia	New York via Southampton	31 Jul 1861	13 Jul 1861	359-374	470841
14	163	Victoria	New York	5 Aug 1861	17 Jun 1861	327-329	470841
14	164	Raleigh	New York	10 Aug 1861	10 Jun 1861	303-306	470841
14	173-174	Louis Napoleon	New York	27 Aug 1861	3 Jul 1861	355-358	470841
14	175-176	Teutonia	New York via Southampton	29 Aug 1861	10 Aug 1861	401-412	470841
14	179-180	John Bertram	New York	9 Sep 1861	31 Jul 1861	391-396	470841
14	180-181	Hammonia	New York via Southampton	11 Sep 1861	24 Aug 1861	421-432	470841
14	185-186	Saxonia	New York via Southampton	25 Sep 1861	7 Sep 1861	445-456	470841
14	191-193	Bavaria	New York via Southampton	10 Oct 1861	18 Sep 1861	461-479	470841
14	194-195	Dr. Barth	New York	12 Oct 1861	31 Aug 1861	437-444	470841

Germans to America vol. and page nos.		Name of the Ship	Route and U.S. Port(s) of Arrival	Date of Arrival	Date of Departure	*HPL* Page numbers	FHL micro-film no.
14	197-198	Teutonia	New York via Southampton	25 Oct 1861	5 Oct 1861	493-503	470841
14	200-201	Borussia	New York via Southampton	5 Nov 1861	19 Oct 1861	509-516	470841
14	206-208	Donau	New York	20 Nov 1861	15 Oct 1861	509-516	470841
14	208-209	Saxonia	New York via Southampton	20 Nov 1861	7 Nov 1861	549-559	470841
14	209-210	Oder	New York	22 Nov 1861	2 Oct 1861	485-492	470841
14	212	Bavaria	New York	6 Dec 1861	16 Nov 1861	569-576	470841
14	214-215	Electric	New York	16 Dec 1861	15 Oct 1861	505-507	470841
14	215-216	Teutonia	New York	23 Dec 1861	30 Nov 1861	589-595	470841
14	216	Borussia	New York	2 Jan 1862	14 Dec 1861	601-607	470841
14	217	Sir Robert Peel	New York	2 Jan 1862	2 Nov 1861	561-563	470841
14	218	Hammonia	New York	10 Jan 1862	missing	missing	-----
14	219	Saxonia	New York	16 Jan 1862	28 Dec 1861	609-615	470841
14	221	Elbe	New York	25 Jan 1862	16 Nov 1861	577-578	470841
14	221	Bavaria	New York	31 Jan 1862	11 Jan 1862	1-3	470842
14	222-223	Lord Brougham	New York	4 Feb 1862	16 Nov 1861	581-583	470841
14	224	Teutonia	New York via Southampton	17 Feb 1862	24 Jan 1862	5-11	470842
14	225	Borussia	New York	3 Mar 1862	8 Feb 1862	13-16	470842
14	225-226	John Bertram	New York	5 Mar 1862	6 Dec 1861	597-598	470841
14	226-227	Hammonia	New York	11 Mar 1862	22 Feb 1862	17-24	470842
14	229-230	Saxonia	New York	28 Mar 1862	8 Mar 1862	29-36	470842
14	233	Prinz Albert	New York	7 Apr 1862	1 Mar 1862	25-27	470842

Germans to America vol. and page nos.		Name of the Ship	Route and U.S. Port(s) of Arrival	Date of Arrival	Date of Departure	*HPL* Page numbers	FHL micro-film no.
14	234-235	Bavaria	New York via Southampton	19 Apr 1862	22 Mar 1862	45-52	470842
14	238-240	Teutonia	New York via Southampton	23 Apr 1862	5 Apr 1862	61-72	470842
14	241	Donau	New York	25 Apr 1862	17 Mar 1862	41-43	470842
14	248	Andrew	New York	1 May 1862	15 Mar 1862	37-39	470842
14	249-251	Hammonia	New York via Southampton	6 May 1862	19 Apr 1862	137-148	470842
14	253	Humboldt	New York	20 May 1862	8 Apr 1862	81-92	470842
14	255-258	Borussia	New York via Southampton	22 May 1862	3 May 1862	197-216	470842
14	261-263	Saxonia	New York via Southampton	5 Jun 1862	17 May 1862	285-304	470842
14	264	Electric	New York	6 Jun 1862	17 Apr 1862	121-136	470842
14	267-268	Oder	New York	9 Jun 1862	15 Apr 1862	105-112	470842
14	272-273	Ocean	New York	11 Jun 1862	15 Apr 1862	113-116	470842
14	277-279	Bavaria	New York via Southampton	19 Jun 1862	31 May 1862	313-324	470842
14	282-284	John Bertram	New York	24 Jun 1862	15 May 1862	273-284	470842
14	284-286	Sir Robert Peel	New York	24 Jun 1862	30 Apr 1862	185-196	470842
14	292-294	Teutonia	New York via Southampton	1 Jul 1862	14 Jun 1862	349-364	470842
14	295-297	New Orleans	New York	5 Jul 1862	15 May 1862	261-272	470842
14	303-305	Borussia	New York via Southampton	15 Jul 1862	28 Jun 1862	385-396	470842
14	314-316	Columbus	New York	29 Jul 1862	14 Jun 1862	365-376	470842
14	316-317	Darmstädter Bank	New York	29 Jul 1862	19 Jun 1862	381-384	470842
14	319-320	Saxonia	New York	29 Jul 1862	12 Jul 1862	417-432	470842
14	320-321	Goethe	New York	30 Jul 1862	4 Jun 1862	343-348	470842

Germans to America vol. and page nos.		Name of the Ship	Route and U.S. Port(s) of Arrival	Date of Arrival	Date of Departure	*HPL* Page numbers	FHL micro-film no.
14	323-325	Bavaria	New York via Southampton	13 Aug 1862	26 Jul 1862	445-460	470842
14	328-329	Prinz Albert	New York	18 Aug 1862	1 Jul 1862	397-404	470842
14	331-333	Donau	New York via Southampton	19 Aug 1862	15 Jul 1862	433-440	470842
14	336-337	Teutonia	New York via Southampton	27 Aug 1862	9 Aug 1862	469-484	470842
14	344-346	Hammonia	New York via Southampton	9 Sep 1862	23 Aug 1862	501-516	470842
14	356-358	Borussia	New York via Southampton	24 Sep 1862	6 Sep 1862	535-550	470842
14	358-359	Deutschland	New York	24 Sep 1862	15 Aug 1862	485-492	470842
14	365-366	Dr. Barth	New York	4 Oct 1862	19 Aug 1862	493-500	470842
14	366-368	Saxonia	New York	8 Oct 1862	20 Sep 1862	571-586	470842
14	374	Louis Napoleon	New York	16 Oct 1862	2 Sep 1862	527-534	470842
14	376-378	Bavaria	New York via Southampton	25 Oct 1862	4 Oct 1862	623-630	470842
14	378-379	Oder	New York	30 Oct 1862	15 Sep 1862	555-562	470842
14	380-382	Electric	New York	5 Nov 1862	17 Sep 1862	563-570	470842
14	383-384	Hammonia	New York via Southampton	10 Nov 1862	18 Oct 1862	659-670	470842
14	390-392	Sir Robert Peel	New York	17 Nov 1862	30 Sep 1862	591-602	470842
14	392-393	Teutonia	New York via Southampton	20 Nov 1862	1 Nov 1862	687-694	470842
14	395-396	Saxonia	New York via Southampton	4 Dec 1862	15 Nov 1862	709-720	470842
14	397-398	Columbus	New York	12 Dec 1862	15 Oct 1862	635-642	470842
14	398-401	Helene	New York	12 Dec 1862	11 Oct 1862	631-632	470842
14	401-403	John Bertram	New York	15 Dec 1862	15 Oct 1862	651-658	470842
14	403-405	Elbe	New York	19 Dec 1862	15 Oct 1862	643-650	470842

Germans to America vol. and page nos.		Name of the Ship	Route and U.S. Port(s) of Arrival	Date of Arrival	Date of Departure	*HPL* Page numbers	FHL micro-film no.
14	406	Bavaria	New York via Southampton	22 Dec 1862	29 Nov 1862	729-736	470842
14	408-410	Donau	New York	27 Dec 1862	4 Nov 1862	701-708	470842
14	413-414	Hammonia	New York	5 Jan 1863	13 Dec 1862	745-748	470842
14	415-416	Union	New York	12 Jan 1863	1 Oct 1862	603-610	470842
14	417	Teutonia	New York via Southampton	17 Jan 1863	27 Dec 1862	753-757	470842
14	418	Saxonia	New York via Southampton	27 Jan 1863	10 Jan 1863	1-9	472894
14	419	Washington	New York	31 Jan 1863	28 Nov 1862	725-727	470842
14	420	Bavaria	New York	16 Feb 1863	24 Jan 1863	11-13	472894
14	421	Humboldt	New York	24 Feb 1863	3 Jan 1863	not listed	472894
14	421-422	Borussia	New York via Southampton	26 Feb 1863	7 Feb 1863	19-26	472894
14	423-424	Teutonia	New York	16 Mar 1863	21 Feb 1863	27-34	472894
14	424-425	Saxonia	New York via Southampton	27 Mar 1863	7 Mar 1863	39-46	472894
14	427	Dr. Barth	New York	10 Apr 1863	4 Feb 1863	15	472894
14	427-428	Bavaria	New York via Southampton	11 Apr 1863	21 Mar 1863	47-54	472894
14	436	Hammonia	New York via Southampton	22 Apr 1863	4 Apr 1863	91-96	472894
14	437	Sir Robert Peel	New York	22 Apr 1863	3 Mar 1863	35-38	472894
14	440-443	Teutonia	New York	6 May 1863	18 Apr 1863	165-184	472894
14	448-450	Donau	New York	21 May 1863	15 Apr 1863	125-136	472894
14	450-452	Borussia	New York via Southampton	22 May 1863	2 May 1863	225-248	472894
14	452-454	John Bertram	New York	23 May 1863	1 Apr 1863	55-66	472894
15	4-6	Hammonia	New York via Southampton	8 Jun 1863	missing	missing	-----

Germans to America vol. and page nos.		Name of the Ship	Route and U.S. Port(s) of Arrival	Date of Arrival	Date of Departure	*HPL* Page numbers	FHL micro-film no.
15	10-13	Deutschland	New York	20 Jun 1863	16 May 1863	307-322	472894
15	13-14	Kepler	New York	20 Jun 1863	1 May 1863	209-216	472894
15	17-18	Elbe	New York	23 Jun 1863	7 May 1863	201-208	472894
15	21-24	Teutonia	New York	23 Jun 1863	3 Jun 1863	355-370	472894
15	26-28	Schiller	New York	29 Jun 1863	4 May 1863	249-256	472894
15	31-33	Bavaria	New York via Southampton	6 Jul 1863	16 Jun 1863	387-396	472894
15	38-40	Humboldt	New York	10 Jul 1863	1 Jun 1863	343-354	472894
15	41-43	Borussia	New York via Southampton	15 Jul 1863	27 Jun 1863	387-396	472894
15	46-47	Landweihinder	New York	27 Jul 1863	15 May 1863	271-278	472894
15	47-48	Hammonia	New York via Southampton	28 Jul 1863	11 Jul 1863	457-472	472894
15	48-49	Bertha	New York	30 Jul 1863	27 Jun 1863	421-428	472894
15	51-52	Emma Ives	New York	31 Jul 1863	17 Jun 1863	409-412	472894
15	58-59	Clio	New York	4 Aug 1863	19 Jun 1863	413-420	472894
15	61-62	Saxonia	New York via Southampton	11 Aug 1863	25 Jul 1863	493-506	472894
15	68-70	Teutonia	New York via Southampton	27 Aug 1863	8 Aug 1863	515-524	472894
15	70-71	Donau	New York	31 Aug 1863	23 Jul 1863	485-492	472894
15	75	Windspiel	New York	3 Sep 1863	16 Jul 1863	473-475	472894
15	75-78	Germania	New York via Southampton	7 Sep 1863	22 Aug 1863	545-564	472894
15	85-86	Sir Isaac Newton	New York	20 Sep 1863	1 Aug 1863	507-510	472894
15	87-88	Bavaria	New York via Southampton	25 Sep 1863	5 Sep 1863	573-588	472894
15	96-97	Prinz Albert	New York	5 Oct 1863	17 Aug 1863	537-544	472894

Germans to America vol. and page nos.		Name of the Ship	Route and U.S. Port(s) of Arrival	Date of Arrival	Date of Departure	*HPL* Page numbers	FHL micro-film no.
15	98-101	Saxonia	New York	6 Oct 1863	19 Sep 1863	609-628	472894
15	110-113	Hammonia	New York	24 Oct 1863	3 Oct 1863	657-676	472894
15	113-114	Sir Robert Peel	New York	24 Oct 1863	1 Sep 1863	565-572	
15	116-118	Keppler	New York	27 Oct 1863	16 Sep 1863	601-608	472894
15	122-123	Oder	New York	30 Oct 1863	16 Sep 1863	593-600	472894
15	124-127	Deutschland	New York	2 Nov 1863	1 Oct 1863	641-656	472894
15	127-131	Germania	New York	2 Nov 1863	17 Oct 1863	713-736	472894
15	133-134	Old Dominion	New York	10 Nov 1863	3 Oct 1863	689-696	472894
15	137-139	John Bertram	New York	21 Nov 1863	3 Oct 1863	677-688	472894
15	139-142	Teutonia	New York via Southampton	21 Nov 1863	31 Oct 1863	745-768	472894
15	145-148	Saxonia	New York	7 Dec 1863	14 Nov 1863	797-816	472894
15	150-152	Bavaria	New York via Southampton	21 Dec 1863	28 Nov 1863	821-832	472894
15	152-153	Hammonia	New York	29 Dec 1863	12 Dec 1863	849-860	472894
15	157-158	Elbe	New York	2 Jan 1864	27 Oct 1863	737-744	472894
15	160-162	Humboldt	New York	13 Jan 1864	31 Oct 1863	777-788	472894
15	164	Teutonia	New York via Southampton	15 Jan 1864	26 Dec 1863	861-863	472894
15	165	Donau	New York	16 Jan 1864	20 Nov 1863	817-819	472894
15	165-166	Washington	New York	20 Jan 1864	15 Oct 1863	705-712	472894
15	166-168	Hammonia	New York	26 Jan 1864	missing	missing	-----
15	170-171	Germania	New York via Southampton	29 Jan 1864	9 Jan 1864	1-4	472895
15	172-173	Dr. Barth	New York	9 Feb 1864	1 Dec 1863	841-848	472894

Germans to America vol. and page nos.		Name of the Ship	Route and U.S. Port(s) of Arrival	Date of Arrival	Date of Departure	*HPL* Page numbers	FHL micro-film no.
15	181-182	Bavaria	New York via Southampton	9 Mar 1864	20 Feb 1864	13-18	472895
15	188-190	Germania	New York	24 Mar 1864	5 Mar 1864	19-30	472895
15	195-198	Teutonia	New York	5 Apr 1864	19 Mar 1864	31-42	472895
15	204-207	Saxonia	New York	19 Apr 1864	missing	missing	-----
15	214-218	Bavaria	New York via Southampton	6 May 1864	16 Apr 1864	103-118	472895
15	226-230	Germania	New York via Southampton	19 May 1864	30 Apr 1864	131-142	472895
15	239-240	Oder	New York	23 May 1864	2 Apr 1864	57-64	472895
15	250-252	Donau	New York	28 May 1864	15 Apr 1864	83-94	472895
15	255-256	Zingara	New York	30 May 1864	missing	missing	-----
15	256-260	Teutonia	New York	1 Jun 1864	14 May 1864	159-174	472895
15	268-270	Levanter	New York	14 Jun 1864	22 Apr 1864	119-130	472895
15	270-274	Saxonia	New York via Southampton	14 Jun 1864	28 May 1864	215-230	472895
15	281-283	John Bertram	New York	18 Jun 1864	7 May 1864	147-158	472895
15	295-299	Bavaria	New York	1 Jul 1864	11 Jun 1864	263-278	472895
15	299-300	Ema Ives	New York	5 Jul 1864	14 May 1864	203-206	472895
15	300-303	New York	New York via Southampton	5 Jul 1864	missing	missing	-----
15	304-308	Germania	New York	11 Jul 1864	25 Jun 1864	347-366	472895
15	314-316	Electric	New York	18 Jul 1864	31 May 1864	239-250	472895
15	319-322	Golden State	New York	19 Jul 1864	18 May 1864	191-202	472895
15	327-330	Borussia	New York	27 Jul 1864	3 Jul 1864	371-386	472895
15	352-354	Saxonia	New York	8 Aug 1864	23 Jul 1864	419-432	472895

Germans to America vol. and page nos.		Name of the Ship	Route and U.S. Port(s) of Arrival	Date of Arrival	Date of Departure	*HPL* Page numbers	FHL micro-film no.
15	354-357	Deutschland	New York	11 Aug 1864	14, 18 Jun 1864	291-302, 319-334	472895
15	362-363	Elbe	New York	15 Aug 1864	15 Jun 1864	303-310	472895
15	267-268	Nord	New York	15 Aug 1864	missing	missing	-----
15	375-377	Humboldt	New York	18 Aug 1864	23 Jun 1864	335-346	472895
15	379-380	Ernst Brockelman	New York	22 Aug 1864	28 May 1864	207-214	472895
15	380-382	Teutonia	New York via Southampton	23 Aug 1864	6 Aug 1864	445-456	472895
15	394-395	Donau	New York	31 Aug 1864	15 Jul 1864	403-414	472895
15	402-405	Germania	New York via Southampton	5 Sep 1864	20 Aug 1864	473-486	472895
15	409-411	Prinz Albert	New York	9 Sep 1864	3 Aug 1864	437-444	472895
15	417-418	Borussia	New York via Southampton	22 Sep 1864	3 Sep 1864	499-506	472895
15	423-426	Saxonia	New York	3 Oct 1864	17 Sep 1864	515-538	472895
15	439-441	Oder	New York	17 Oct 1864	15 Aug 1864	457-464	472895
15	441-444	Teutonia	New York	19 Oct 1864	1 Oct 1864	547-562	472895
15	447-448	Keppler	New York	25 Oct 1864	2 Sep 1864	490-498	472895
15	454-455	Anna Delius	New York	27 Oct 1864	19 Aug 1864	465-472	472895
16	1-5	Germania	New York	1 Nov 1864	15 Oct 1864	575-598	472895
16	5-7	Dr. Barth	New York	3 Nov 1864	1 Oct 1864	563-574	472895
16	7-9	John Bertram	New York	5 Nov 1864	17 Sep 1864	539-546	472895
16	16-17	Junior	New York	10 Nov 1864	16 Sep 1864	507-514	472895
16	24-27	Borussia	New York via Southampton	23 Nov 1864	29 Oct 1864	649-672	472895
16	30-33	Deutschland	New York	29 Nov 1864	24 Oct 1864	633-648	472895

Germans to America vol. and page nos.		Name of the Ship	Route and U.S. Port(s) of Arrival	Date of Arrival	Date of Departure	*HPL* Page numbers	FHL micro-film no.
16	39-41	Bavaria	New York	7 Dec 1864	12 Nov 1864	673-688	472895
16	44-47	Electric	New York	11 Dec 1864	20 Oct 1864	603-618	472895
16	47-49	Saxonia	New York	19 Dec 1864	10 Dec 1864	709-720	472895
16	61	Borussia	New York via Southampton	30 Jan 1865	7 Jan 1865	1-6	472896
16	64-66	Albert	New York	15 Feb 1865	15 Nov 1864	689-700	472895
16	66-68	Saxonia	New York	20 Feb 1865	4 Feb 1865	7-16	472896
16	74-76	Borussia	New York via Southampton	22 Mar 1865	4 Mar 1865	17-28	472896
16	79-82	Teutonia	New York	6 Apr 1865	18 Mar 1865	33-44	472896
16	87-90	Germania	New York via Southampton	17 Apr 1865	1 Apr 1865	45-60	472896
16	97-98	Prinz Albert	New York	1 May 1865	14 Mar 1865	29-32	472896
16	98-99	Bavaria	New York via Southampton	2 May 1865	15 Apr 1865	83-98	472896
16	111-115	Saxonia	New York	15 May 1865	29 Apr 1865	151-170	472896
16	121-122	Dr. Barth	New York	19 May 1865	1 Apr 1865	61-68	472896
16	126-127	Donau	New York	22 May 1865	15 Apr 1865	99-110	472896
16	137-141	Teutonia	New York via Southampton	2 Jun 1865	15 May 1865	251-270	472896
16	141-143	John Bertram	New York	3 Jun 1865	20 Apr 1865	127-138	472896
16	152-156	Germania	New York	12 Jun 1865	27 May 1865	327-350	472896
16	156-159	Deutschland	New York	14 Jun 1865	1 May 1865	175-190	472896
16	171-175	Bavaria	New York	19 Jun 1865	3 Jun 1865	379-406	472896
16	175-178	Electric	New York	20 Jun 1865	16 May 1865	303-314	472896
16	178-180	Newton	New York	20 Jun 1865	1 May 1865	199-210	472896

Germans to America vol. and page nos.		Name of the Ship	Route and U.S. Port(s) of Arrival	Date of Arrival	Date of Departure	*HPL* Page numbers	FHL micro-film no.
16	185-186	Oder	New York	26 Jun 1865	15 May 1865	271-278	472896
16	188-191	Borussia	New York	27 Jun 1865	10 Jun 1865	411-426	472896
16	204-207	Saxonia	New York	10 Jul 1865	24 Jun 1865	451-476	472896
16	218-220	Fortuna	New York	17 Jul 1865	16 May 1865	315-326	472896
16	227-230	Eugenie	New York	20 Jul 1865	1 Jun 1865	359-370	472896
16	232-236	Teutonia	New York	27 Jul 1865	8 Jul 1865	489-510	472896
16	236-240	Bavaria	New York	31 Jul 1865	15 Jul 1865	533-552	472896
16	254-258	Germania	New York	7 Aug 1865	22 Jul 1865	511-532	472896
16	261-262	Meridian	New York	10 Aug 1865	15 Jun 1865	443-450	472896
16	274276	Humboldt	New York	18 Aug 1865	15 Jun 1865	431-442	472896
16	278-287	Borussia	New York	22 Aug 1865	5 Aug 1865	589-608	472896
16	287-289	Prinz Albert	New York	27 Aug 1865	15 Jul 1865	563-574	472896
16	292-294	Donau	New York	30 Aug 1865	15 Jul 1865	553-562	472896
16	302-306	Saxonia	New York	4 Sep 1865	19 Aug 1865	651-676	472896
16	312-315	Teutonia	New York	11 Sep 1865	26 Aug 1865	685-710	472896
16	341-345	Germania	New York	20 Sep 1865	2 Sep 1865	711-734	472896
16	345-347	Dr. Barth	New York	23 Sep 1865	2 Aug 1865	579-588	472896
16	357-361	Bavaria	New York	28 Sep 1865	9 Sep 1865	747-770	472896
16	361-364	Deutschland	New York	28 Sep 1865	15 Aug 1865	637-650	472896
16	376-380	Allemania	New York	2 Oct 1865	15 Sep 1865	791-812	472896
16	382-384	Gellert	New York	2 Oct 1865	15 Aug 1865	625-636	472896

Germans to America vol. and page nos.		Name of the Ship	Route and U.S. Port(s) of Arrival	Date of Arrival	Date of Departure	*HPL* Page numbers	FHL micro-film no.
16	407-411	Borussia	New York	20 Oct 1865	30 Sep 1865	833-850	472896
16	412-416	Teutonia	New York	26 Oct 1865	7 Oct 1865	895-916	472896
16	423-425	Keppler	New York	28 Oct 1865	2 Sep 1865	735-746	472896
16	439-444	Saxonia	New York	1 Nov 1865	14 Oct 1865	962-985	472896
16	451-453	Copernicus	New York	2 Nov 1865	16 Sep 1865	813-824	472896
17	3-4	Newton	New York	4 Nov 1865	16 Sep 1865	825-832	472896
17	4-9	Germania	New York	6 Nov 1865	21 Oct 1865	1014-1037	472896
17	25-27	Oder	New York	11 Nov 1865	15 Sep 1865	783-790	472896
17	38-42	Bavaria	New York	16 Nov 1865	28 Oct 1865	1062-1083a	472896
17	48-50	John Bertram	New York	20 Nov 1865	2 Oct 1865	883-894	472896
17	54-57	Harry Bluff	New York	20 Nov 1865	2 Oct 1865	851-866	472896
17	75-79	Allemannia	New York via Southampton	29 Nov 1865	11 Nov 1865	1140-1161	472896
17	83-86	Valley Forge	New York	1 Dec 18ß65	12 Oct 1865	937-949	472896
17	92-95	Wizard King	New York	6 Dec 1865	18 Oct 1865	998-1013	472896
17	100-104	Teutonia	New York	12 Dec 1865	25 Nov 1865	1190-1211	472896
17	105-107	Delft Haven	New York	14 Dec 1865	24 Oct 1865	1050-1061	472896
17	118-122	Saxonia	New York	28 Dec 1865	7 Dec 1865	1220-1241	472896
17	133-134	Thatcher Magoun	New York	6 Jan 1866	20 Nov 1865	1162-1167	472896
17	135-137	Washington	New York	9 Jan 1866	3 Nov 1865	1098-1105	472896
17	138-140	Deutschland	New York	12 Jan 1866	21 Nov 1865	1180-1189	472896
17	145-147	Borussia	New York	16 Jan 1866	23 Dec 1865	1242-1249	472896

Germans to America vol. and page nos.		Name of the Ship	Route and U.S. Port(s) of Arrival	Date of Arrival	Date of Departure	*HPL* Page numbers	FHL micro-film no.
17	152-155	Eugenie	New York	23 Jan 1866	15 Oct 1865	986-997	472896
17	160-161	Germania	New York	26 Jan 1866	6 Jan 1866	1-10	472897
17	165-168	Albert	New York	2 Feb 1866	17 Nov 1865	1168-1179	472896
17	168-170	Bavaria	New York via Southampton	8 Feb 1866	20 Jan 1866	11-20	472897
17	173-174	Prinz Albert	New York	10 Feb 1866	7 Dec 1865	1212-1214	472896
17	179-181	Allemania	New York	21 Feb 1866	3 Feb 1866	21-34	472897
17	188-191	Borussia	New York	8 Mar 1866	17 Feb 1866	35-52	472897
17	197-199	Donau	New York	14 Mar 1866	missing	missing	-----
17	205-208	Humboldt	New York	16 Mar 1866	10 Nov 1865	1128-1139	472896
17	208-212	Germania	New York	19 Mar 1866	3 Mar 1866	53-76	472897
17	225	Dr. Barth	New York	2 Apr 1866	missing	missing	-----
17	226-230	Bavaria	New York	5 Apr 1866	17 Mar 1866	99-120	472897
17	231-233	Hertha	New York	6 Apr 1866	21 Oct 1865	1038-1049	472896
17	250-254	Saxonia	New York	16 Apr 1866	30 Mar 1866	121-142	472897
17	258-263	Teutonia	New York	23 Apr 1866	7 Apr 1866	176-195	472897
17	268-272	Allemannia	New York	30 Apr 1866	14 Apr 1866	206-227	472897
17	289-294	Borussia	New York	7 May 1866	21 Apr 1866	338-359	472897
17	312-314	Electric	New York	14 May 1866	15 Mar 1866	77-98	472897
17	320-322	Herschell	New York	15 May 1866	1 Apr 1866	163-175	472897
17	329-331	Oder	New York	17 May 1866	31 Mar 1866	143-150	472897
17	331	Eidswold	New York	21 May 1866	missing	missing	-----

Germans to America vol. and page nos.		Name of the Ship	Route and U.S. Port(s) of Arrival	Date of Arrival	Date of Departure	*HPL* Page numbers	FHL micro-film no.
17	331-336	Bavaria	New York	22 May 1866	5 May 1866	404-428	472897
17	341-344	Deutschland	New York	22 May 1866	15 Apr 1866	228-243	472897
17	360-365	Saxonia	New York	26 May 1866	12 May 1866	450-471	472897
17	386-388	Undine	New York	2 Jun 1866	18 Apr 1866	296-305	472897
17	404-406	Eugenie	New York	5 Jun 1866	18 Apr 1866	306-317	472897
17	419-423	Palmerston	New York	7 Jun 1866	23 Apr 1866	318-337	472897
17	423-425	Prinz Albert	New York	7 Jun 1866	1 May 1866	386-394	472897
17	434-439	Allemannia	New York	11 Jun 1866	26 May 1866	601-626	472897
17	447-448	Henriette	New York	12 Jun 1866	15 Apr 1866	244-251	472897
18	8-13	Teutonia	New York	14 Jun 1866	19 May 1866	517-540	472897
18	18-22	Borussia	New York	18 Jun 1866	2 Jun 1866	65-675	472897
18	33-34	Florentin	New York	20 Jun 1866	15 May 1866	487-491	472897
18	43-47	Germania	New York	25 Jun 1866	28 Apr 1866	362-385	472897
18	53-58	Bavaria	New York	2 Jul 1866	15 Jun 1866	740-765	472897
18	63-64	Alpha	New York	5 Jul 1866	16 May 1866	504-511	472897
18	66-68	Apollo	New York	6 Jul 1866	15 May 1866	492-497b	472897
18	68-70	John Bertram	New York	7 Jul 1866	25 May 1866	631-642	472897
18	70-74	Saxonia	New York	9 Jul 1866	23 Jun 1866	786-799	472897
18	93-96	Teutonia	New York	17 Jul 1866	30 Jun 1866	808-829	472897
18	102-106	Allemannia	New York	21 Jul 1866	7 Jul 1866	830-852	472897
18	111-113	Jessie	New York	25 Jul 1866	2 Jun 1866	676-683	472897

Germans to America vol. and page nos.		Name of the Ship	Route and U.S. Port(s) of Arrival	Date of Arrival	Date of Departure	*HPL* Page numbers	FHL micro-film no.
18	120-123	Borussia	New York	30 Jul 1866	14 Jul 1866	853-870	472897
18	129	Hugo Georg	New York	30 Jul 1866	2 Jun 1866	704-707	472897
18	136-137	Dr. Barth	New York	3 Aug 1866	15 Jun 1866	766-773	472897
18	142-143	Ann & Lizzy	New York	6 Aug 1866	15 Jun 1866	732-739	472897
18	145-148	Germania	New York	6 Aug 1866	9 Jun 1866	708-731	472897
18	154-156	Emil	New York	15 Aug 1866	15 Jun 1866	774-781	472897
18	158-160	Bavaria	New York	20 Aug 1866	28 Jul 1866	903-914	472897
18	160-162	Saxonia	New York	21 Aug 1866	4 Aug 1866	923-936	472897
18	176-178	Teutonia	New York	28 Aug 1866	11 Aug 1866	937-951	472897
18	186-190	Allemannia	New York	3 Sep 1866	18 Aug 1866	952-973	472897
18	190-191	Lord Brougham	New York	3 Sep 1866	30 Jun 1866	800-807	472897
18	194-195	Electric	New York	7 Sep 1866	31 July 1866	915-922	472897
18	202	Victoria	New York	10 Sep 1866	14 Jul 1866	881-884	472897
18	203-204	Oder	New York	11 Sep 1866	14 Jul 1866	871-880	472897
18	208-211	Borussia	New York	22 Sep 1866	1 Sep 1866	986-1007	472897
18	231-233	Eugenie	New York	29 Sep 1866	18 Aug 1866	974-985	472897
18	233-238	Allemannia	New York	2 Oct 1866	missing	missing	-----
18	246-249	Saxonia	New York	5 Oct 1866	15 Sep 1866	1017-1040	472897
18	262-265	Teutonia	New York	11 Oct 1866	22 Sep 1866	1061-1078	472897
18	274-277	Bavaria	New York	15 Oct 1866	29 Sep 1866	1079-1100	472897
18	283-284	Palmerston	New York	20 Oct 1866	1 Sep 1866	1008-1016	472897

Germans to America vol. and page nos.		Name of the Ship	Route and U.S. Port(s) of Arrival	Date of Arrival	Date of Departure	*HPL* Page numbers	FHL micro-film no.
18	300-302	Deutschland	New York	25 Oct 1866	15 Sep 1866	1049-1060	472897
18	304-309	Allemannia	New York	29 Oct 1866	13 Oct 1866	1129-1156	472897
18	318-320	Herschel	New York	3 Nov 1866	15 Sep 1866	1041-1048	472897
18	331-335	Borussia	New York	7 Nov 1866	20 Oct 1866	1195-1214	472897
18	346-350	Saxonia	New York	12 Nov 1866	27 Oct 1866	1215-1246	472897
18	355-358	John Bertram	New York	15 Nov 1866	1 Oct 1866	1101-1116	472897
18	374-380	Teutonia	New York	22 Nov 1866	3 Nov 1866	1253-1274	472897
18	380-384	Germania	New York	26 Nov 1866	10 Nov 1866	1295-1316	472897
18	395-397	Jessie	New York	3 Dec 1866	15 Oct 1866	1157-1163	472897
18	403-405	Dr. Barth	New York	7 Dec 1866	16 Oct 1866	1165-1176	472897
18	405-408	Bavaria	New York	13 Dec 1866	24 Nov 1866	1325-1342	472897
18	411-414	Neckar	New York	17 Dec 1866	15 Oct 1866	1177-1194	472897
18	419-421	Allemannia	New York	26 Dec 1866	8 Dec 1866	1346a-1363	472897
18	422-424	Prinz Albert	New York	27 Dec 1866	31 Oct 1866	1241-1252	472897
19	12-13	Geestemunde	New York	8 Jan 1867	3 Nov 1866	1275-1282	472897
19	15-16	Saxonia	New York via Southampton	12 Jan 1867	22 Dec 1866	1364-1373	472897
19	20-21	Germania	New York	23 Jan 1867	5 Jan 1867	1-5	472898
19	25-27	John Lawrence	New York	28 Jan 1867	6 Nov 1866	1283-1294	472897
19	29-30	Electric	New York	29 Jan 1867	17 Nov 1866	1317-1324	472897
19	34	Victoria	New York	14 Feb 1867	6 Dec 1866	1343-1345	472897
19	41-42	Allemannia	New York	21 Feb 1867	2 Feb 1867	16-25	472898

Germans to America vol. and page nos.		Name of the Ship	Route and U.S. Port(s) of Arrival	Date of Arrival	Date of Departure	*HPL* Page numbers	FHL micro-film no.
19	51-55	Teutonia	New York	8 Mar 1867	16 Feb 1867	26-35	472898
19	62-65	Hammonia	New York	16 Mar 1867	2 Mar 1867	36-53	472898
19	79	Galena	New York	27 Mar 1867	missing	missing	-----
19	110-111	Dr. Barth	New York	4 May 1867	15 Mar 1867	62-69	472898
19	124-128	Teutonia	New York	10 May 1867	20 Apr 1867	236-255	472898
19	132-136	Hammonia	New York	13 May 1867	27 Apr 1867	260-281	472898
19	143-148	Saxonia	New York	17 May 1867	16 Mar 1867	70-87	472898
19	165-169	Palmerston	New York	20 May 1867	1 Apr 1867	122-137	472898
19	190-195	Germania	New York	27 May 1867	23 Mar 1867	88-103	472898
19	212-216	Bavaria	New York	31 May 1867	19 Jan 1867	7-15	472898
19	227-230	Electric	New York	4 Jun 1867	1 May 1867	299-314	472898
19	232-235	John Bertram	New York	4 Jun 1867	15 Apr 1867	192-204	472898
19	239-243	Borussia	New York	5 Jun 1867	6 Apr 1867	150-171	472898
19	257-262	Allemannia	New York	10 Jun 1867	25 May 1867	507-528	472898
19	262-264	Herschel	New York	10 Jun 1867	1 May 1867	315-326	472898
19	264-266	Victoria	New York	10 Jun 1867	1 May 1867	327-334	472898
19	279-284	Cimbria	New York	13 Jun 1867	13 Apr 1867	172-191	472898
19	318-319	Eulalia	New York	22 Jun 1867	16 May 1867	445-452	472898
19	325-330	Hammonia	New York	24 Jun 1867	8 Jun 1867	579-600	472898
19	341-343	Sir John Lawrence	New York	25 Jun 1867	15 May 1867	433-444	472898
19	360-364	Teutonia	New York	1 Jul 1867	15 Jun 1867	605-624	472898

Germans to America vol. and page nos.		Name of the Ship	Route and U.S. Port(s) of Arrival	Date of Arrival	Date of Departure	*HPL* Page numbers	FHL micro-film no.
19	368-372	Saxonia	New York	6 Jul 1867	22 Jun 1867	645-666	472898
19	387-390	Germania	New York	15 Jul 1867	29 Jun 1867	667-684	472898
19	394-397	Humboldt	New York	18 Jul 1867	1 Jun 1867	567-578	472898
19	397-400	Allemannia	New York	20 Jul 1867	6 Jul 1867	700-717	472898
19	420-422	Borussia	New York	29 Jul 1867	13 Jul 1867	718-727	472898
19	424-427	Shakespeare	New York	30 Jul 1867	15 Jun 1867	625-640	472898
19	436-439	Cimbria	New York	5 Aug 1867	20 Jul 1867	740-759	472898
19	451-452	Teutonia	New York	14 Aug 1867	27 Jul 1867	760-769	472898
19	453-456	Hammonia	New York	15 Aug 1867	3 Aug 1867	782-803	472898
20	10-12	Saxonia	New York	26 Aug 1867	10 Aug 1867	804-817	472898
20	18-21	Germania	New York	30 Aug 1867	17 Aug 1867	828-849	472898
20	23-25	Prinz Albert	New York	30 Aug 1867	30 Jun 1867	685-696	472898
20	25-27	Reichstag	New York	31 Aug 1867	19 Jul 1867	728-739	472898
20	45-47	Allemannia	New York	9 Sep 1867	24 Aug 1867	850-868	472898
20	49	Raleigh	New York	9 Sep 1867	13 Jul 1867	pages not numbered	472898
20	54-57	Cimbria	New York	13 Sep 1867	31 Aug 1867	869-894	472898
20	63-65	Dr. Barth	New York	16 Sep 1867	2 Aug 1867	770-781	472898
20	83-85	Teutonia	New York	23 Sep 1867	7 Sep 1867	905-918	472898
20	88-89	John Bertram	New York	24 Sep 1867	15 Aug 1867	818-825	472898
20	95-100	Hammonia	New York	30 Sep 1867	15 Sep 1867	919-941	472898
20	115-118	Saxonia	New York	8 Oct 1867	21 Sep 1867	961-975	472898

Germans to America vol. and page nos.		Name of the Ship	Route and U.S. Port(s) of Arrival	Date of Arrival	Date of Departure	*HPL* Page numbers	FHL micro-film no.
20	136-141	Borussia	New York	23 Oct 1867	5 Oct 1867	1031-1050	472898
20	146-147	Washington	New York	24 Oct 1867	1 Sep 1867	895-902	472898
20	150-154	Allemannia	New York	28 Oct 1867	12 Oct 1867	1053-1072	472898
20	165-169	Cimbria	New York	2 Nov 1867	19 Oct 1867	1099-1118	472898
20	169-171	Eugenie	New York	2 Nov 1867	15 Sep 1867	942-954	472898
20	175-178	Germania	New York	5 Nov 1867	28 Sep 1867	976-991	472898
20	183-184	John Lawrence	New York	8 Nov 1867	18 Sep 1867	954-960	472898
20	191-195	Hammonia	New York	9 Nov 1867	26 Oct 1867	1129-1152	472898
20	214-217	Herschel	New York	20 Nov 1867	2 Oct 1867	1022-1030	472898
20	224-228	Saxonia	New York	25 Nov 1867	9 Nov 1867	1185-1205	472898
20	228-233	Palmerston	New York	26 Nov 1867	1 Oct 1867	1002-1030	472898
20	238-239	Teutonia	New Orleans via Southampton	27 Nov 1867	1 Nov 1867	1152-1156	472898
20	252-254	Borussia	New York	12 Dec 1867	23 Nov 1867	1210-1222	472898
20	261-263	Lord Brougham	New York	18 Dec 1867	15 Oct 1867	1073-1083	472898
20	265-268	Humboldt	New York	23 Dec 1867	16 Oct 1867	1084-1094	472898
20	268-270	Cimbria	New York	24 Dec 1867	7 Dec 1867	1225-1237	472898
20	270-273	Electric	New York	24 Dec 1867	1 Nov 1867	1172-1184	472898
20	275	Franklin	New York	26 Dec 1867	16 Oct 1867	1095-1098	472898
20	282-283	Hammonia	New York	6 Jan 1868	21 Dec 1867	1238-1243	472898
20	289-290	Shakespeare	New York	17 Jan 1868	15 Nov 1867	1206-1209	472898
20	291-294	Leibnitz	New York	21 Jan 1868	1 Nov 1867	1157-1174	472898

Germans to America vol. and page nos.		Name of the Ship	Route and U.S. Port(s) of Arrival	Date of Arrival	Date of Departure	*HPL* Page numbers	FHL micro-film no.
20	295	Germania	New York	23 Jan 1868	8 Jan 1868	1-5	472899
20	301-302	Allemannia	New York	6 Feb 1868	22 Jan 1868	6-10	472899
20	302	Prinz Albert	New York	6 Feb 1868	7 Dec 1867	1223-1224	472898
20	309-310	Cimbria	New York	18 Feb 1868	5 Feb 1868	11-19	472899
20	334-337	Germania	New York	21 Mar 1868	4 Mar 1868	33-46	472899
20	346-349	Allemannia	New York	26 Mar 1868	11 Mar 1868	50-63	472899
20	349-351	Borussia	New York	27 Mar 1868	7 Mar 1868	49	472899
20	358-362	Cimbria	New York	31 Mar 1868	18 Mar 1868	68-85	472899
20	368-372	Saxonia	New York	9 Apr 1868	25 Mar 1868	86-104	472899
20	382-386	Hammonia	New York	15 Apr 1868	1 Apr 1868	105-123	472899
20	400-404	Teutonia	New York	25 Apr 1868	8 Apr 1868	177-194	472899
20	416-420	Germania	New York	2 May 1868	15 Apr 1868	198-215	472899
20	429-434	Allemannia	New York	7 May 1868	22 Apr 1868	258-281	472899
20	448-452	Cimbria	New York	12 May 1868	29 Mar 1868	286-305	472899
20	452-453	Herschel	New York	12 May 1868	16 Mar 1868	64-67	472899
21	5-10	Bavaria	New York	18 May 1868	2 May 1868	336-355	472899
21	26-31	Saxonia	New York	21 May 1868	6 May 1868	378-397	472899
21	33-34	Eugenie	New York	23 May 1868	1 Mar 1868	29-32	472899
21	34-38	Hammonia	New York	23 May 1868	12 May 1868	415-434	472899
21	49-51	John Bertram	New York	25 May 1868	1 Apr 1868	124-135	472899
21	71-75	Borussia	New York	2 Jun 1868	16 May 1868	453-471	472899

Germans to America vol. and page nos.		Name of the Ship	Route and U.S. Port(s) of Arrival	Date of Arrival	Date of Departure	*HPL* Page numbers	FHL micro-film no.
21	88-91	Palmerston	New York	6 Jun 1868	16 Apr 1868	231-244	472899
21	92-95	Teutonia	New York	6 Jun 1868	20 May 1868	472-489	472899
21	118-122	Germania	New York	10 Jun 1868	27 May 1868	496-513	472899
21	137-142	Allemannia	New York	17 Jun 1868	3 Jun 1868	528-550	472899
21	145-148	Electric	New York	19 Jun 1868	15 May 1868	435-447	472899
21	150-153	Humboldt	New York	20 Jun 1868	2 May 1868	356-366	472899
21	163-167	Holsatia	New York	22 Jun 1868	10 Jun 1868	571-589	472899
21	168-170	Prinz Albert	New York	23 Jun 1868	1 May 1868	306-314	472899
21	170-175	Bavaria	New York	24 Jun 1868	9 Jun 1868	551-570	472899
21	194-197	Cymbria	New York	30 Jun 1868	17 Jun 1868	597-617	472899
21	225-230	Saxonia	New York	8 Jul 1868	24 Jun 1868	618-637	472899
21	231-234	Borussia	New York	13 Jul 1868	27 Jun 1868	648-659	472899
21	241-245	Hammonia	New York	14 Jul 1868	1 Jul 1868	660-678	472899
21	260-262	Reichstag	New York	17 Jul 1868	32 May 1868	517-527	472899
21	278-282	Germania	New York	21 Jul 1868	8 Jul 1868	679-696	472899
21	291-295	Allemannia	New York	29 Jul 1868	15 Jul 1868	707-725	472899
21	307-309	Mazatlan	New York	1 Aug 1868	16 Jun 1868	590-596	472899
21	309-313	Holsatia	New York	3 Aug 1868	22 Jul 1868	726-744	472899
21	323-328	Cimbria	New York	11 Aug 1868	29 Jul 1868	747-767	472899
21	348-352	Saxonia	New York via Southampton	19 Aug 1868	5 Aug 1868	768-786	472899
21	359-360	Dr. Barth	New York	24 Aug 1868	9 Jul 1868	697-706	472899

Germans to America vol. and page nos.		Name of the Ship	Route and U.S. Port(s) of Arrival	Date of Arrival	Date of Departure	*HPL* Page numbers	FHL micro-film no.
21	362-366	Hammonia	New York	25 Aug 1868	12 Aug 1868	794-816	472899
21	380-383	Germania	New York	2 Sep 1868	19 Aug 1868	821-840	472899
21	391-393	Shakespeare	New York	9 Sep 1868	5 Aug 1868	787-793	472899
21	393-395	Allemannia	New York	10 Sep 1868	26 Aug 1868	841-854	472899
21	402-405	Holsatia	New York	14 Sep 1868	2 Sep 1868	866-883	472899
21	412-413	Borussia	New York	16 Sep 1868	29 Aug 1868	855-858	472899
21	429-431	Cimbria	New York	22 Sep 1868	9 Sep 1868	889-904	472899
21	444-448	Westphalia	New York	28 Sep 1868	16 Sep 1868	905-925	472899
22	2-3	Herschel	New York	2 Oct 1868	18 Aug 1868	817-820	472899
22	10-12	Hammonia	New York	6 Oct 1868	23 Sep 1868	939-952	472899
22	20	Glenalladale	New York	10 Oct 1868	missing	missing	-----
22	25-26	John Bertram	New York	12 Oct 1868	2 Sep 1868	884-888	472899
22	28-32	Germania	New York	15 Oct 1868	30 Sep 1868	956-874	472899
22	42-45	Teutonia	New York	20 Oct 1868	3 Oct 1868	1008-1022	472899
22	46-50	Allemannia	New York	21 Oct 1868	7 Oct 1868	1023-1041	472899
22	62-64	Gutenberg	New York	26 Oct 1868	16 Sep 1868	926-934	472899
22	65-70	Hamburg	New York	27 Oct 1868	missing	missing	-----
22	77-82	Cimbria	New York	4 Nov 1868	21 Oct 1868	1096-1118	472899
22	90-95	Westphalia	New York	10 Nov 1868	28 Oct 1868	1125-1144	472899
22	103-108	Hammonia	New York	19 Nov 1868	4 Nov 1868	1191-1210	472899
22	118-120	Germania	New York	24 Nov 1868	11 Nov 1868	1211-1220	472899

Germans to America vol. and page nos.		Name of the Ship	Route and U.S. Port(s) of Arrival	Date of Arrival	Date of Departure	*HPL* Page numbers	FHL micro-film no.
22	120-122	Humboldt	New York	24 Nov 1868	1 Oct 1868	987-998	472899
22	127-128	Bavaria	New Orleans via Havre	27 Nov 1868	1 Nov 1868	1185-1190	472899
22	128-133	Borussia	New York	27 Nov 1868	31 Oct 1868	1145-1162	472899
22	147-149	Holsatia	New York	8 Dec 1868	14 Oct 1868	1044a-1067	472899
22	156-158	Cimbria	New York	18 Dec 1868	2 Dec 1868	1250-1256	472899
22	161-162	Westphalia	New York	23 Dec 1868	9 Dec 1868	1257-1262	472899
22	163-166	Electric	New York	26 Dec 1868	1 Nov 1868	1163-1173	472899
22	166-168	Eugenie	New York	28 Dec 1868	15 Oct 1868	1078-1089	472899
22	172	Teutonia	New Orleans via Havana and Havre	31 Dec 1868	1 Dec 1868	1246-1249	472899
22	173-175	Prinz Albert	New York	4 Jan 1869	15 Oct 1868	1068-1077	472899
22	177-180	Reichstag	New York	6 Jan 1869	1 Nov 1868	1174-1184	472899
22	180-181	Allemannia	New York	11 Jan 1869	23 Dec 1868	1265-1268	472899
22	189-192	Hammonia	New York	20 Jan 1869	6 Jan 1869	1-11	472900
22	195	Saxonia	New Orleans via Havre	26 Jan 1869	31 Dec 1868	1269-1270	472899
22	196	Holsatia	New York	29 Jan 1869	13 Jan 1869	12-14	472900
22	197-198	Cimbria	New York	5 Feb 1869	20 Jan 1869	15-18	472900
22	202-203	Westphalia	New York via Havre	10 Feb 1869	27 Jan 1869	19-22	472900
22	205-206	Allemannia	New York via Havre	20 Feb 1869	3 Feb 1869	25-29	472900
22	208-209	Hammonia	New York via Havre	27 Feb 1869	10 Feb 1869	30-35	472900
22	214-215	Bavaria	New Orleans	4 Mar 1869	1 Feb 1869	23-24	472900
22	215-217	Holsatia	New York	4 Mar 1869	17 Feb 1869	36-45	472900

Germans to America vol. and page nos.		Name of the Ship	Route and U.S. Port(s) of Arrival	Date of Arrival	Date of Departure	*HPL* Page numbers	FHL micro-film no.
22	219-220	Cimbria	New York	12 Mar 1869	24 Feb 1869	46-55	472900
22	229-233	Germania	New York via Havre	18 Mar 1869	3 Mar 1869	60-75	472900
22	240-244	Westphalia	New York via Havre	25 Mar 1869	10 Mar 1869	76-94	472900
22	253-254	Teutonia	New Orleans via Havana and Havre	31 Mar 1869	1 Mar 1869	56-59	472900
22	255-259	Saxonia	New York via Havre	2 Apr 1869	14 Mar 1869	100-120	472900
22	270-273	Hammonia	New York via Havre	6 Apr 1869	24 Mar 1869	122-137	472900
22	290-295	Allemannia	New York via Havre	17 Apr 1869	31 Mar 1869	138-156	472900
22	303-307	Holsatia	New York via Havre	21 Apr 1869	7 Apr 1869	185-205	472900
22	321-327	Germania	New York via Havre	29 Apr 1869	14 Apr 1869	237-260	472900
22	349-354	Cimbria	New York	5 May 1869	21 Apr 1869	295-316	472900
22	388-393	Westphalia	New York	11 May 1869	28 Apr 1869	319-324	472900
22	393-394	Prinz Albert	New York	12 May 1869	15 Mar 1869	95-99	472900
22	410-414	Bavaria	New York	17 May 1869	1 May 1869	343-365	472900
22	419-424	Hammonia	New York	19 May 1869	5 May 1869	373-395	472900
22	430-434	Borussia	New York	24 May 1869	8 May 1869	396-415	472900
22	446-449	Reichstag	New York	24 May 1869	15 Apr 1869	275-286	472900
22	460-463	Eugenie	New York	27 May 1869	15 Apr 1869	264-274	472900
22	467-471	Allemannia	New York via Havre	28 May 1869	12 May 1869	435-454	472900
23	2-6	Holsatia	New York via Havre	1 Jun 1869	19 May 1869	467-485	472900
23	14-19	Saxonia	New York	5 Jun 1869	22 May 1869	494-517	472900
23	25-29	Germania	New York via Havre	9 Jun 1869	26 May 1869	518-535	472900

Germans to America vol. and page nos.		Name of the Ship	Route and U.S. Port(s) of Arrival	Date of Arrival	Date of Departure	*HPL* Page numbers	FHL micro-film no.
23	52-56	Teutonia	New York	14 Jun 1869	29 May 1869	542-563	472900
23	57-61	Cimbria	New York	15 Jun 1869	2 Jun 1869	573-592	472900
23	64-66	Mathilde	New York	16 Jun 1869	8 May 1869	416-425	472900
23	79-83	Westphalia	New York via Havre	23 Jun 1869	9 Jun 1869	595a-611	472900
23	89-91	Bavaria	New York	28 Jun 1869	12 Jun 1869	617-627	472900
23	91-92	Herrmann	New York	28 Jun 1869	2 May 1869	366-369	472900
23	96-99	Hammonia	New York via Havre	29 Jun 1869	16 Jun 1869	629a-643	472900
23	104-105	Cimbria	New York via Havre	4 Jul 1869	missing	missing	-----
23	106-108	Lord Brougham	New York	6 Jul 1869	14 May 1869	454-463	472900
23	110-114	Silesia	New York via Havre	6 Jul 1869	23 Jun 1869	650-666	472900
23	119-121	Friedeburg	New York	7 Jul 1869	31 May 1869	564-572	472900
23	138-139	Caroline	New York	13 Jul 1869	26 May 1869	536-541	472900
23	144-147	Allemannia	New York via Havre	15 Jul 1869	30 Jun 1869	667-684	472900
23	157-160	Holsatia	New York	20 Jul 1869	7 Jul 1869	690-704	472900
23	177-180	Germania	New York	29 Jul 1869	14 Jul 1869	708-721	472900
23	184-186	Cimbria	New York via Havre	4 Aug 1869	21 Jul 1869	722-732	472900
23	190-191	Dr. Barth	New York	6 Aug 1869	17 Jun 1869	644-649	472900
23	199-202	Westphalia	New York via Havre	11 Aug 1869	28 Jul 1869	733-747	472900
23	210-213	Hammonia	New York via Havre	18 Aug 1869	4 Aug 1869	754-769	472900
23	213-214	Shakespeare	New York	18 Aug 1869	1 Jul 1869	685-689	472900
23	227-230	Silesia	New York	24 Aug 1869	11 Aug 1869	770-789	472900

Germans to America vol. and page nos.		Name of the Ship	Route and U.S. Port(s) of Arrival	Date of Arrival	Date of Departure	*HPL* Page numbers	FHL micro-film no.
23	246-250	Saxonia	New York via Havre	2 Sep 1869	18 Aug 1869	800-821	472900
23	258-261	Holsatia	New York	8 Sep 1869	25 Aug 1869	822-839	472900
23	271-274	Allemannia	New York via Havre	17 Sep 1869	1 Sep 1869	840-857	472900
23	274-276	Palmerston	New York	18 Sep 1869	1 Aug 1869	748-753	472900
23	285-286	Herschel	New York	23 Sep 1869	14 Aug 1869	796-799	472900
23	290-293	Cimbria	New York via Havre	24 Sep 1869	8 Sep 1869	862-880	472900
23	306-310	Westphalia	New York via Havre	29 Sep 1869	15 Sep 1869	883-905	472900
23	322-326	Hammonia	New York	8 Oct 1869	22 Sep 1869	913-931	472900
23	334-337	Silesia	New York via Havre	12 Oct 1869	29 Sep 1869	940-961	472900
23	344-347	Teutonia	New York	16 Oct 1869	2 Oct 1869	975-987	472900
23	349-350	Reichstag	New York	18 Oct 1869	1 Sep 1869	858-861	472900
23	352-357	Holsatia	New York	19 Oct 1869	6 Oct 1869	994-1016	472900
23	357-359	Saxonia	New Orleans via Havre	19 Oct 1869	25 Sep 1869	932-939	472900
23	372-377	Allemannia	New York	28 Oct 1869	13 Oct 1869	1023-1045	472900
23	378-379	Prinz Albert	New York	29 Oct 1869	15 Sep 1869	906-910	472900
23	385-389	Cimbria	New York	3 Nov 1869	20 Oct 1869	1060-1082	472900
23	398-403	Westphalia	New York	9 Nov 1869	27 Oct 1869	1090-1111	472900
23	412-413	Bavaria	New Orleans via Havana and Havre	19 Nov 1869	23 Oct 1869	1083-1089	472900
23	413-419	Borussia	New York	19 Nov 1869	30 Oct 1869	1112-1135	472900
23	421-424	Hammonia	New York	19 Nov 1869	3 Nov 1869	1147-1163	472900
23	435-437	Silesia	New York	24 Nov 1869	10 Nov 1869	1164-1174	472900

Germans to America vol. and page nos.		Name of the Ship	Route and U.S. Port(s) of Arrival	Date of Arrival	Date of Departure	*HPL* Page numbers	FHL micro-film no.
23	449-450	Holsatia	New York	2 Dec 1869	17 Nov 1869	1183-1190	472900
23	459-460	Allemannia	New York	10 Dec 1869	24 Nov 1869	1195-1204	472900
23	463-466	Friedeburg	New York	13 Dec 1869	15 Oct 1869	1046-1057	472900
23	466-467	Cimbria	New York via Havre	15 Dec 1869	1 Dec 1869	1203a-1208	472900
23	467-468	Eugenie	New York	15 Dec 1869	5 Oct 1869	988-990	472900
23	468-469	Teutonia	New Orleans via Havana and Havre	17 Dec 1869	20 Nov 1869	1191-1194	472900
23	469	Frankfurt	New Orleans via Havana and Havre	20 Dec 1869	missing	missing	-----
23	471-473	Dr. Barth	New York	24 Dec 1869	1 Nov 1869	1136-1146	472900
23	474	Westphalia	New York	25 Dec 1869	8 Dec 1869	1209-1214	472900
23	476-477	Hammonia	New York via Havre	30 Dec 1869	15 Dec 1869	1215-1219	472900
24	2-3	Silesia	New York	5 Jan 1870	missing	missing	-----
24	3-5	Shakespeare	New York	6 Jan 1870	11 Nov 1869	1175-1182	472900
24	5-6	Saxonia	New Orleans via Havana and Havre	11 Jan 1870	18 Dec 1869	1220	472900
24	8-11	John Bertram	New York	15 Jan 1870	30 Sep 1869	962-974	472900
24	12-13	Holsatia	New York	21 Jan 1870	5 Jan 1870	1-4	472901
24	14-15	Allemannia	New York	27 Jan 1870	12 Jan 1870	5-8	472901
24	19	Bavaria	New Orleans via Havana and Havre	11 Feb 1870	15 Jan 1870	9-16	472901
24	20-21	Westphalia	New York via Havre	12 Feb 1870	26 Jan 1870	25-28	472901
24	23-24	Hammonia	New York via Havre	16 Feb 1870	2 Feb 1870	29-33	472901
24	30-32	Holsatia	New York	3 Mar 1870	16 Feb 1870	34-49	472901
24	35-36	Silesia	New York	9 Mar 1870	23 Feb 1870	50-56	472901
24	40-43	Cimbria	New York	16 Mar 1870	2 Mar 1870	57-68	472901

Germans to America vol. and page nos.		Name of the Ship	Route and U.S. Port(s) of Arrival	Date of Arrival	Date of Departure	*HPL* Page numbers	FHL micro-film no.
24	46-49	Saxonia	New York via Havre	26 Mar 1870	9 Mar 1870	69-74, 75-82 follow pg 110	472901
24	56-60	Hammonia	New York via Havre	30 Mar 1870	16 Mar 1870	89-110	472901
24	70-73	Allemannia	New York via Havre	6 Apr 1870	23 Mar 1870	120-139	472901
24	81-82	Teutonia	New Orleans via Havana and Havre	9 Apr 1870	12 Mar 1870	85-88	472901
24	90-95	Holsatia	New York via Havre	13 Apr 1870	30 Mar 1870	140-163	472901
24	106-107	Prinz Albert	New York	20 Apr 1870	19 Mar 1870	111-119	472901
24	107-112	Silesia	New York via Havre	20 Apr 1870	6 Apr 1870	181-203	472901
24	124-129	Cimbria	New York via Havre	27 Apr 1870	13 Apr 1870	213-237	472901
24	142-147	Saxonia	New York	6 May 1870	20 Apr 1870	262-280, 281-282	472901
24	158-163	Hammonia	New York via Havre	11 May 1870	27 Apr 1870	283-303	472901
24	172-174	Reichstag	New York	18 May 1870	1 Apr 1870	167-178	472901
24	174-177	Borussia	New York	19 May 1870	30 Apr 1870	304-315	472901
24	185-189	Allemannia	New York via Havre	20 May 1870	4 May 1870	329-350	472901
24	210-215	Holsatia	New York via Havre	25 May 1870	11 May 1870	374-397	472901
24	224-229	Bavaria	New York via Havre	28 May 1870	7 May 1870	353-373	472901
24	244-247	Friedeburg	New York	31 May 1870	14 Apr 1870	238-250	472901
24	247-252	Silesia	New York via Havre	31 May 1870	18 May 1870	411-435	472901
24	290-294	Westphalia	New York	9 Jun 1870	25 May 1870	441-463	472901
24	305-309	Teutonia	New York via Havre	14 Jun 1870	28 May 1870	464-478	472901
24	309-312	Cimbria	New York via Havre	15 Jun 1870	1 Jun 1870	483-499	472901
24	325-328	Shakespeare	New York	21 Jun 1870	1 May 1870	316-328	472901
24	332-334	Gutenberg	New York	23 Jun 1870	14 May 1870	403-410	472901
24	334-337	Hammonia	New York via Havre	23 Jun 1870	8 Jun 1870	500-510-512	472901

Germans to America vol. and page nos.		Name of the Ship	Route and U.S. Port(s) of Arrival	Date of Arrival	Date of Departure	*HPL* Page numbers	FHL micro-film no.
24	348-352	Allemannia	New York	30 Jun 1870	15 Jun 1870	510a, 513-531	472901
24	367-370	Holsatia	New York via Havre	6 Jul 1870	22 May 1870	538-553	472901
24	384-388	Silesia	New York via Havre	13 Jul 1870	29 May 1870	558-576	472901
24	398-399	Herschel	New York	18 Jul 1870	1 Jun 1870	479-482	472901
24	403-405	Westphalia	New York via Havre	20 Jul 1870	6 Jul 1870	583-598	472901
24	412-415	Cimbria	New York via Havre	27 Jul 1870	13 Jul 1870	599-614	472901
24	420-423	Hammonia	New York	1 Aug 1870	20 Jul 1870	637-654	472901
24	430	Asia	Philadelphia	8 Aug 1870	missing	missing	-----
24	437-438	Eugenie	New York	15 Aug 1870	15 Jun 1870	532-536	472901
24	443-444	John Bertram	New York	24 Aug 1870	1 Jul 1870	577-579a	472901
24	448-449	Prinz Albert	New York	27 Aug 1870	15 Jul 1870	618-626	472901
24	493-496	Silesia	New York	18 Oct 1870	7 Oct 1870	655-673	472901
24	514-518	Allemannia	New York	7 Nov 1870	19 Oct 1870	674-697	472901
24	523-528	Thuringia	New York	9 Nov 1870	26 Oct 1870	698-722	472901
24	530-535	Cimbria	New York	14 Nov 1870	2 Nov 1870	723-744	472901
24	549-551	Westphalia	New York	23 Nov 1870	9 Nov 1870	745-755	472901
24	562-565	Silesia	New York	9 Dec 1870	23 Nov 1870	779-793	472901
24	568-570	Thuringia	New York	21 Dec 1870	7 Dec 1870	805-814	472901
25	1-3	Allemannia	New Orleans via Havana	2 Jan 1871	5 Dec 1870	794-804	472901
25	4-5	Cimbria	New York	6 Jan 1871	21 Dec 1870	826-833	472901
25	5-8	Doctor Barth	New York	7 Jan 1871	19 Nov 1870	768-778	472901
25	11-12	Holsatia	New York	30 Jan 1871	13 Jan 1871	1-4a	472902
25	14-15	Thuringia	New York	10 Feb 1871	25 Jan 1871	5-12	472902
25	19-20	Cimbria	New York	2 Mar 1871	13 Feb 1871	13-19	472902

Germans to America vol. and page nos.		Name of the Ship	Route and U.S. Port(s) of Arrival	Date of Arrival	Date of Departure	*HPL* Page numbers	FHL micro-film no.
25	23-24	Westphalia	New York	11 Mar 1871	23 Feb 1871	20-26	472902
25	28-29	Holsatia	New York	18 Mar 1871	1 Mar 1871	27-32	472902
25	32-34	Thuringia	New York	22 Mar 1871	8 Mar 1871	34-42	472902
25	37-39	Silesia	New York	28 Mar 1871	15 Mar 1871	44-51	472902
25	49-52	Allemannia	New York	5 Apr 1871	22 Mar 1871	62-76	472902
25	52-55	Cimbria	New York	10 Apr 1871	29 Mar 1871	81-92	472902
25	67-70	Westphalia	New York	17 Apr 1871	5 Apr 1871	97-111	472902
25	73-74	Prinz Albert	New York	20 Apr 1871	13 Mar 1871	43	472902
25	76-78	Holsatia	New York	26 Apr 1871	13 Apr 1871	113-123	472902
25	89-93	Thuringia	New York	3 May 1871	19 Apr 1871	128-147	472902
25	109-114	Silesia	New York	8 May 1871	26 Apr 1871	158-179	472902
25	126-127	Herschel	New York	15 May 1871	2 Apr 1871	93-96	472902
25	131-138	Germania	New York	18 May 1871	3 May 1871	182-212	472902
25	147-151	Cimbria	New York	22 May 1871	10 May 1871	214-237	472902
25	173-178	Westphalia	New York	30 May 1871	17 May 1871	259-280	472902
25	194-200	Holsatia	New York	5 Jun 1871	24 May 1871	281-306	472902
25	204-205	John Bertram	New York	6 Jun 1871	15 Apr 1871	124-127	472902
25	224-229	Thuringia	New York	13 Jun 1871	31 May 1871	309-332	472902
25	246-251	Silesia	New York	20 Jun 1871	7 Jun 1871	338-361	472902
25	272-276	Germania	New York	28 Jun 1871	14 Jun 1871	364-382	472902
25	288-291	Cimbria	New York	3 Jul 1871	21 Jun 1871	383-395	472902
25	310-312	Palmerston	New York	14 Jul 1871	12 May 1871	248-258	472902
25	313-316	Vandalia	New York	15 Jul 1871	28 Jun 1871	398-417	472902
25	327-330	Hammonia	New York	18 Jul 1871	5 Jul 1871	424-441	472902

Germans to America vol. and page nos.		Name of the Ship	Route and U.S. Port(s) of Arrival	Date of Arrival	Date of Departure	*HPL* Page numbers	FHL micro-film no.
25	337-341	Westphalia	New York	24 Jul 1871	12 Jul 1871	443-466	472902
25	344-345	Eugenie	New York	26 Jul 1871	2 Jun 1871	333-337	472902
25	355	Rosa	New York	31 Jul 1871	missing	missing	-----
25	358-361	Holsatia	New York via Havre	2 Aug 1871	19 Jul 1871	473-490	472902
25	369-372	Thuringia	New York	9 Aug 1871	26 Jul 1871	491-504	472902
25	382-384	Prinz Albert	New York	16 Aug 1871	30 Jun 1871	418-423	472902
25	384-386	Allemannia	New York via Havre	17 Aug 1871	2 Aug 1871	511-523	472902
25	399-402	Silesia	New York	22 Aug 1871	9 Aug 1871	524-544	472902
25	414-416	Hammonia	New York via Havre	31 Aug 1817	16 Aug 1871	548-562	472902
25	431-432	Doctor Barth	New York	4 Sep 1871	15 Jul 1871	467-468	472902
25	434-435	Vandalia	New York via Havre	5 Sep 1871	19 Aug 1871	563-570	472902
25	436-439	Westphalia	New York via Havre	6 Sep 1871	23 Aug 1871	571-590	472902
25	452-453	Herschel	New York	13 Sep 1871	1 Aug 1871	508-510	472902
25	453-456	Holsatia	New York via Havre	14 Sep 1871	30 Aug 1871	598-616	472902
25	472-475	Thuringia	New York	19 Sep 1871	6 Sep 1871	630-646	472902
25	487-489	Saxonia	New York via Havre	25 Sep 1871	2 Sep 1871	617-623	472902
25	490-493	Cimbria	New York	27 Sep 1871	13 Sep 1871	647-666	472902
25	494-496	Allemannia	New York	30 Sep 1871	16 Sep 1871	667-678	472902
26	9-12	Silesia	New York via Southampton	5 Oct 1871	20-Sep-71	679-702	472902
26	30-33	Hammonia	New York	12 Oct 1871	27 Sep 1871	719-734	472902
26	41-45	Westphalia	New York	18 Oct 1871	4 Oct 1871	743-770	472902
26	45	Washington	New York	19 Oct 1871	15 Aug 1871	546-547	472902
26	55-57	Germania	New Orleans via Havre	23 Oct 1871	23 Sep 1871	703-714	472902
26	58-62	Holsatia	New York	25 Oct 1871	11 Oct 1871	800-819	472902

Germans to America vol. and page nos.		Name of the Ship	Route and U.S. Port(s) of Arrival	Date of Arrival	Date of Departure	*HPL* Page numbers	FHL micro-film no.
26	62-67	Vandalia	New York	25 Oct 1871	8 Oct 1871	773-799	472902
26	74	Mozart	New York	28 Oct 1871	2 Sep 1871	624-626	472902
26	84-88	Thuringia	New York via Havre	2 Nov 1871	18 Oct 1871	832-859	472902
26	102-106	Cimbria	New York via Havre	9 Nov 1871	25 Oct 1871	872-873	472902
26	106-113	Allemannia	New York	11 Nov 1871	28 Oct 1871	874-893	472902
26	125-129	Silesia	New York via Havre	15 Nov 1871	1 Nov 1871	933-953	472902
26	140-142	Electric	New York	23 Nov 1871	1 Oct 1871	735-742	472902
26	155-158	Westphalia	New York	1 Dec 1871	15 Nov 1871	964-980	472902
26	164-166	Hammonia	New Orleans via Havana, Havre, and Santander	4 Dec 1871	4 Nov 1871	954-960	472902
26	171-174	Holsatia	New York	7 Dec 1871	22 Nov 1871	994-1008	472902
26	177-179	Thuringia	New York via Havre	14 Dec 1871	29 Nov 1871	1016-1024	472902
26	185-186	Vandalia	New Orleans via Havana, Havre, and Santander	23 Dec 1871	25 Nov 1871	1011-1015	472902
26	186-187	Cimbria	New York via Havre	25 Dec 1871	6 Dec 1871	1035-1041	472902
26	193-195	Palmerston	New York	27 Dec 1871	15 Oct 1871	820-831	472902
26	198-200	Prinz Albert	New York	29 Dec 1871	31 Oct 1871	922-932	472902
26	201-203	Doctor Barth	New York	3 Jan 1872	15 Nov 1871	981-988	472902
26	209-210	Silesia	New York	9 Jan 1872	13 Dec 1871	1042-1047	472902
26	212-213	Westphalia	New York	15 Jan 1872	23 Dec 1871	1050-1053	472902
26	215-216	Germania	New Orleans via Havana, Havre, and Santander	20 Jan 1872	16 Dec 1871	1048-1049	472902
26	217-218	Holsatia	New York via Havre	23 Jan 1872	3 Jan 1872	1-6	472903
26	219-220	Thuringia	New York	30 Jan 1872	10 Jan 1872	7-13	472903
26	223-224	Hammonia	New York via Havre	3 Feb 1872	17 Jan 1872	17-24	472903

Germans to America vol. and page nos.		Name of the Ship	Route and U.S. Port(s) of Arrival	Date of Arrival	Date of Departure	*HPL* Page numbers	FHL micro-film no.
26	228-230	Cimbria	New York via Havre	16 Feb 1872	31 Jan 1872	25-35	472903
26	235	Saxonia	New Orleans via Havana, Havre, and Santander	19 Feb 1872	13 Jan 1872	14-16	472903
26	237-239	Allemannia	New York	23 Feb 1872	7 Feb 1872	36-42	472903
26	245-247	Silesia	New York	29 Feb 1872	14 Feb 1872	45a-56	472903
26	255-257	Westphalia	New York via Havre	8 Mar 1872	21 Feb 1872	57-68	472903
26	261-262	Vandalia	New Orleans via Havana, Havre, and Santander	11 Mar 1872	10 Feb 1872	43-44a	472903
26	267-270	Holsatia	New York via Havre	15 Mar 1872	28 Feb 1872	69-83	472903
26	282-287	Thuringia	New York	25 Mar 1872	6 Mar 1872	84-106	472903
26	299-304	Hammonia	New York via Havre	28 Mar 1872	13 Mar 1872	111-132	472903
26	318-323	Cimbria	New York	4 Apr 1872	20 Mar 1872	142-163	472903
26	349-354	Silesia	New York via Havre	11 Apr 1872	27 Mar 1872	164-185	472903
26	376-381	Westphalia	New York via Havre	18 Apr 1872	3 Apr 1872	195-217	472903
26	385-388	Electric	New York	20 Apr 1872	15 Mar 1872	133-141	472903
26	402-407	Holsatia	New York via Havre	24 Apr 1872	10 Apr 1872	261-283	472903
26	441-445	Thuringia	New York via Havre	30 Apr 1872	17 Apr 1872	321-341	472903
27	1-9	Allemannia	New York	4 May 1872	20 Apr 1872	342-375	472903
27	23-24	Saxonia	New Orleans via Havana, Havre and Santander	6 May 1872	6 Apr 1872	232-236	472903
27	30-35	Hammonia	New York	9 May 1872	24 Apr 1872	378-400	472903
27	74-79	Cimbria	New York via Havre	16 May 1872	1 May 1872	401-423	472903
27	97-99	Prinz Albert	New York	18 May 1872	1 Apr 1872	186-194	472903
27	114-121	Vandalia	New York	20 May 1872	4 May 1872	439-468	472903
27	133-138	Silesia	New York via Havre	21 May 1872	8 May 1872	482-496	472903

Germans to America vol. and page nos.		Name of the Ship	Route and U.S. Port(s) of Arrival	Date of Arrival	Date of Departure	*HPL* Page numbers	FHL micro-film no.
27	171-177	Westphalia	New York via Havre	28 May 1872	15 May 1872	502-526	472903
27	196-198	Hattie M	New York	4 Jun 1872	15 Apr 1872	302-307	472903
27	198-201	Louise	New York	4 Jun 1872	15 Apr 1872	308-320	472903
27	201-202	St. Olaf	New York	4 Jun 1872	11 Apr 1872	284-289	472903
27	206-209	Doctor Barth	New York	5 Jun 1872	1 May 1872	424-433	472903
27	209-214	Holsatia	New York via Havre	5 Jun 1872	22 May 1872	543-565	472903
27	221-228	Germania	New York	8 Jun 1872	25 May 1872	568-599	472903
27	268-272	Thuringia	New York	12 Jun 1872	29 May 1872	604-624	472903
27	276-281	Allemannia	New York	15 Jun 1872	1 Jun 1872	625-647	472903
27	296-297	Dryaden	New York	20 Jun 1872	1 May 1872	434-438	472903
27	297-301	Hammonia	New York	20 Jun 1872	5 Jun 1872	648-667	472903
27	322-326	Cimbria	New York via Havre	27 Jun 1872	12 Jun 1872	669-686	472903
27	329	Pauline David	Philadelphia	28 Jun 1872	missing	missing	-----
27	336-340	Silesia	New York via Havre	2 Jul 1872	19 Jun 1872	705-726	472903
27	365-367	Messenger	New York	10 Jul 1872	15 May 1872	527-535	472903
27	374-378	Vandalia	New York via Havre	13 Jul 1872	26 Jun 1872	732-750	472903
27	386-390	Westphalia	New York via Havre	17 Jul 1872	3 Jul 1872	751-772	472904
27	405-409	Holsatia	New York via Havre	24 Jul 1872	10 Jul 1872	776-796	472904
27	422-426	Thuringia	New York via Havre	31 Jul 1872	17 Jul 1872	801-818	472904
28	10-11	Lady Bowen	New York	6 Aug 1872	14 Jun 1872	697-704	472903
28	13-15	Hammonia	New York via Havre	8 Aug 1872	24 Jul 1872	823-836	472904
28	34-38	Cimbria	New York via Havre	14 Aug 1872	31 Jul 1872	846-866	472904
28	57-59	Vandalia	New York via Havre	24 Aug 1872	7 Aug 1872	876-890	472904
28	64-69	Silesia	New York via Havre	28 Aug 1872	14 Aug 1872	891-915	472904

Germans to America vol. and page nos.		Name of the Ship	Route and U.S. Port(s) of Arrival	Date of Arrival	Date of Departure	*HPL* Page numbers	FHL micro-film no.
28	88-91	Frisia	New York via Havre	5 Sep 1872	21 Aug 1872	921-940	472904
28	103-104	Washington	New York	11 Sep 1872	17 Jul 1872	797-800	472904
28	104-108	Westphalia	New York via Havre	11 Sep 1872	28 Aug 1872	944-965	472904
28	120-124	Holsatia	New York via Havre	18 Sep 1872	2 Sep 1872	966-992	472904
28	140	Prinz Albert	New York	23 Sep 1872	missing	missing	-----
28	142-147	Thuringia	New York via Havre	24 Sep 1872	11 Sep 1872	998-1020	472904
28	148	Electric	New York	26 Sep 1872	17 Aug 1872	916-919	472904
28	169-174	Hammonia	New York via Havre	2 Oct 1872	18 Sep 1872	1029-1053	472904
28	189-193	Cimbria	New York via Havre	10 Oct 1872	25 Sep 1872	1056-1080	472904
28	209-211	Saxonia	New Orleans via Havana, Havre, and Santander	14 Oct 1872	14 Sep 1872	1021-1028	472904
28	221-225	Silesia	New York	15 Oct 1872	2 Oct 1872	1084-1109	472904
28	242-250	Allemannia	New York	21 Oct 1872	5 Oct 1872	1111-1140	472904
28	271-276	Frisia	New York	29 Oct 1872	9 Oct 1872	1152-1176	472904
28	278-284	Westphalia	New York via Havre	30 Oct 1872	16 Oct 1872	1189-1214	472904
28	303-308	Holsatia	New York via Havre	7 Nov 1872	23 Oct 1872	1225-1248	472904
28	326-335	Germania	New York	13 Nov 1872	26 Oct 1872	1265-1299	472904
28	336-342	Thuringia	New York via Havre	13 Nov 1872	30 Oct 1872	1308-1332	472904
28	344-351	Hammonia	New York	16 Nov 1872	2 Nov 1872	1343-1370	472904
28	358-360	Vandalia	New Orleans via Havana, Havre, and Santander	18 Nov 1872	19 Oct 1872	1215-1222	472904
28	361-363	Cimbria	New York via Havre	20 Nov 1872	6 Nov 1872	1374-1396	472904
28	376-381	Silesia	New York	3 Dec 1872	13 Nov 1872	1407-1429	472904
28	387-390	Frisia	New York via Havre	7 Dec 1872	20 Nov 1872	1433-1448	472904
28	397-399	Westphalia	New York via Havre	12 Dec 1872	27 Nov 1872	1469-1480	472904

Germans to America vol. and page nos.		Name of the Ship	Route and U.S. Port(s) of Arrival	Date of Arrival	Date of Departure	*HPL* Page numbers	FHL micro-film no.
28	408-411	John Bertram	New York	16 Dec 1872	15 Oct 1872	1177-1188	472904
28	413-415	Doctor Barth	New York	21 Dec 1872	1 Nov 1872	1333-1342	472904
28	416-417	Holsatia	New York via Havre	21 Dec 1872	4 Dec 1872	1485-1492	472904
28	423-425	Thuringia	New York	29 Dec 1872	11 Dec 1872	1496-1502	472904
29	9-10	Hammonia	New York via Havre	4 Jan 1873	18 Dec 1872	1503-1508a	472904
29	13-14	Cimbria	New York via Havre	10 Jan 1873	25 Dec 1872	1511-1514	472904
29	19	Silesia	New York via Havre	17 Jan 1873	1 Jan 1873	1-5	472905
29	25-26	Frisia	New York via Havre	25 Jan 1873	8 Jan 1873	6-10	472905
29	27-28	Prinz Albert	New York	28 Jan 1873	20 Nov 1872	1449-1455	472904
29	29-30	Westphalia	New York via Havre	3 Feb 1873	15 Jan 1873	11-19	472905
29	34-35	Thuringia	New York via Havre	7 Feb 1873	22 Jan 1873	21-24	472905
29	38-40	Hammonia	New York via Havre	13 Feb 1873	29 Jan 1873	25-31	472905
29	46-47	Cimbria	New York via Havre	20 Feb 1873	5 Feb 1873	35-42	472905
29	51-52	Silesia	New York via Havre	27 Feb 1873	12 Feb 1873	45-50	472905
29	58-60	Frisia	New York via Havre	7 Mar 1873	19 Feb 1873	51-60	472905
29	64-65	Westphalia	New York via Havre	14 Mar 1873	26 Feb 1873	63-73	472905
29	71-74	Thuringia	New York via Havre	20 Mar 1873	5 Mar 1873	74-90	472905
29	88-92	Hammonia	New York via Havre	27 Mar 1873	12 Mar 1873	91-111	472905
29	109	Athena	New York	4 Apr 1873	missing	missing	-----
29	120-125	Holsatia	New York via Havre	9 Apr 1873	missing	missing	-----
29	141-145	Frisia	New York via Havre	16 Apr 1873	2 Apr 1873	204-222	472905
29	145-150	Silesia	New York via Havre	16 Apr 1873	26 Mar 1873	135-155	472905
29	152-157	Saxonia	New York	17 Apr 1873	1 Apr 1873	172-192	472905
29	207-212	Westphalia	New York via Havre	23 Apr 1873	9 Apr 1873	239-260	472905

Germans to America vol. and page nos.		Name of the Ship	Route and U.S. Port(s) of Arrival	Date of Arrival	Date of Departure	*HPL* Page numbers	FHL micro-film no.
29	233-238	Thuringia	New York via Havre	30 Apr 1873	16 Apr 1873	309-333	472905
29	264-269	Hammonia	New York via Havre	8 May 1873	23 Apr 1873	334-355	472905
29	287-294	Vandalia	New York	13 May 1873	26 Apr 1873	363-394	472905
29	296-301	Holsatia	New York via Havre	15 May 1873	30 Apr 1873	397-419	472905
29	342-348	Silesia	New York via Havre	20 May 1873	7 May 1873	434-458	472905
29	388-393	Frisia	New York via Havre	29 May 1873	14 May 1873	474-496	472905
29	403-405	Prinz Albert	New York	31 May 1873	15 Apr 1873	300-308	472905
30	14-22	Saxonia	New York	4 Jun 1873	17 May 1873	497-530	472905
30	22-27	Westphalia	New York via Havre	4 Jun 1873	21 May 1873	539-560	472905
30	48-52	Thuringia	New York via Havre	11 Jun 1873	28 May 1873	569-591	472905
30	81-85	Cimbria	New York via Havre	19 Jun 1873	4 Jun 1873	592-608	472905
30	97-99	Vandalia	New York	24 Jun 1873	7 Jun 1873	612-623a	472905
30	101-103	Hammonia	New York via Havre	26 Jun 1873	11 Jun 1873	639-651	472905
30	121-124	Holsatia	New York	2 Jul 1873	18 Jun 1873	661-680	472905
30	137-141	Silesia	New York via Havre	10 Jul 1873	25 Jun 1873	696-712	472905
30	147-149	Ariadne	New York	14 Jul 1873	19 May 1873	531-538	472905
30	158-161	Frisia	New York via Havre	16 Jul 1873	2 Jul 1873	713-738	472906
30	173-176	Westphalia	New York via Havre	23 Jul 1873	9 Jul 1873	754-772	472906
30	186-188	Thuringia	New York via Havre	30 Jul 1873	15 Jul 1873	773-798	472906
30	198-200	Cimbria	New York via Havre	6 Aug 1873	23 Jul 1873	802-816	472906
30	219-221	Hammonia	New York via Havre	15 Aug 1873	30 Jul 1873	817-835	472906
30	229-231	Holsatia	New York via Havre	21 Aug 1873	6 Aug 1873	839-857	472906
30	245-247	Silesia	New York via Southampton	28 Aug 1873	13 Aug 1873	858-875a	472906
30	259-262	Frisia	New York via Havre	3 Sep 1873	20 Aug 1873	883-903	472906

Germans to America vol. and page nos.		Name of the Ship	Route and U.S. Port(s) of Arrival	Date of Arrival	Date of Departure	*HPL* Page numbers	FHL micro-film no.
30	273	Athena	New York	10 Sep 1873	missing	missing	-----
30	273-276	Westphalia	New York via Southampton	10 Sep 1873	27 Aug 1873	907-927	472906
30	294-297	Thuringia	New York via Southampton	18 Sep 1873	3 Sep 1873	928-947	472906
30	310-312	Cimbria	New York via Southampton	25 Sep 1873	10 Sep 1873	950-965	472906
30	329-330	Goethe	New York	1 Oct 1873	11 Sep 1873	966-971	472906
30	330-333	Holsatia	New York via Southampton	1 Oct 1873	17 Sep 1873	972-990	472906
30	333	Prinz Albert	New York	1 Oct 1873	16 Aug 1873	879	472906
30	348-352	Silesia	New York via Southampton	8 Oct 1873	24 Sep 1873	997-1015	472906
30	362-365	Frisia	New York via Southampton	16 Oct 1873	1 Oct 1873	1016-1034	472906
30	372-375	Saxonia	New York	22 Oct 1873	4 Oct 1873	1035-1046a	472906
30	375-378	Westphalia	New York via Southampton	22 Oct 1873	8 Oct 1873	1051-1069	472906
30	394-399	Thuringia	New York via Southampton	29 Oct 1873	15 Oct 1873	1082-1107	472906
30	417-422	Cimbria	New York via Southampton	6 Nov 1873	22 Oct 1873	1115-1138	472906
30	433-438	Holsatia	New York via Southampton	13 Nov 1873	29 Oct 1873	1168-1191	472906
30	439-444	Hammonia	New York	14 Nov 1873	1 Nov 1873	1192-1217	472906
30	457-464	Bavaria	New York	19 Nov 1873	25 Oct 1873	1141-1167	472906
30	464-466	Silesia	New York via Southampton	19 Nov 1873	5 Nov 1873	1232-1243	472906
30	473-475	Frisia	New York via Southampton	26 Nov 1873	12 Nov 1873	1246-1256	472906
30	475-476	Goethe	New York	26 Nov 1873	13 Nov 1873	1257-1263	472906
31	9-10	Westphalia	New York via Southampton	6 Dec 1873	19 Nov 1873	1266-1272	472906
31	13-14	Thuringia	New York via Southampton	10 Dec 1873	26 Nov 1873	1281-1287	472906
31	20	Saxonia	New Orleans via Havana and Southampton	18 Dec 1873	18 Nov 1873	1264-1265	472906
31	21-22	Pommerania	New York via Southampton	19 Dec 1873	3 Dec 1873	1288-1294	472906

Germans to America vol. and page nos.		Name of the Ship	Route and U.S. Port(s) of Arrival	Date of Arrival	Date of Departure	*HPL* Page numbers	FHL micro-film no.
31	25	Holsatia	New York via Southampton	26 Dec 1873	10 Dec 1873	1298-1301	472906
31	30-31	Thuringia	New York via Havre	28 Dec 1873	26 Nov 1873	1281-1287	472906
31	32	Cimbria	New York via Southampton	3 Jan 1874	17 Dec 1873	1305-1308	472906
31	35	Hammonia	New York via Havre	12 Jan 1874	24 Dec 1873	1309-1311	472906
31	36	Silesia	New York via Havre	15 Jan 1874	31 Dec 1873	1312-1314	472906
31	37-38	Herder	New York	26 Jan 1874	8 Jan 1874	7-10	472907
31	38-39	Westphalia	New York via Havre	30 Jan 1874	14 Jan 1874	11-13	472907
31	39-40	Thuringia	New York via Havre	4 Feb 1874	21 Jan 1874	14-17	472907
31	40	Goethe	New York	6 Feb 1874	22 Jan 1874	18-21	472907
31	41-42	Pommerania	New York via Havre	11 Feb 1874	28 Jan 1874	22-25	472907
31	45	Holsatia	New York via Havre	19 Feb 1874	4 Feb 1874	28-30	472907
31	45-46	Schiller	New York	20 Feb 1874	5 Feb 1874	31-33	472907
31	47	Hammonia	New York via Havre	28 Feb 1874	11 Feb 1874	35-38	472907
31	50-51	Frisia	New York via Havre	11 Mar 1874	25 Feb 1874	47-50	472907
31	53-54	Goethe	New York	19 Mar 1874	5 Mar 1874	61-64	472907
31	54-56	Thuringia	New York via Havre	19 Mar 1874	4 Mar 1874	51-60	472907
31	60-62	Westphalia	New York via Havre	26 Mar 1874	11 Mar 1874	66-78	472907
31	66-70	Pommerania	New York via Havre	2 Apr 1874	18 Mar 1874	82-99	472907
31	74-76	Holsatia	New York via Havre	10 Apr 1874	25 Mar 1874	100-109	472907
31	85-87	Hammonia	New York via Havre	17 Apr 1874	1 Apr 1874	110-123	472907
31	101-103	Frisia	New York via Havre	24 Apr 1874	8 Apr 1874	137-149	472907
31	112-117	Thuringia	New York via Havre	30 Apr 1874	15 Apr 1874	166-187	472907
31	130-134	Westphalia	New York via Havre	6 May 1874	22 Apr 1874	202-223	472907
31	147-150	Herder	New York	13 May 1874	30 Apr 1874	244-259	472907

Germans to America vol. and page nos.		Name of the Ship	Route and U.S. Port(s) of Arrival	Date of Arrival	Date of Departure	*HPL* Page numbers	FHL micro-film no.
31	151-154	Pommerania	New York via Havre	13 May 1874	29 Apr 1874	226-243	472907
31	161-165	Holsatia	New York via Havre	21 May 1874	6 May 1874	262-282	472907
31	178-180	Goethe	New York	26 May 1874	14 May 1874	314-327	472907
31	182-185	Silesia	New York via Havre	26 May 1874	13 May 1874	295-313	472907
31	197-200	Frisia	New York via Havre	4 Jun 1874	20 May 1874	328-341	472907
31	207-209	Thuringia	New York via Havre	10 Jun 1874	27 May 1874	346-354	472907
31	209-211	Lessing	New York	11 Jun 1874	28 May 1874	355-363	472907
31	217-220	Westphalia	New York via Havre	18 Jun 1874	3 Jun 1874	367-383	472907
31	228-229	Herder	New York	24 Jun 1874	11 Jun 1874	397-404	472907
31	229-230	Pommerania	New York via Havre	24 Jun 1874	10 Jun 1874	386-396	472907
31	231	Graf Bismarck	New York via Havre	25 Jun 1874	missing	missing	-----
31	238-240	Holsatia	New York via Havre	1 Jul 1874	17 Jun 1874	405-416	472907
31	247-248	Silesia	New York via Havre	8 Jul 1874	24 Jun 1874	417-428	472907
31	253-254	Schiller	New York	15 Jul 1874	1 Jul 1874	452-459	472907
31	256-257	Hammonia	New York via Havre	17 Jul 1874	1 Jul 1874	429-451	472907
31	262-263	Goethe	New York	21 Jul 1874	9 Jul 1874	477-482	472907
31	263-264	Frisia	New York via Havre	22 Jul 1874	8 Jul 1874	466-476	472907
31	270-271	Thuringia	New York via Havre	29 Jul 1874	15 Jul 1874	483-492	472907
31	276-277	Westphalia	New York via Havre	5 Aug 1874	22 Jul 1874	493-501	472907
31	282-283	Pommerania	New York via Havre	13 Aug 1874	29 Jul 1874	508-516	472907
31	287-289	Holsatia	New York via Havre	19 Aug 1874	5 Aug 1874	517-527	472907
31	289-290	Herder	New York	20 Aug 1874	6 Aug 1874	531-536	472907
31	296-297	Cimbria	New York via Havre	27 Aug 1874	12 Aug 1874	539-563	472907
31	304-306	Schiller	New York	1 Sep 1874	20 Aug 1874	601-620	472907

Germans to America vol. and page nos.		Name of the Ship	Route and U.S. Port(s) of Arrival	Date of Arrival	Date of Departure	*HPL* Page numbers	FHL micro-film no.
31	306-308	Hammonia	New York via Havre	2 Sep 1874	19 Aug 1874	590-599b	472907
31	308	Teutonia	New York via Havre	3 Sep 1874	15 Aug 1874	564-589	472907
31	313-315	Frisia	New York via Havre	9 Sep 1874	26 Aug 1874	623-639	472907
31	323-324	Goethe	New York	15 Sep 1874	3 Sep 1874	653-661	472907
31	326-328	Thuringia	New York via Havre	16 Sep 1874	2 Sep 1874	640-652	472907
31	334-335	Pommerania	New York via Havre	23 Sep 1874	9 Sep 1874	669-681	472907
31	342-343	Lessing	New York	29 Sep 1874	17 Sep 1874	693-701	472907
31	344-345	Silesia	New York via Havre	29 Sep 1874	16 Sep 1874	682-692	472907
31	351-353	Holsatia	New York	7 Oct 1874	23 Sep 1874	711-723	472907
31	358-359	Herder	New York	14 Oct 1874	1 Oct 1874	736-743	472907
31	360-362	Cimbria	New York	16 Oct 1874	30 Sep 1874	724-735	472907
31	366-369	Frisia	New York via Havre	22 Oct 1874	7 Oct 1874	747-760	472907
31	378-379	Schiller	New York	28 Oct 1874	15 Oct 1874	788-802	472907
31	380-382	Thuringia	New York via Havre	29 Oct 1874	14 Oct 1874	773-787	472907
31	389-391	Suevia	New York via Havre	6 Nov 1874	21 Oct 1874	803-818	472907
31	395-397	Goethe	New York	12 Nov 1874	29 Oct 1874	842-854	472907
31	398-402	Westphalia	New York via Havre	13 Nov 1874	28 Oct 1874	821-841	472907
31	405-407	Pommerania	New York via Havre	17 Nov 1874	4 Nov 1874	855-865	472907
31	412-413	Silesia	New York via Havre	27 Nov 1874	11 Nov 1874	871-878	472907
31	416-417	Holsatia	New York via Havre	3 Dec 1874	18 Nov 1874	887-894	472907
31	418-419	Klopstock	New York	5 Dec 1874	missing	missing	-----
31	422	Schiller	New York	9 Dec 1874	26 Nov 1874	921-927	472907
31	423	Cimbria	New York via Havre	12 Dec 1874	25 Nov 1874	901-905	472907
31	425	Frisia	New York via Havre	17 Dec 1874	2 Dec 1874	928-932	472907

Germans to America vol. and page nos.		Name of the Ship	Route and U.S. Port(s) of Arrival	Date of Arrival	Date of Departure	*HPL* Page numbers	FHL micro-film no.
31	428	Lessing	New York	24 Dec 1874	10 Dec 1874	937-939	472907
31	428-429	Westphalia	New York via Havre	24 Dec 1874	9 Dec 1874	933-936	472907
32	1	Suevia	New York via Havre	4 Jan 1875	16 Dec 1874	940-943	472907
32	2	Pommerania	New York via Havre	7 Jan 1875	23 Dec 1874	944-946	472907
32	2	Goethe	New York	8 Jan 1875	24 Dec 1874	947-949	472907
32	5	Silesia	New York via Havre	22 Jan 1875	6 Jan 1875	1-4	472908
32	6	Holsatia	New York via Havre	1 Feb 1875	13 Jan 1875	5-8	472908
32	6-7	Klopstock	New York	1 Feb 1875	14 Jan 1875	9-11	472908
32	8	Schiller	New York	4 Feb 1875	21 Jan 1875	16-18	472908
32	8-9	Cimbria	New York	6 Feb 1875	20 Jan 1875	12-15	472908
32	11-12	Frisia	New York via Havre	18 Feb 1875	3 Feb 1875	19-25	472908
32	13-14	Lessing	New York	26 Feb 1875	11 Feb 1875	30-36	472908
32	14-15	Suevia	New York via Havre	26 Feb 1875	10 Feb 1875	26-29	472908
32	16-17	Pommerania	New York via Havre	4 Mar 1875	17 Feb 1875	37-45	472908
32	19-20	Herder	New York	11 Mar 1875	25 Feb 1875	54-59	472908
32	22	Silesia	New York via Havre	19 Mar 1875	24 Feb 1875	46-53	472908
32	26-28	Cimbria	New York via Havre	24 Mar 1875	10 Mar 1875	69-80	472908
32	28-29	Holsatia	New York via Havre	24 Mar 1875	3 Mar 1875	60-68	472908
32	32-35	Klopstock	New York via Halifax	29 Mar 1875	11 Mar 1875	81-95	472908
32	38-39	Westphalia	New York via Havre	1 Apr 1875	17 Mar 1875	96-104	472908
32	41-42	Goethe	New York	6 Apr 1875	25 Mar 1875	119-126	472908
32	42-44	Frisia	New York via Havre	7 Apr 1875	24 Mar 1875	107-118	472908
32	48-50	Schiller	New York	14 Apr 1875	1 Apr 1875	146-157	472908
32	50-51	Suevia	New York via Havre	16 Apr 1875	31 Mar 1875	127-134	472908

Germans to America vol. and page nos.		Name of the Ship	Route and U.S. Port(s) of Arrival	Date of Arrival	Date of Departure	*HPL* Page numbers	FHL micro-film no.
32	56-59	Pommerania	New York via Havre	21 Apr 1875	7 Apr 1875	158-174	472908
32	65-67	Holsatia	New York via Havre	28 Apr 1875	14 Apr 1875	179-190	472908
32	67-69	Lessing	New York	28 Apr 1875	15 Apr 1875	191-205	472908
32	76-79	Cimbria	New York via Havre	6 May 1875	21 Apr 1875	206-221	472908
32	85-88	Westphalia	New York via Havre	13 May 1875	28 Apr 1875	222-240	472908
32	94-97	Frisia	New York via Havre	19 May 1875	5 May 1875	241-262	472908
32	102-105	Thuringia	New York via Havre	26 May 1875	12 May 1875	275-295	472908
32	111-112	Pommerania	New York via Havre	2 Jun 1875	19 May 1875	300-316	472908
32	117-119	Gellert	New York via Havre	9 Jun 1875	26 May 1875	317-333	472908
32	128-129	Suevia	New York via Havre	17 Jun 1875	2 Jun 1875	334-350	472908
32	133-134	Herder	New York via Havre	23 Jun 1875	9 Jun 1875	355-363	472908
32	137-139	Cimbria	New York via Havre	1 Jul 1875	16 Jun 1875	364-376	472908
32	143-144	Klopstock	New York via Havre	7 Jul 1875	23 Jun 1875	377-389	472908
32	148-149	Frisia	New York via Havre	14 Jul 1875	30 Jun 1875	397-405	472908
32	152-153	Wieland	New York via Havre	21 Jul 1875	7 Jul 1875	408-417	472908
32	157-158	Pommerania	New York via Havre	27 Jul 1875	14 Jul 1875	421-431	472908
32	161-162	Suevia	New York via Havre	4 Aug 1875	21 Jul 1875	432-442	472908
32	166	Gellert	New York via Havre	11 Aug 1875	28 Jul 1875	443-451	472908
32	170	Marie	New York	16 Aug 1875	missing	missing	-----
32	171	Cimbria	New York via Havre	18 Aug 1875	4 Aug 1875	452-463	472908
32	174-176	Klopstock	New York via Cherbourg and Halifax	27 Aug 1875	11 Aug 1875	468-477	472908
32	179-180	Frisia	New York via Havre	1 Sep 1875	18 Aug 1875	478-489	472908
32	183-184	Wieland	New York via Havre	8 Sep 1875	25 Aug 1875	490-499	472908
32	188-190	Pommerania	New York via Havre	14 Sep 1875	1 Sep 1875	500-511	472908

Germans to America vol. and page nos.		Name of the Ship	Route and U.S. Port(s) of Arrival	Date of Arrival	Date of Departure	*HPL* Page numbers	FHL micro-film no.
32	192-194	Suevia	New York via Havre	22 Sep 1875	8 Sep 1875	518-530	472908
32	198-200	Gellert	New York via Havre	28 Sep 1875	15 Sep 1875	532-544	472908
32	203-205	Hammonia	New York via Havre	7 Oct 1875	22 Sep 1875	547-556	472908
32	209-210	Klopstock	New York via Havre	14 Oct 1875	29 Sep 1875	557-566	472908
32	212-214	Frisia	New York via Havre	21 Oct 1875	6 Oct 1875	571-585	472908
32	218-220	Wieland	New York via Havre	28 Oct 1875	13 Oct 1875	600-610	472908
32	223-224	Pommerania	New York via Havre	3 Nov 1875	20 Oct 1875	613-626	472908
32	228-230	Suevia	New York via Havre	12 Nov 1875	27 Oct 1875	627-639	472908
32	233-234	Gellert	New York via Havre	22 Nov 1875	3/4 Nov 1875	640-648	472908
32	236-237	Herder	New York via Havre	27 Nov 1875	10 Nov 1875	651b-657	472908
32	241	Klopstock	New York via Havre	6 Dec 1875	17 Nov 1875	669-672	472908
32	242-243	Frisia	New York via Havre	8 Dec 1875	24 Nov 1875	673-676	472908
32	244	Wieland	New York via Havre	16 Dec 1875	1 Dec 1875	677-680	472908
32	245	Pommerania	New York via Havre	23 Dec 1875	8 Dec 1875	683-686	472908
32	247	Suevia	New York via Havre	3 Jan 1876	15 Dec 1875	687-689	472908
32	248	Gellert	New York via Havre	5 Jan 1876	22 Dec 1875	690-692	472908
32	250	Klopstock	New York via Havre	20 Jan 1876	5 Jan 1876	1-4	472909
32	250-251	Frisia	New York via Havre	29 Jan 1876	12 Jan 1876	5-7	472909
32	252	Wieland	New York via Havre	7 Feb 1876	19 Jan 1876	8-10	472909
32	253	Pommerania	New York via Havre	11 Feb 1876	26 Jan 1876	11-13	472909
32	254	Herder	New York via Havre	21 Feb 1876	2 Feb 1876	14-16	472909
32	256	Suevia	New York via Havre	28 Feb 1876	9 Feb 1876	19-22	472909
32	258	Gellert	New York via Havre	4 Mar 1876	16 Feb 1876	23-28	472909
32	259-260	Klopstock	New York via Havre	11 Mar 1876	23 Feb 1876	29-32	472909

Germans to America vol. and page nos.		Name of the Ship	Route and U.S. Port(s) of Arrival	Date of Arrival	Date of Departure	*HPL* Page numbers	FHL micro-film no.
32	261	Lessing	New York via Havre	20 Mar 1876	1 Mar 1876	33-38	472909
32	263-265	Wieland	New York via Havre	24 Mar 1876	8 Mar 1876	44-53	472909
32	267	Hammonia	Philadelphia	27 Mar 1876	11 Mar 1876	54-55	472909
32	268-269	Cimbria	New York via Havre	31 Mar 1876	15 Mar 1876	56-65	472909
32	272-273	Suevia	New York via Havre	6 Apr 1876	22 Mar 1876	66-72	472909
32	277-278	Gellert	New York via Havre	12 Apr 1876	29 Mar 1876	73-81	472909
32	282-284	Pommerania	New York via Havre	19 Apr 1876	5 Apr 1876	82-95	472909
32	293-294	Lessing	New York via Havre	4 May 1876	19 Apr 1876	143-151a	472909
32	302-304	Wieland	New York via Havre	11 May 1876	26 Apr 1876	154-170	472909
32	309-312	Frisia	New York via Havre and Plymouth	16 May 1876	3 May 1876	173-192	472909
32	314-316	Goethe	New York via Havre and Plymouth	20 May 1876	12 Apr 1876	117-128	472909
32	317-320	Suevia	New York via Havre	25 May 1876	10 May 1876	197-215	472909
32	320	Kate	Philadelphia	27 May 1876	missing	missing	-----
32	326-328	Gellert	New York via Havre	31 May 1876	17 May 1876	321-234	472909
32	334-336	Pommerania	New York via Havre	7 Jun 1876	24 May 1876	246-261	472909
32	339-340	Hammonia	New York via Havre	14 Jun 1876	31 May 1876	262-275	472909
32	344-345	Lessing	New York via Havre	21 Jun 1876	7 Jun 1876	276-284	472909
32	351-352	Wieland	New York via Havre	28 Jun 1876	14 Jun 1876	293-307	472909
32	358-359	Frisia	New York via Havre	5 Jul 1876	21 Jun 1876	316-325	472909
32	362-363	Cimbria	New York via Havre	12 Jul 1876	28 Jun 1876	328-335	472909
32	369-371	Pommerania	New York via Havre	25 Jul 1876	12 Jul 1876	355-363a	472909
32	372-374	Gellert	New York via Havre	29 Jul 1876	5 Jul 1876	340-354	472909
32	376-377	Suevia	New York via Havre	3 Aug 1876	19 Jul 1876	364-380	472909
32	382	Hammonia	New York via Havre	9 Aug 1876	26 Jul 1876	381-389	472909

Germans to America vol. and page nos.		Name of the Ship	Route and U.S. Port(s) of Arrival	Date of Arrival	Date of Departure	*HPL* Page numbers	FHL micro-film no.
32	385-386	Wieland	New York via Havre	15 Aug 1876	2 Aug 1876	391-397	472909
32	390-391	Frisia	New York via Havre	22 Aug 1876	9 Aug 1876	398-413	472909
32	395-396	Cimbria	New York via Havre	29 Aug 1876	16 Aug 1876	414-424	472909
32	400-401	Gellert	New York via Havre	6 Sep 1876	23 Aug 1876	425-436	472909
32	404-405	Pommerania	New York via Havre	13 Sep 1876	30 Aug 1876	439-451	472909
32	410-412	Suevia	New York via Havre	21 Sep 1876	6 Sep 1876	452-465	472909
32	415-416	Lessing	New York via Havre	27 Sep 1876	13 Sep 1876	472-482	472909
33	1-2	Wieland	New York via Havre	4 Oct 1876	20 Sep 1876	483-492	472909
33	5-6	Frisia	New York via Havre	11 Oct 1876	27 Sep 1876	508-517	472909
33	10-11	Cimbria	New York via Havre	20 Oct 1876	4 Oct 1876	518-528	472909
33	16-17	Gellert	New York via Havre	26 Oct 1876	11 Oct 1876	542-553	472909
33	21-22	Pommerania	New York via Havre	1 Nov 1876	18 Oct 1876	556-565	472909
33	25-26	Suevia	New York via Havre	9 Nov 1876	25 Oct 1876	568-577	472909
33	28-29	Lessing	New York via Havre	15 Nov 1876	1 Nov 1876	580-587	472909
33	31-32	Wieland	New York via Havre	21 Nov 1876	8 Nov 1876	591-597	472909
33	34-35	Herder	New York via Havre	1 Dec 1876	15 Nov 1876	598-604	472909
33	38-39	Frisia	New York via Havre	8 Dec 1876	22 Nov 1876	607-614	472909
33	40	Gellert	New York via Havre	16 Dec 1876	29 Nov 1876	618-622	472909
33	42	Pommerania	New York via Havre	25 Dec 1876	6 Dec 1876	629-632	472909
33	44	Suevia	New York via Havre	30 Dec 1876	13 Dec 1876	633-637	472909
33	44-45	Frisia	New York via Havre	1 Jan 1877	22 Dec 1876	607-614	472909
33	45-46	Lessing	New York via Havre	6 Jan 1877	20 Dec 1876	645-647	472909
33	48-49	Herder	New York via Havre	24 Jan 1877	4 Jan 1877	1-3	472910
33	49	Wieland	New York via Havre	27 Jan 1877	10 Jan 1877	4-6	472910

Germans to America vol. and page nos.		Name of the Ship	Route and U.S. Port(s) of Arrival	Date of Arrival	Date of Departure	*HPL* Page numbers	FHL micro-film no.
33	51-52	Gellert	New York via Havre	10 Feb 1877	24 Jan 1877	13-15	472910
33	53-54	Pommerania	New York via Havre	16 Feb 1877	31 Jan 1877	16-18	472910
33	55-56	Suevia	New York via Havre	24 Feb 1877	7 Feb 1877	19-21	472910
33	57	Hammonia	New York via Havre	2 Mar 1877	14 Feb 1877	22-24	472910
33	59-60	Herder	New York via Havre	9 Mar 1877	21 Mar 1877	27-30	472910
33	61	Wieland	New York via Havre	14 Mar 1877	28 Feb 1877	31-34	472910
33	63-64	Frisia	New York via Havre	20 Mar 1877	7 Mar 1877	35-41	472910
33	68	Gellert	New York via Havre	4 Apr 1877	21 Mar 1877	54-59	472910
33	71-72	Suevia	New York via Havre	12 Apr 1877	28 Mar 1877	60-65	472910
33	75-76	Hammonia	New York via Havre	18 Apr 1877	4 Apr 1877	81-88	472910
33	82-84	Herder	New York via Havre	25 Apr 1877	11 Apr 1877	89-100	472910
33	90-91	Wieland	New York via Havre	2 May 1877	18 Apr 1877	101-111	472910
33	95-97	Frisia	New York via Havre	8 May 1877	25 Apr 1877	119-129	472910
33	101-102	Pommerania	New York via Havre	16 May 1877	2 May 1877	137-149	472910
33	107-109	Gellert	New York via Havre	23 May 1877	9 May 1877	161-173	472910
33	115-117	Suevia	New York via Havre	31 May 1877	16 May 1877	174-187	472910
33	121-122	Hammonia	New York via Havre	6 Jun 1877	23 May 1877	192-201	472910
33	126-128	Herder	New York via Havre	14 Jun 1877	30 May 1877	203-211	472910
33	132-133	Wieland	New York via Havre	19 Jun 1877	6 Jun 1877	218-228	472910
33	138-139	Frisia	New York via Havre	26 Jun 1877	13 Jun 1877	237-244a	472910
33	143-144	Pommerania	New York via Havre	3 Jul 1877	20 Jun 1877	268-281	472910
33	148	Gellert	New York via Havre	11 Jul 1877	27 Jun 1877	284-291	472910
33	152-153	Suevia	New York via Havre	19 Jul 1877	4 Jul 1877	295-302	472910
33	156-157	Lessing	New York via Havre	25 Jul 1877	11 Jul 1877	310-316	472910

Germans to America vol. and page nos.		Name of the Ship	Route and U.S. Port(s) of Arrival	Date of Arrival	Date of Departure	*HPL* Page numbers	FHL micro-film no.
33	160-161	Herder	New York via Havre	1 Aug 1877	18 Jul 1877	317-323	472910
33	165-166	Hammonia	New York via Havre	8 Aug 1877	25 Jul 1877	333-340a	472910
33	169-170	Pommerania	New York via Havre	15 Aug 1877	1 Aug 1877	341-349	472910
33	173-174	Wieland	New York via Havre	21 Aug 1877	8 Aug 1877	356-363	472910
33	179-180	Gellert	New York via Havre	28 Aug 1877	15 Aug 1877	364-374	472910
33	185-187	Suevia	New York via Havre	6 Sep 1877	22 Aug 1877	386-395	472910
33	189-190	Lessing	New York via Havre	11 Sep 1877	29 Aug 1877	396-404	472910
33	193-194	Frisia	New York via Havre	18 Sep 1877	5 Sep 1877	405-414	472910
33	198	Herder	New York via Havre	26 Sep 1877	12 Sep 1877	422-428	472910
33	202-203	Pommerania	New York via Havre	3 Oct 1877	19 Sep 1877	429-437	472910
33	208-209	Wieland	New York via Havre	10 Oct 1877	26 Sep 1877	454-461	472910
33	213-214	Gellert	New York via Havre	16 Oct 1877	3 Oct 1877	462-470	472910
33	216-217	Suevia	New York via Havre	27 Oct 1877	10 Oct 1877	478-487	472910
33	220-221	Lessing	New York via Havre	2 Nov 1877	17 Oct 1877	495-503	472910
33	225-226	Frisia	New York via Havre	8 Nov 1877	24 Oct 1877	511-519	472910
33	230	Herder	New York via Havre	19 Nov 1877	31 Oct 1877	520-528	472910
33	232-233	Pommerania	New York via Havre	23 Nov 1877	7 Nov 1877	533-543; 545b	472910
33	236	Wieland	New York via Havre	28 Nov 1877	14 Nov 1877	546-549	472910
33	240-241	Cimbria	New York via Havre	8 Dec 1877	21 Nov 1877	559-562	472910
33	241-242	Gellert	New York via Havre	13 Dec 1877	28 Nov 1877	563-566	472910
33	245	Frisia	New York via Havre	19 Dec 1877	5 Dec 1877	567-570	472910
33	247-248	Lessing	New York via Havre	26 Dec 1877	12 Dec 1877	575-577	472910
33	250	Pommerania	New York via Havre	2 Jan 1878	19 Dec 1877	578-580	472910
33	252	Herder	New York via Havre	10 Jan 1878	26 Dec 1877	585-587	472910

Germans to America vol. and page nos.		Name of the Ship	Route and U.S. Port(s) of Arrival	Date of Arrival	Date of Departure	*HPL* Page numbers	FHL micro-film no.
33	253	Cimbria	New York via Havre	17 Jan 1878	2 Jan 1878	1-3	472911
33	255	Wieland	New York via Havre	23 Jan 1878	9 Jan 1878	13-15	472911
33	257	Frisia	New York via Havre	30 Jan 1878	16 Jan 1878	16-18	472911
33	259	Lina	New York	7 Feb 1878	missing	missing	-----
33	259-260	Gellert	New York via Havre	8 Feb 1878	23 Jan 1878	29-31	472911
33	261	Holsatia	New York via Havre	14 Feb 1878	30 Jan 1878	32-34	472911
33	263-264	Lessing	New York via Havre	21 Feb 1878	6 Feb 1878	46-49	472911
33	265-266	Cimbria	New York via Havre	28 Feb 1878	13 Feb 1878	50-53	472911
33	269-270	Herder	New York via Havre	8 Mar 1878	20 Feb 1878	58-63	472911
33	272-273	Suevia	New York via Havre	15 May 1878	27 Feb 1878	77-80	472911
33	275-276	Gellert	New York via Havre	21 Mar 1878	6 Mar 1878	81-88	472911
33	280-281	Frisia	New York via Havre	27 Mar 1878	13 Mar 1878	89-94	472911
33	286-287	Holsatia	New York via Havre	3 Apr 1878	20 Mar 1878	95-102	472911
33	290-292	Lessing	New York via Havre	10 Apr 1878	27 Mar 1878	103-110	472911
33	297-299	Wieland	New York via Havre	16 Apr 1878	3 Apr 1878	119-129	472911
33	306-307	Suevia	New York via Havre	25 Apr 1878	10 Apr 1878	141-151	472911
33	313-314	Pommerania	New York via Havre	30 Apr 1878	17 Apr 1878	152-158	472911
33	324-326	Frisia	New York via Havre	15 May 1878	1 May 1878	173-187	472911
33	331-333	Herder	New York via Havre	21 May 1878	8 May 1878	190-203	472911
33	340-341	Lessing	New York via have	29 May 1878	15 May 1878	204-214	472911
33	347-348	Wieland	New York via Havre	5 Jun 1878	22 May 1878	229-254	472911
33	354-355	Pommerania	New York via Havre	11 Jun 1878	29 May 1878	255-264	472911
33	361-362	Suevia	New York via Havre	20 Jun 1878	5 Jun 1878	265-272	472911
33	365	Gellert	New York via Havre	25 Jun 1878	12 Jun 1878	273-280	472911

Germans to America vol. and page nos.		Name of the Ship	Route and U.S. Port(s) of Arrival	Date of Arrival	Date of Departure	*HPL* Page numbers	FHL micro-film no.
33	371-372	Frisia	New York via Havre	3 Jul 1878	19 Jun 1878	281-290	472911
33	375-376	Herder	New York via Havre	10 Jul 1878	26 Jun 1878	309-317	472911
33	379-380	Lessing	New York via Havre	17 Jul 1878	3 Jul 1878	318-331	472911
33	384-385	Wieland	New York via Havre	23 Jul 1878	10 Jul 1878	338-347	472911
33	390	Pommerania	New York via Havre	31 Jul 1878	17 Jul 1878	355-363	472911
33	395-396	Suevia	New York via Havre	7 Aug 1878	24 Jul 1878	375-384	472911
33	399-400	Gellert	New York via Havre	13 Aug 1878	31 Jul 1878	385-395	472911
33	405-406	Frisia	New York via Havre	21 Aug 1878	7 Aug 1878	406-415	472911
33	409-410	Herder	New York via Havre	28 Aug 1878	14 Aug 1878	418-427	472911
33	415-416	Lessing	New York via Havre	4 Sep 1878	21 Aug 1878	430-439	472911
33	421-422	Wieland	New York via Havre	10 Sep 1878	28 Aug 1878	442-452	472911
33	432-434	Pommerania	New York via Havre	17 Sep 1878	4 Sep 1878	453-466	472911
33	440-441	Suevia	New York via Havre	26 Sep 1878	11 Sep 1878	473-483	472911
34	2-3	Gellert	New York via Havre	3 Oct 1878	18 Sep 1878	484-492	472911
34	7-8	Frisia	New York via Havre	9 Oct 1878	25 Sep 1878	497-505	472911
34	13-14	Herder	New York via Havre	18 Oct 1878	2 Oct 1878	506-516	472911
34	19-20	Lessing	New York via Havre	24 Oct 1878	9 Oct 1878	534-541	472911
34	27-29	Wieland	New York via Havre	30 Oct 1878	16 Oct 1878	542-552	472911
34	31-33	Pommerania	New York via Havre	6 Nov 1878	23 Oct 1878	557-566	472911
34	38-39	Suevia	New York via Havre	14 Nov 1878	30 Oct 1878	567-573	472911
34	40-41	Gellert	New York via Havre	20 Nov 1878	6 Nov 1878	574-580	472911
34	47-48	Frisia	New York via Havre	27 Nov 1878	13 Nov 1878	597-604	472911
34	51-52	Herder	New York via Havre	3 Dec 1878	20 Nov 1878	605-609	472911
34	55-56	Lessing	New York via Havre	11 Dec 1878	27 Nov 1878	611-614	472911

Germans to America vol. and page nos.		Name of the Ship	Route and U.S. Port(s) of Arrival	Date of Arrival	Date of Departure	*HPL* Page numbers	FHL micro-film no.
34	58-59	Cimbria	New York via Havre	17 Dec 1878	4 Dec 1878	615-618a	472911
34	61	Wieland	New York via Havre	26 Dec 1878	11 Dec 1878	619-621	472911
34	65	Suevia	New York via Havre	7 Jan 1879	18 Dec 1878	622-624	472911
34	66	Frisia	New York via Havre	11 Jan 1879	25 Dec 1878	625-626	472911
34	68	Herder	New York via Havre	20 Jan 1879	1 Jan 1879	1-3	472912
34	69	Gellert	New York via Havre	25 Jan 1879	8 Jan 1879	4-6	472912
34	72	Cimbria	New York via Havre	1 Feb 1879	16 Jan 1879	7-9	472912
34	74	Lessing	New York via Havre	6 Feb 1879	22 Jan 1879	10-12	472912
34	77-78	Wieland	New York via Havre	15 Feb 1879	29 Jan 1879	13-15	472912
34	80-81	Suevia	New York via Havre	24 Feb 1879	5 Feb 1879	16-18	472912
34	82-83	Frisia	New York via Havre	27 Feb 1879	12 Feb 1879	19-23	472912
34	87	Herder	New York via Havre	6 Mar 1879	19 Feb 1879	24-27	472912
34	91-92	Gellert	New York via Havre	14 Mar 1879	26 Feb 1879	28-31	472912
34	95-96	Lessing	New York via Havre	20 Mar 1879	5 Mar 1879	32-37	472912
34	102	Wieland	New York via Havre	27 Mar 1879	12 Mar 1879	42-46	472912
34	106-108	Silesia	New York via Havre	5 Apr 1879	19 Mar 1879	47-53	472912
34	117-118	Suevia	New York via Havre	11 Apr 1879	26 Mar 1879	54-61	472912
34	123-125	Herder	New York via Havre	16 Apr 1879	2 Apr 1879	62-73a	472912
34	135-136	Frisia	New York via Havre	23 Apr 1879	9 Apr 1879	77-87	472912
34	143-145	Gellert	New York via Havre	2 May 1879	16 Apr 1879	88-97	472912
34	152-154	Lessing	New York via Havre	7 May 1879	23 Apr 1879	103-115	472912
34	161-162	Wieland	New York via Havre	13 May 1879	30 Apr 1879	116-129	472912
34	172-174	Silesia	New York via Havre	22 May 1879	7 May 1879	130-147	472912
34	186-189	Suevia	New York via Havre	31 May 1879	14 May 1879	152-168	472912

Germans to America vol. and page nos.		Name of the Ship	Route and U.S. Port(s) of Arrival	Date of Arrival	Date of Departure	*HPL* Page numbers	FHL micro-film no.
34	192-194	Herder	New York via Havre	4 Jun 1879	21 May 1879	174-183a	472912
34	200-202	Frisia	New York via Havre	10 Jun 1879	28 May 1879	184-196	472912
34	207-209	Gellert	New York via Havre	18 Jun 1879	4 Jun 1879	199-209	472912
34	215-217	Lessing	New York via Havre	25 Jun 1879	11 Jun 1879	212-223	472912
34	226-227	Silesia	New York via Havre	3 Jul 1879	18 Jun 1879	224-233	472912
34	232-233	Cimbria	New York via Havre	10 Jul 1879	25 Jun 1879	239-249	472912
34	239-240	Suevia	New York via Havre	17 Jul 1879	2 Jul 1879	250-257	472912
34	245-246	Frisia	New York via Havre	22 Jul 1879	9 Jul 1879	261-271	472912
34	251-252	Herder	New York via Havre	30 Jul 1879	16 Jul 1879	272-283	472912
34	259-260	Gellert	New York via Havre	6 Aug 1879	23 Jul 1879	289-297	472912
34	265-266	Westphalia	New York via Havre	13 Aug 1879	30 Jul 1879	298-306	472912
34	267	Betty Stoirer	New York	15 Aug 1879	missing	missing	-----
34	269	Astronom	New York	16 Aug 1879	missing	missing	-----
34	269-271	Herder	New York via Havre	16 Aug 1879	missing	missing	-----
34	273-274	Lessing	New York via Havre	20 Aug 1879	6 Aug 1879	307-316a	472912
34	282	Silesia	New York via Havre	28 Aug 1879	13 Aug 1879	317-324	472912
34	288-289	Frisia	New York via Havre	3 Sep 1879	20 Aug 1879	325-338	472912
34	297-298	Wieland	New York via Havre	10 Sep 1879	27 Aug 1879	339-351	472912
34	311-312	Westphalia	New York via Havre	23 Sep 1879	10 Sep 1879	369-379	472912
34	320-322	Gellert	New York via Havre	1 Oct 1879	17 Sep 1879	380-389	472912
34	330-332	Lessing	New York via Havre	8 Oct 1879	24 Sep 1879	392-402	472912
34	333	Silesia	New York	10 Oct 1879	missing	missing	-----
34	344-345	Suevia	New York via Havre	16 Oct 1879	1 Oct 1879	404-414	472912
34	352-354	Wieland	New York via Havre	22 Oct 1879	8 Oct 1879	419-431	472912

Germans to America vol. and page nos.		Name of the Ship	Route and U.S. Port(s) of Arrival	Date of Arrival	Date of Departure	*HPL* Page numbers	FHL micro-film no.
34	360-362	Herder	New York via Havre	29 Oct 1879	15 Oct 1879	432-441	472912
34	369-370	Frisia	New York via Havre	5 Nov 1879	22 Oct 1879	446-456	472912
34	380-382	Westphalia	New York via Havre	11 Nov 1879	22 or 29 Oct 1879	456a-472	472912
34	388-389	Gellert	New York via Havre	19 Nov 1879	5 Nov 1879	477-485	472912
34	395-396	Lessing	New York via Havre	26 Nov 1879	12 Nov 1879	487-496	472912
34	405-406	Suevia	New York via Havre	4 Dec 1879	19 Nov 1879	499-505	472912
34	411-412	Wieland	New York via Havre	10 Dec 1879	26 Nov 1879	507-513	472912
34	416-417	Frisia	New York via Havre	17 Dec 1879	3 Dec 1879	514-519	472912
34	420-421	Herder	New York via Havre	26 Dec 1879	10 Dec 1879	520-524	472912
35	2	Westphalia	New York via Havre	3 Jan 1880	17 Dec 1879	525-529	472912
35	4-5	Gellert	New York via Havre	12 Jan 1880	24 Dec 1879	530-532	472912
35	7	Lessing	New York via Havre	15 Jan 1880	31 Dec 1879	533-537	472912
35	10-11	Suevia	New York via Havre	22 Jan 1880	7 Jan 1880	1-3	472913
35	13-14	Wieland	New York via Havre	29 Jan 1880	14 Jan 1880	4-9	472913
35	17-18	Frisia	New York via Havre	6 Feb 1880	21 Jan 1880	10-17	472913
35	23	Westphalia	New York via Havre	14 Feb 1880	28 Jan 1880	18-26	472913
35	27	Wilhelm	New York	20 Feb 1880	missing	missing	-----
35	27-28	Gellert	New York via Havre	24 Feb 1880	4 Feb 1880	27-34	472913
35	34-35	Lessing	New York via Havre	26 Feb 1880	11 Feb 1880	35-47	472913
35	42-44	Silesia	New York via Havre	8 Mar 1880	18 Feb 1880	48-61	472913
35	49-50	Suevia	New York via Havre	12 Mar 1880	25 Feb 1880	62-73	472913
35	58-61	Wieland	New York via Havre	19 Mar 1880	3 Mar 1880	74-93	472913
35	74-77	Frisia	New York via Havre	25 Mar 1880	10 Mar 1880	94-113	472913

Germans to America vol. and page nos.		Name of the Ship	Route and U.S. Port(s) of Arrival	Date of Arrival	Date of Departure	*HPL* Page numbers	FHL micro-film no.
35	96-98	Westphalia	New York via Havre	31 Mar 1880	17 Mar 1880	114-131	472913
35	120-123	Gellert	New York via Havre	8 Apr 1880	24 Mar 1880	134-150	472913
35	134-137	Lessing	New York via Havre	16 Apr 1880	31 Mar 1880	151-166	472913
35	153-160	Herder	New York	22 Apr 1880	7 Apr 1880	167-201a	472913
35	198-200	Allemannia	New York	29 Apr 1880	11 Apr 1880	202-217	472913
35	206-211	Suevia	New York via Havre	29 Apr 1880	14 Apr 1880	218-247	472913
35	230-231	Wieland	New York	1 May 1880	18 or 20 Apr 1880	248-260	472913
35	236-240	Frisia	New York via Havre	5 May 1880	21 Apr 1880	261-290	472913
35	264-269	Westphalia	New York via Havre	12 May 1880	28 Apr 1880	296-328	472913
35	292-298	Gellert	New York via Havre	19 May 1880	5 May 1880	329-361	472913
35	316-320	Silesia	New York	22 May 1880	9 May 1880	366-393	472913
35	333-337	Lessing	New York via Havre	26 May 1880	12 May 1880	394-422	472913
35	351-356	Herder	New York via Havre	2 Jun 1880	19 May 1880	423-453	472913
35	385-389	Suevia	New York via Havre	9 Jun 1880	26 May 1880	460-487	472913
35	394-397	Allemannia	New York	14 Jun 1880	30 May 1880	488-507	472913
35	405-408	Wieland	New York via Havre	15 Jun 1880	2 Jun 1880	508-532	472913
35	426-430	Frisia	New York via Havre	23 Jun 1880	9 Jun 1880	535-561	472913
35	442-446	Westphalia	New York via Havre	30 Jun 1880	16 Jun 1880	562-586	472913
36	14-17	Gellert	New York via Havre	7 Jul 1880	23 Jun 1880	593-622	472913
36	30-34	Herder	New York via Havre	14 Jul 1880	30 Jun 1880	623-648	472913
36	47-51	Cimbria	New York via Havre	22 Jul 1880	7 Jul 1880	651-676	472914
36	60-64	Suevia	New York via Havre	28 Jul 1880	14 Jul 1880	677-705	472914
36	81-85	Wieland	New York via Havre	4 Aug 1880	21 Jul 1880	712-739	472914

Germans to America vol. and page nos.		Name of the Ship	Route and U.S. Port(s) of Arrival	Date of Arrival	Date of Departure	*HPL* Page numbers	FHL micro-film no.
36	95-99	Frisia	New York via Havre	11 Aug 1880	28 Jul 1880	740-764	472914
36	117-121	Westphalia	New York via Havre	18 Aug 1880	4 Aug 1880	767-793	472914
36	139-143	Gellert	New York via Havre	25 Aug 1880	11 Aug 1880	796-820	472914
36	156-158	Silesia	New York	28 Aug 1880	15 Aug 1880	821-838	472914
36	164-166	Herder	New York via Havre	1 Sep 1880	18 Aug 1880	839-862	472914
36	170-172	Cimbria	New York	4 Sep 1880	22 Aug 1880	864-876	472914
36	182-186	Lessing	New York via Havre	8 Sep 1880	25 Aug 1880	877-898	472914
36	201-203	Suevia	New York	13 Sep 1880	29 Aug 1880	899-915	472914
36	209-212	Wieland	New York via Havre	15 Sep 1880	1 Sep 1880	916-935	472914
36	223-225	Allemannia	New York	21 Sep 1880	5 Sep 1880	941-951	472914
36	226-228	Frisia	New York via Havre	22 Sep 1880	8 Sep 1880	952-972	472914
36	248-249	Vandalia	New York	27 Sep 1880	12 Sep 1880	973-980	472914
36	253-257	Westphalia	New York via Havre	29 Sep 1880	15 Sep 1880	981-1006	472914
36	266-268	Frisia	New York via Havre	3 Oct 1880	Missing	Missing	Missing
36	279-283	Gellert	New York via Havre	6 Oct 1880	22 Sep 1880	1011-1036	472914
36	300-303	Silesia	New York	8 Oct 1880	26 Sep 1880	1040-1054	472914
36	310-313	Herder	New York via Havre	12 Oct 1880	29 Sep 1880	1055-1075	472914
36	318-322	Cimbria	New York	15 Oct 1880	3 Oct 1880	1078-1096	472914
36	334-339	Lessing	New York via Havre	20 Oct 1880	6 Oct 1880	1099-1127	472914
36	351-355	Suevia	New York	22 Oct 1880	10 Oct 1880	1131-1148	472914
36	358-361	Wieland	New York via Havre	26 Oct 1880	13 Oct 1880	1149-1171	472914
36	396-399	Allemannia	New York	3 Nov 1880	19 Oct 1880	1178-1197	472914
36	415-417	Vandalia	New York	8 Nov 1880	24 Oct 1880	1216-1231	472914
36	419-424	Westphalia	New York via Havre	10 Nov 1880	27 Oct 1880	1232-1256	472914

Germans to America vol. and page nos.		Name of the Ship	Route and U.S. Port(s) of Arrival	Date of Arrival	Date of Departure	*HPL* Page numbers	FHL micro-film no.
36	448-453	Gellert	New York via Havre	19 Nov 1880	4 Nov 1880	1257-1285	472914
36	467-470	Silesia	New York via Havre	29 Nov 1880	10 or 11 Nov 1880	1286-1312	472914
37	7-8	Cimbria	New York via Havre	2 Dec 1880	14 Nov 1880	1313-1321	472914
37	11-13	Herder	New York via Havre	4 Dec 1880	17 Nov 1880	1322-1341	472914
37	31-33	Lessing	New York via Havre	10 Dec 1880	24 Nov 1880	1344-1360	472914
37	46-48	Suevia	New York via Havre	17 Dec 1880	1 Dec 1880	1361-1377	472914
37	56-58	Frisia	New York via Havre	22 Dec 1880	8 Dec 1880	1384-1399	472914
37	67-68	Westphalia	New York via Havre	31 Dec 1880	15 Dec 1880	1400-1413	472914
37	75-76	Silesia	New York via Havre	6 Jan 1881	22 Dec 1880	1414-1426	472914
37	81-82	Cimbria	New York via Havre	13 Jan 1881	29 Dec 1880	1427-1435	472914
37	85-87	Gellert	New York via Havre	18 Jan 1881	5 Jan 1881	1-14	472915
37	95-97	Herder	New York via Havre	26 Jan 1881	12 Jan 1881	15-29	472915
37	108-110	Lessing	New York via Havre	5 Feb 1881	19 Jan 1881	30-47	472915
37	115-117	Suevia	New York via Havre	11 Feb 1881	26 Jan 1881	48-61	472915
37	121-123	Frisia	New York via Havre	19 Feb 1881	2 Feb 1881	62-79	472915
37	138-140	Wieland	New York via Havre	25 Feb 1881	9 Feb 1881	80-98	472915
37	149	Silesia	New York via Havre	1 Mar 1881	13 Feb 1881	99-108	472915
37	151-154	Westphalia	New York via Havre	3 Mar 1881	16 Feb 1881	109-129	472915
37	170-175	Gellert	New York via Havre	8 Mar 1881	23 Feb 1881	130-154	472915
37	193-195	Cimbria	New York via Havre	14 Mar 1881	27 Feb 1881	155-175	472915
37	199-205	Herder	New York via Havre	16 Mar 1881	2 Mar 1881	176-205	472915
37	236-244	Lessing	New York via Havre	23 Mar 1881	9 Mar 1881	206-237	472915
37	258-265	Suevia	New York via Havre	26 Mar 1881	13 Mar 1881	238-269	472915

Germans to America vol. and page nos.		Name of the Ship	Route and U.S. Port(s) of Arrival	Date of Arrival	Date of Departure	*HPL* Page numbers	FHL micro-film no.
37	284-290	Frisia	New York via Havre	31 Mar 1881	16 Mar 1881	270-294	472915
37	321-327	Vandalia	New York via Havre	6 Apr 1881	20 Mar 1881	295-324	472915
37	334-342	Wieland	New York via Havre	7 Apr 1881	23 Mar 1881	325-359	472915
37	356-364	Silesia	New York via Havre	9 Apr 1881	3 Apr 1881	392-430	472915
37	391-399	Westphalia	New York via Havre	12 Apr 1881	30 Mar 1881	360-391	472915
38	54-61	Gellert	New York via Havre	21 Apr 1881	6 Apr 1881	431-460a	472915
38	75-83	Cimbria	New York via Havre	23 Apr 1881	10 Apr 1881	463-493	472915
38	127-135	Herder	New York via Havre	28 Apr 1881	13 Apr 1881	494-526	472915
38	168-174	Lessing	New York via Havre	4 May 1881	20 Apr 1881	529-557	472915
38	214-221	Suevia	New York via Havre	9 May 1881	24 Apr 1881	567-603	472915
38	229-234	Frisia	New York via Havre	11 May 1881	27 Apr 1881	604-626	472915
38	284-292	Wieland	New York via Havre	18 May 1881	4 May 1881	627-665	472915
38	327-335	Vandalia	New York via Havre	23 May 1881	8 May 1881	672-707	472915
38	346-351	Westphalia	New York via Havre	25 May 1881	11 May 1881	708-734	472915
39	9-13	Cimbria	New York via Havre	1 Jun 1881	18 May 1881	735-761	472915
39	60-68	Silesia	New York via Havre	6 Jun 1881	22 May 1881	772-810	472915
39	70	Glad Tidings	Baltimore	7 Jun 1881	missing	missing	-----
39	91-96	Herder	New York via Havre	9 Jun 1881	25 May 1881	811-840	472915
39	136-141	Lessing	New York via Havre	16 Jun 1881	1 Jun 1881	841-870	472915
39	170-176	Suevia	New York via Havre	20 Jun 1881	5 Jun 1881	874-909	472915
39	187-190	Frisia	New York via Havre	22 Jun 1881	8 Jun 1881	910-930	472915
39	216-219	Australia	New York	27 Jun 1881	8 Jun 1881	931-950	472915
39	229-235	Wieland	New York via Havre	28 Jun 1881	15 Jun 1881	951-978	472915
39	273-277	Westphalia	New York via Havre	6 Jul 1881	22 Jun 1881	1021-1045	472915

Germans to America vol. and page nos.		Name of the Ship	Route and U.S. Port(s) of Arrival	Date of Arrival	Date of Departure	*HPL* Page numbers	FHL micro-film no.
39	309-313	Cimbria	New York via Havre	13 Jul 1881	29 Jun 1881	1046-1069	472915
39	329-333	Silesia	New York	18 Jul 1881	3 Jul 1881	1070-1091	472916
39	339-343	Herder	New York via Havre	21 Jul 1881	6 Jul 1881	1092-1116	472916
39	361-364	Lessing	New York via Havre	28 Jul 1881	13 Jul 1881	1117-1141	472916
39	374-377	Suevia	New York	1 Aug 1881	17 Jul 1881	1145-1162	472916
39	377-383	Vandalia	New York	1 Aug 1881	19 Jun 1881	979-1014	472915
39	383-386	Frisia	New York via Havre	3 Aug 1881	20 Jul 1881	1170-1189	472916
40	19-23	Wieland	New York via Havre	11 Aug 1881	27 Jul 1881	1190-1210	472916
40	38-42	Westphalia	New York via Havre	16 Aug 1881	3 Aug 1881	1224-1247	472916
40	42-45	Australia	New York via Havre	18 Aug 1881	30 Jul 1881	1211-1221	472916
40	60-64	Cimbria	New York via Havre	24 Aug 1881	10 Aug 1881	1250-1273	472916
40	95-97	Silesia	New York via Havre	29 Aug 1881	14 Aug 1881	1274-1287	472916
40	108-111	Herder	New York via Havre	31 Aug 1881	17 Aug 1881	1288-1311	472916
40	122-126	Lessing	New York via Havre	7 Sep 1881	24 Aug 1881	1322-1345	472916
40	127-128	Allemannia	New York via Havre	9 Sep 1881	21 Aug 1881	1315-1321	472916
40	159-162	Suevia	New York	12 Sep 1881	28 Aug 1881	1346-1370	472916
40	164-168	Frisia	New York via Havre	14 Sep 1881	31 Aug 1881	1371-1391	472916
40	186-189	America	New York via Newcastle	17 Sep 1881	31 Aug 1881	1392-1404	472916
40	191	Cashier	Baltimore	19 Sep 1881	missing	missing	-----
40	193-195	Vandalia	New York via Havre	19 Sep 1881	4 Sep 1881	1405-1423	472916
40	205-210	Wieland	New York via Havre	21 Sep 1881	missing	missing	-----
40	234-238	Westphalia	New York via Havre	29 Sep 1881	14 Sep 1881	1455-1480	472916
40	270-275	Cimbria	New York via Havre	6 Oct 1881	21 Sep 1881	1485-1509	472916
40	293-298	Silesia	New York via Havre	10 Oct 1881	25 Sep 1881	1513-1538	472916

Germans to America vol. and page nos.		Name of the Ship	Route and U.S. Port(s) of Arrival	Date of Arrival	Date of Departure	*HPL* Page numbers	FHL micro-film no.
40	306	Kentigern	Baltimore	12 Oct 1881	missing	missing	-----
40	312-316	Herder	New York via Havre	13 Oct 1881	28 Sep 1881	1539-1565	472916
40	337-340	Allemannia	New York	18 Oct 1881	2 Oct 1881	1568-1582	472916
40	348-354	Lessing	New York via Havre	20 Oct 1881	5 Oct 1881	1603-1632	472916
40	363-367	Australia	New York	22 Oct 1881	4 Oct 1881	1583-1599	472916
40	393-400	Suevia	New York	26 Oct 1881	9 Oct 1881	1635-1671	472916
40	409-413	Frisia	New York via Havre	31 Oct 1881	12 Oct 1881	1672-1692	472916
41	10-14	Vandalia	New York	2 Nov 1881	16 Oct 1881	1694-1719	472916
41	14-19	Wieland	New York via Havre	2 Nov 1881	19 Oct 1881	1720-1744b	472916
41	44-47	Rhenania	New York	7 Nov 1881	23 Oct 1881	1751-1765	472916
41	51-57	Westphalia	New York via Havre	9 Nov 1881	26 Oct 1881	1766-1790	472916
41	79-86	Bohemia	New York via Havre	16 Nov 1881	30 Oct 1881	1791-1828	472916
41	86-92	Cimbria	New York via Havre	16 Nov 1881	2 Nov 1881	1850-1878	472916
41	94-98	America	New York	18 Nov 1881	31 Oct 1881	1831-1849	472916
41	112-118	Silesia	New York via Havre	25 Nov 1881	9 Nov 1881	1879-1916	472916
41	144-146	Gellert	New York via Havre	12 Dec 1881	23 Nov 1881	1980-1993	472916
41	154-156	Suevia	New York	12 Dec 1881	20 Nov 1881	1959-1977	472916
41	159	Claudius	New York	15 Dec 1881	missing	missing	-----
41	160-163	Wieland	New York via Havre and Plymouth	16 Dec 1881	30 Nov 1881	2013-2026	472916
41	170-171	Vandalia	New York	19 Dec 1881	27 Nov 1881	2006-2012	472916
41	171-173	Australia	New York	21 Dec 1881	30 Nov 1881	2027-2037	472916
41	184-188	Westphalia	New York via Havre	23 Dec 1881	8 Dec 1881	2038-2051	472916
41	201-202	Cimbria	New York via Havre	31 Dec 1881	14 Dec 1881	2054-2075	472916
41	210	Bohemia	New York	4 Jan 1882	19 Dec 1881	2076-2084	472916

Germans to America vol. and page nos.		Name of the Ship	Route and U.S. Port(s) of Arrival	Date of Arrival	Date of Departure	*HPL* Page numbers	FHL micro-film no.
41	211	Frisia	New York via Havre	4 Jan 1882	21 Dec 1881	2085-2094	472916
41	212-214	Cassius	New York via Falmouth	6 Jan 1882	24 Nov 1881	1994-2005	472916
41	225	Silesia	New York via Havre	16 Jan 1882	28 Dec 1881	2102-2111	472916
41	226-227	Polynesia	New York	17 Jan 1882	22 Dec 1881	2096-2101	472916
41	227-228	Gellert	New York via Havre	19 Jan 1882	4 Jan 1882	1-21	472917
41	232	America	New York	23 Jan 1882	31 Dec 1881	2112-2116	472916
41	237-239	Suevia	New York	27 Jan 1882	11 Jan 1882	24-46	472917
41	250-252	Wieland	New York via Havre	6 Feb 1882	18 Jan 1882	48-71	472917
41	259-261	Westphalia	New York via Havre	10 Feb 1882	25 Jan 1882	72-91	472917
41	267-268	Vandalia	New York	16 Feb 1882	29 Jan 1882	92-103	472917
41	269-271	Lessing	New York via Havre	17 Feb 1882	1 Feb 1882	104-118	472917
41	279-281	Australia	New York	20 Feb 1882	1 Feb 1882	119-133	472917
41	292-296	Cimbria	New York via Havre	25 Feb 1882	8 Feb 1882	134-156	472917
41	305-311	Silesia	New York via Havre	1 Mar 1882	15 Feb 1882	157-190	472917
41	331-336	Gellert	New York via Havre	8 Mar 1882	22 Feb 1882	192-220	472917
41	361-367	Suevia	New York	18 Mar 1882	1 Mar 1882	221-252	472917
41	384-386	Bohemia	New York	21 Mar 1882	5 Mar 1882	253-271	472917
41	402-405	Wieland	New York via Havre	22 Mar 1882	8 Mar 1882	290-315	472917
41	409-412	India	New York	24 Mar 1882	5 Mar 1882	274-287	472917
42	9-13	Vandalia	New York	28 Mar 1882	12 Mar 1882	316-343	472917
42	17-22	Westphalia	New York via Havre	29 Mar 1882	15 Mar 1882	344-368	472917
42	72-75	Allemannia	New York	7 Apr 1882	19 Mar 1882	369-383	472917
42	75-81	Lessing	New York via Havre	7 Apr 1882	22 Mar 1882	384-411	472917
42	109-112	Albingia	New York	12 Apr 1882	26 Mar 1882	412-426	472917

Germans to America vol. and page nos.		Name of the Ship	Route and U.S. Port(s) of Arrival	Date of Arrival	Date of Departure	*HPL* Page numbers	FHL micro-film no.
42	112-117	Cimbria	New York via Havre	12 Apr 1882	29 Mar 1882	427-450	472917
42	154-162	Silesia	New York	17 Apr 1882	2 Apr 1882	472-506	472918
42	183-189	Gellert	New York via Havre	19 Apr 1882	5 Apr 1882	507-534	472918
42	199-203	Polynesia	New York	20 Apr 1882	30 Mar 1882	451-471	472917
42	231-235	Rhenania	New York	27 Apr 1882	9 Apr 1882	559-573	472918
42	239-245	Suevia	New York	28 Apr 1882	12 Apr 1882	574-602	472918
42	264-270	Frisia	New York	1 May 1882	16 Apr 1882	603-628	472918
42	303-309	Wieland	New York via Havre	4 May 1882	19 Apr 1882	629-656	472918
42	320-327	Bohemia	New York	8 May 1882	23 Apr 1882	660-696	472918
42	351-355	Westphalia	New York via Havre	11 May 1882	26 Apr 1882	697-720	472918
42	391-396	Polaria	New York	15 May 1882	26 Apr 1882	721-747	472918
42	407-414	Vandalia	New York	16 May 1882	30 Apr 1882	748-783	472918
42	423-429	Lessing	New York via Havre	18 May 1882	3 May 1882	784-813	472918
43	33-36	Albingia	New York	23 May 1882	7 May 1882	819-833	472918
43	36-42	Herder	New York via Havre	23 May 1882	10 May 1882	834-862	472918
43	57-62	Cimbria	New York	26 May 1882	14 May 1882	863-890	472918
43	93-98	Gellert	New York via Havre	31 May 1882	17 May 1882	904-931	472918
43	105-108	India	New York	31 May 1882	14 May 1882	891-903	472918
43	141-146	Silesia	New York	3 Jun 1882	21 May 1882	934-968	472918
43	156-159	Suevia	New York	8 Jun 1882	24 May 1882	969-990	472918
43	172-175	Frisia	New York	10 Jun 1882	28 May 1882	991-1008	472918
43	192-195	Wieland	New York via Havre	15 Jun 1882	31 May 1882	1009-1026	472918
43	196-199	Polynesia	New York	17 Jun 1882	31 May 1882	1027-1045	472918
43	217-221	Bohemia	New York	22 Jun 1882	4 Jun 1882	1047-1083	472918

Germans to America vol. and page nos.		Name of the Ship	Route and U.S. Port(s) of Arrival	Date of Arrival	Date of Departure	*HPL* Page numbers	FHL micro-film no.
43	244-246	Vandalia	New York	27 Jun 1882	11 Jun 1882	1113-1134	472918
43	251-255	Lessing	New York via Havre	29 Jun 1882	14 Jun 1882	1135-1158	472918
43	268-270	Albingia	New York	5 Jul 1882	18 Jun 1882	1159-1168	472918
43	270-273	Herder	New York via Havre	5 Jul 1882	21 Jun 1882	1192-1209	472918
43	273-275	Australia	New York	6 Jul 1882	18 Jun 1882	1169-1188	472918
43	290-292	Cimbria	New York	10 Jul 1882	25 Jun 1882	1210-1226	472918
43	296-299	Gellert	New York via Havre	12 Jul 1882	28 Jun 1882	1227-1245	472918
43	316-319	Silesia	New York	17 Jul 1882	2 Jul 1882	1267-1282	472919
43	329-332	Polaria	New York	21 Jul 1882	29 Jun 1882	1246-1264	472918
43	339-343	Suevia	New York	21 Jul 1882	5 Jul 1882	1283-1305	472919
43	356-361	Wieland	New York via Havre	26 Jul 1882	12 Jul 1882	1309-1339	472919
43	381-384	Westphalia	New York via Havre	2 Aug 1882	19 Jul 1882	1350-1366	472919
43	406-408	Vandalia	New York	7 Aug 1882	23 Jul 1882	1369-1379	472919
43	408-411	Frisia	New York via Havre	9 Aug 1882	26 Jul 1882	1380-1395	472919
44	19-23	Herder	New York via Havre	15 Aug 1882	2 Aug 1882	1413-1437	472919
44	23-25	Polynesia	New York	15 Aug 1882	30 Jul 1882	1400-1412	472919
44	36-38	Cimbria	New York	19 Aug 1882	6 Aug 1882	1440-1453	472919
44	47-49	Gellert	New York via Havre	24 Aug 1882	9 Aug 1882	1454-1475	472919
44	65-68	Silesia	New York	26 Aug 1882	13 Aug 1882	1476-1492	472919
44	69	British America	Baltimore	28 Aug 1882	missing	missing	-----
44	78-82	Suevia	New York	31 Aug 1882	16 Aug 1882	1493-1511, 1516-1519	472919
44	103-105	Australia	New York	6 Sep 1882	19 Aug 1882	1527-1540	472919
44	112-116	Wieland	New York	7 Sep 1882	23 Aug 1882	1541-1568	472919

Germans to America vol. and page nos.		Name of the Ship	Route and U.S. Port(s) of Arrival	Date of Arrival	Date of Departure	*HPL* Page numbers	FHL micro-film no.
44	126	Bremen	New York	11 Sep 1882	missing	missing	-----
44	132-136	Westphalia	New York via Havre	12 Sep 1882	30 Aug 1882	1583-1602	472919
44	153	Amelia	New York	16 Sep 1882	missing	missing	-----
44	158-160	Vandalia	New York	19 Sep 1882	3 Sep 1882	1603-1619	472919
44	160-163	Frisia	New York via Havre	20 Sep 1882	6 Sep 1882	1637-1656	472919
44	173-174	Polaria	New York	21 Sep 1882	3 Sep 1882	1620-1631	472919
44	187-192	Herder	New York via Havre	26 Sep 1882	13 Sep 1882	1659-1689	472919
44	204-207	Cimbria	New York	30 Sep 1882	17 Sep 1882	1692-1708	472919
44	214-217	Habsburg	New York	2 Oct 1882	missing	missing	-----
44	224-229	Vandalia	New York	3 Oct 1882	missing	missing	-----
44	230-233	Gellert	New York via Havre	4 Oct 1882	20 Sep 1882	1713-1732	472919
44	254-257	Silesia	New York	7 Oct 1882	24 Sep 1882	1747-1762	472919
44	258-260	India	New York	9 Oct 1882	21 Sep 1882	1733-1744	472919
44	267-271	Suevia	New York	12 Oct 1882	27 Sep 1882	1763-1786	472919
44	298-305	Wieland	New York via Havre	19 Oct 1882	4 Oct 1882	1791-1819	472919
44	313-320	Bohemia	New York	23 Oct 1882	8 Oct 1882	1843-1877	472919
44	320-324	Polynesia	New York	23 Oct 1882	5 Oct 1882	1822-1840	472919
44	331-335	Westphalia	New York via Havre	24 Oct 1882	11 Oct 1882	1878-1902	472919
44	375-378	Frisia	New York via Havre	8 Nov 1882	18 Oct 1882	1933-1951	472919
44	382-385	Australia	New York	9 Nov 1882	19 Oct 1882	1956-1974	472919
44	388-392	Allemannia	New York	10 Nov 1882	22 Oct 1882	1979-1994	472919
44	393-399	Cimbria	New York via Havre	13 Nov 1882	25 Oct 1882	1995-2023	472919
45	8-Jan	Lessing	New York	16 Nov 1882	29 Oct 1882	2024-2058	472919
45	27-30	Polaria	New York	23 Nov 1882	1 Nov 1882	2087-2122	472919

Germans to America vol. and page nos.		Name of the Ship	Route and U.S. Port(s) of Arrival	Date of Arrival	Date of Departure	*HPL* Page numbers	FHL micro-film no.
45	30-33	Silesia	New York	23 Nov 1882	5 Nov 1882	2116-2143	472919
45	39-42	Suevia	New York	27 Nov 1882	8 Nov 1882	2144-2166	472919
45	53-58	Gellert	New York via Havre and Plymouth	2 Dec 1882	1 Nov 1882	2059-2086	472919
45	71-74	Wieland	New York via Havre	7 Dec 1882	15 Nov 1882	2169-2193	472919
45	77-78	India	New York	12 Dec 1882	19 Nov 1882	2194-2206	472919
45	83-86	Rugia	New York	13 Dec 1882	22 Nov 1882	2207-2231	472919
45	87-88	Bohemia	New York	15 Dec 1882	26 Nov 1882	2232-2240	472919
45	90-91	Frisia	New York via Havre	15 Dec 1882	29 Nov 1882	2241-2252	472919
45	101-102	Vandalia	New York	21 Dec 1882	3 Dec 1882	2254-2261	472919
45	106-107	Cimbria	New York via Havre	22 Dec 1882	6 Dec 1882	2262-2275	472919
45	113-115	Silesia	New York via Havre	29 Dec 1882	13 Dec 1882	2286-2299	472919
45	116-117	Polynesia	New York	30 Dec 1882	7 Dec 1882	2276-2285	472919
45	121-122	Gellert	New York via Havre	5 Jan 1883	22 Dec 1882	2307-2316	472919
45	133-134	Australia	New York	15 Jan 1883	21 Dec 1882	2300-2306	472919
45	136-137	Wieland	New York	15 Jan 1883	30 Dec 1882	2317-2328	472919
45	137-138	Rugia	New York via Havre	18 Jan 1883	3 Jan 1883	1-11	472920
45	143-144	Frisia	New York	27 Jan 1883	10 Jan 1883	12-22	472920
45	157-158	Westphalia	New York via Havre	8 Feb 1883	24 Jan 1883	41-50	472920
45	170	Polaria	New York	15 Feb 1883	18 Jan 1883	35-39	472920
45	171-172	Silisia	New York via Havre	19 Feb 1883	31 Jan 1883	51-60	472920
45	178	Bohemia	New York	23 Feb 1883	4 Feb 1883	64-70	472920
45	197-200	Vandalia	New York	2 Mar 1883	12 Feb 1883	88-95	472920
45	208-210	Wieland	New York via Havre	5 Mar 1883	14 Feb 1883	96-113	472920
45	211-212	Polynesia	New York	6 Mar 1883	8 Feb 1883	82-87	472920

Germans to America vol. and page nos.		Name of the Ship	Route and U.S. Port(s) of Arrival	Date of Arrival	Date of Departure	*HPL* Page numbers	FHL micro-film no.
45	224-227	Suevia	New York	10 Mar 1883	21 Feb 1883	123-140	472920
45	227-231	Hammonia	New York via Havre	12 Mar 1883	28 Feb 1883	141-163	472920
45	236-237	Australia	New York	13 Mar 1883	20 Feb 1883	114-122	472920
45	257-259	Rugia	New York	19 Mar 1883	4 Mar 1883	164-175	472920
45	260-263	Gellert	New York	21 Mar 1883	7 Mar 1883	181-202	472920
45	286-290	Westphalia	New York via Havre	27 Mar 1883	14 Mar 1883	203-230	472920
45	301-305	California	New York	30 Mar 1883	15 Mar 1883	231-253	472920
45	313-315	Silesia	New York via Havre	2 Apr 1883	18 Mar 1883	254-270	472920
45	318-321	Frisia	New York via Havre	4 Apr 1883	21 Mar 1883	276-293	472920
45	353-358	Wieland	New York via Havre	13 Apr 1883	28 Mar 1883	294-305	472920
45	387-393	Bohemia	New York	16 Apr 1883	1 Apr 1883	322-353	472920
45	415-423	Rhaetia	New York via Havre	19 Apr 1883	4 Apr 1883	354-388	472920
46	5-12	Polaria	New York	20 Apr 1883	4 Apr 1883	389-417	472920
46	28-33	Suevia	New York	23 Apr 1883	8 Apr 1883	427-454	472920
46	34-39	Hammonia	New York via Havre	25 Apr 1883	11 Apr 1883	455-477	472920
46	63-69	Gellert	New York via Havre	1 May 1883	18 Apr 1883	500-527	472920
46	90-94	Polynesia	New York	4 May 1883	12 Apr 1883	478-499	472920
46	121-125	Rugia	New York	7 May 1883	22 Apr 1883	533-560	472920
46	127-130	Westphalia	New York via Havre	8 May 1883	25 Apr 1883	561-581	472920
46	146-150	Australia	New York	14 May 1883	26 Apr 1883	583-604	472920
46	165-170	Frisia	New York via Havre	16 May 1883	2 May 1883	626-652	472920
46	202-209	California	New York	23 May 1883	6 May 1883	664-696	472920
46	224-229	Wieland	New York	23 May 1883	9 May 1883	697-722	472920
46	274-279	Suevia	New York	31 May 1883	16 May 1883	723-753	472920

Germans to America vol. and page nos.		Name of the Ship	Route and U.S. Port(s) of Arrival	Date of Arrival	Date of Departure	*HPL* Page numbers	FHL micro-film no.
46	298-302	Bohemia	New York via Havre	5 Jun 1883	20 May 1883	769-800	472920
46	302-306	Hammonia	New York	5 Jun 1883	23 May 1883	806-831	472920
46	312-314	India	New York	6 Jun 1883	19 May 1883	756-768	472920
46	330-334	Rhaetia	New York via Havre	11 Jun 1883	27 May 1883	858-891	472920
46	343-347	Gellert	New York via Havre	12 Jun 1883	30 May 1883	892-918	472920
46	348-352	Polaria	New York	13 Jun 1883	24 May 1883	832-857	472920
46	380-383	Westphalia	New York via Havre	19 Jun 1883	6 Jun 1883	948-973	472920
46	391-394	Polynesia	New York	22 Jun 1883	3 Jun 1883	923-944	472920
46	398-401	Rugia	New York	23 Jun 1883	10 Jun 1883	974-996	472920
46	410-413	Frisia	New York via Havre	26 Jun 1883	13 Jun 1883	997-1012	472920
47	25-28	California	New York	13 Jul 1883	28 Jun 1883	1086-1100	472920
47	31-33	Suevia	New York	13 Jul 1883	27 Jun 1883	1066-1085	472920
47	40-41	Silesia	New York	16 Jul 1883	1 Jul 1883	1103-1117	472921
47	54-55	Bohemia	New York via Havre	23 Jul 1883	8 Jul 1883	1143-1156	472921
47	63-65	Gellert	New York via Havre	24 Jul 1883	11 Jul 1883	1157-1171	472921
47	77-78	Rhaetia	New York via Havre	28 Jul 1883	15 Jul 1883	1172-1186	472921
47	85-87	Polaria	New York	2 Aug 1883	15 Jul 1883	1187-1198	472921
47	98-101	Frisia	New York via Havre	7 Aug 1883	25 Jul 1883	1219-1241	472921
47	111-113	Rugia	New York	11 Aug 1883	29 Jul 1883	1257-1269	472921
47	118	Bremen	New York	15 Aug 1883	missing	missing	-----
47	122-124	India	New York	16 Aug 1883	29 Jul 1883	1245-1256	472921
47	149-150	Polynesia	New York	25 Aug 1883	7 Aug 1883	1270a-1275a	472921
47	152-156	Suevia	New York	25 Aug 1883	8 Aug 1883	1276a-1301	472921
47	167-169	Silesia	New York via Havre	27 Aug 1883	12 Aug 1883	1310-1322	472921

Germans to America vol. and page nos.		Name of the Ship	Route and U.S. Port(s) of Arrival	Date of Arrival	Date of Departure	*HPL* Page numbers	FHL micro-film no.
47	169-174	Hammonia	New York via Havre	28 Aug 1883	16 Aug 1883	1323-1346	472921
47	181-182	Australia	New York	31 Aug 1883	11 Aug 1883	1302-1309	472921
47	197-201	Gellert	New York via Havre	5 Sep 1883	22 Aug 1883	1363-1388	472921
47	201-203	California	New York	7 Sep 1883	22 Aug 1883	1349-1362	472921
47	215-217	Bohemia	New York	10 Sep 1883	26 Aug 1883	1389-1402	472921
47	223-226	Westphalia	New York via Havre	11 Sep 1883	29 Aug 1883	1403-1422	472921
47	249-252	Frisia	New York via Havre	18 Sep 1883	5 Sep 1883	1443-1464	472921
47	252-254	Rhaetia	New York via Havre	18 Sep 1883	2 Sep 1883	1425-1442	472921
47	275-279	Rugia	New York	25 Sep 1883	12 Sep 1883	1485-1515	472921
47	284-287	Polaria	New York	26 Sep 1883	6 Sep 1883	1467-1485a	472921
47	302-306	Gellert	New York via Havre	1 Oct 1883	missing	missing	-----
47	324-328	Suevia	New York	5 Oct 1883	19 Sep 1883	1523-1550	472921
47	332-335	Silesia	New York via Havre	8 Oct 1883	23 Sep 1883	1552-1572	472921
47	338-343	Hammonia	New York	9 Oct 1883	26 Sep 1883	1586-1610	472921
47	349-351	India	New York	12 Oct 1883	23 Sep 1883	1573-1585	472921
47	366	Sebastian Bach	New York	15 Oct 1883	missing	missing	-----
47	366-372	Lessing	New York	16 Oct 1883	3 Oct 1883	1613a-1641	472921
47	372	China	New York	17 Oct 1883	missing	missing	-----
47	400-405	Westphalia	New York	23 Oct 1883	10 Oct 1883	1660-1685	472921
47	405-408	Polynesia	New York	25 Oct 1883	6 Oct 1883	1642-1659	472921
47	420-425	Bohemia	New York	29 Oct 1883	14 Oct 1883	1704-1732	472921
47	433-435	Australia	New York	30 Oct 1883	11 Oct 1883	1686-1703	472921
48	18-24	Frisia	New York via Havre	5 Nov 1883	24 Oct 1883	1792-1818	472921
48	26-30	Rhaetia	New York	5 Nov 1883	21 Oct 1883	1763-1783	472921

Germans to America vol. and page nos.		Name of the Ship	Route and U.S. Port(s) of Arrival	Date of Arrival	Date of Departure	*HPL* Page numbers	FHL micro-film no.
48	55-61	Rugia	New York	17 Nov 1883	31 Oct 1883	1851-1886	472921
48	64-70	California	New York	19 Nov 1883	30 Oct 1883	1819-1850	472921
48	74-76	Silesia	New York	20 Nov 1883	4 Nov 1883	1887-1908	472921
48	80-83	Hammonia	New York	22 Nov 1883	7 Nov 1883	1924-1946	472921
48	96-99	Lessing	New York via Havre	26 Nov 1883	14 Nov 1883	1947-1974	472921
48	102-103	Polaria	New York	28 Nov 1883	7 Nov 1883	1909-1923	472921
48	112-114	Moravia	New York via Havre	5 Dec 1883	18 Nov 1883	1975-1992	472921
48	114-117	Westphalia	New York via Havre	5 Dec 1883	21 Nov 1883	2010-2030	472921
48	127-129	Gellert	New York via Havre	11 Dec 1883	28 Nov 1883	2033-2053	472921
48	129-132	India	New York	12 Dec 1883	21 Nov 1883	1996-2009	472921
48	144-145	Bohemia	New York via Havre	18 Dec 1883	2 Dec 1883	2068-2076	472921
48	148-149	Rhaetia	New York via Havre	21 Dec 1883	5 Dec 1883	2077-2087	472921
48	151-152	Polynesia	New York	22 Dec 1883	1 Dec 1883	2054-2067	472921
48	160-162	Wieland	New York	27 Dec 1883	12 Dec 1883	2101-2114	472921
48	164-165	Australia	New York	2 Jan 1884	11 Dec 1883	2090-2100	472921
48	166-167	Rugia	New York	3 Jan 1884	19 Dec 1883	2115-2127	472921
48	171	California	New York	8 Jan 1884	23 Dec 1883	2131-2137	472921
48	174-175	Frisia	New York	14 Jan 1884	30 Dec 1883	2138-2146	472921
48	176	Victoria	New York	14 Jan 1884	missing	missing	-----
48	178-179	Lessing	New York	21 Jan 1884	6 Jan 1884	1-12	472922
48	182-183	Westphalia	New York via Havre	23 Jan 1884	9 Jan 1884	13-20	472922
48	189-190	Gellert	New York	29 Jan 1884	16 Jan 1884	37-50	472922
48	190	Polaria	New York	29 Jan 1884	9 Jan 1884	21-28	472922
48	194	India	New York	5 Feb 1884	15 Jan 1884	29-36	472922

Germans to America vol. and page nos.		Name of the Ship	Route and U.S. Port(s) of Arrival	Date of Arrival	Date of Departure	*HPL* Page numbers	FHL micro-film no.
48	197-198	Rhaetia	New York via Havre	8 Feb 1884	20 Jan 1884	53-60	472922
48	204-205	Moravia	New York	11 Feb 1884	23 Jan 1884	61-69	472922
48	209-210	Rugia	New York	13 Feb 1884	30 Jan 1884	78-94	472922
48	214	Polynesia	New York	15 Feb 1884	24 Jan 1884	70-77	472922
48	217-218	Wieland	New York	19 Feb 1884	3 Feb 1884	95-106	472922
48	218-220	Frisia	New York	20 Feb 1884	6 Feb 1884	109-123	472922
48	235-238	Bohemia	New York	29 Feb 1884	13 Feb 1884	124-148	472922
48	239-241	California	New York	3 Mar 1884	14 Feb 1884	149-165	472922
48	244-246	Lessing	New York via Havre	4 Mar 1884	17 Feb 1884	166-183; 192-195	472922
48	246-248	Westphalia	New York	6 Mar 1884	20 Feb 1884	184-191: 196-202	472922
48	259-262	Gellert	New York	12 Mar 1884	27 Feb 1884	203-229	472922
48	281-282	Australia	New York	20 Mar 1884	28 Feb 1884	230-241	472922
48	286-292	Rhaetia	New York	21 Mar 1884	5 Mar 1884	244-279	472922
48	314-318	Moravia	New York	27 Mar 1884	12 Mar 1884	298-337	472922
48	341-343	Polaria	New York	31 Mar 1884	9 Mar 1884	283-297	472922
48	346-349	Wieland	New York	31 Mar 1884	16 Mar 1884	338-365	472922
48	352-356	Rugia	New York	2 Apr 1884	19 Mar 1884	366-397	472922
48	383-388	Hammonia	New York via Havre	7 Apr 1884	23 Mar 1884	411-438	472922
48	388-393	Frisia	New York	8 Apr 1884	26 Mar 1884	439-465	472922
48	393-395	India	New York	8 Apr 1884	20 Mar 1884	398-410	472922
48	415-421	Lessing	New York via Havre	12 Apr 1884	30 Mar 1884	466-495	472922
49	14-20	Bohemia	New York	18 Apr 1884	2 Apr 1884	497-533	472922
49	51-58	Gellert	New York via Havre	21 Apr 1884	6 Apr 1884	556-586	472922
49	62-66	Polynesia	New York	21 Apr 1884	3 Apr 1884	534-555	472922

Germans to America vol. and page nos.		Name of the Ship	Route and U.S. Port(s) of Arrival	Date of Arrival	Date of Departure	*HPL* Page numbers	FHL micro-film no.
49	68-74	Westphalia	New York	22 Apr 1884	9 Apr 1884	592-619	472922
49	88-94	California	New York	24 Apr 1884	10 Apr 1884	620-648	472922
49	107-113	Rhaetia	New York	30 Apr 1884	16 Apr 1884	649-681	472922
49	132-137	Wieland	New York	2 May 1884	20 Apr 1884	683-709	472922
49	144-150	Moravia	New York	6 May 1884	23 Apr 1884	717-754	472922
49	175-176	Australia	New York	12 May 1884	24 Apr 1884	755-773	472922
49	193-199	Rugia	New York	15 May 1884	30 Apr 1884	774-811	472922
49	224-230	Hammonia	New York via Havre	19 May 1884	4 May 1884	814-841	472922
49	233-237	Frisia	New York	20 May 1884	7 May 1884	879-905	472922
49	272-277	Polaria	New York	25 May 1884	4 May 1884	842-871	472922
49	281-286	Lessing	New York	27 May 1884	11 May 1884	906-934	472922
49	292-298	Bohemia	New York	29 May 1884	14 May 1884	935-972	472922
49	316-318	India	New York	2 Jun 1884	15 May 1884	973-986	472922
49	318-322	Westphalia	New York	2 Jun 1884	21 May 1884	1022-1049	472922
49	324-329	Gellert	New York via Havre	3 Jun 1884	18 May 1884	989-1016	472922
49	360-364	Rhaetia	New York	11 Jun 1884	28 May 1884	1050-1084	472922
49	375-377	Wieland	New York	13 Jun 1884	1 Jun 1884	1106-1120	472922
49	384-386	Polynesia	New York	14 Jun 1884	29 May 1884	1084a-1105	472922
49	389-392	Suevia	New York	18 Jun 1884	4 Jun 1884	1121-1142	472922
49	392-394	California	New York	19 Jun 1884	5 Jun 1884	1145-1160	472922
49	407-409	Moravia	New York	24 Jun 1884	11 Jun 1884	1161-1189	472922
49	414-417	Hammonia	New York via Havre	27 Jun 1884	15 Jun 1884	1190-1214	472922
50	11-13	Rugia	New York	3 Jul 1884	18 Jun 1884	1215-1234	472922
50	18-20	Australia	New York	7 Jul 1884	19 Jun 1884	1238-1249	472922

Germans to America vol. and page nos.		Name of the Ship	Route and U.S. Port(s) of Arrival	Date of Arrival	Date of Departure	*HPL* Page numbers	FHL micro-film no.
50	20-23	Gellert	New York	7 Jul 1884	25 Jun 1884	1265-1282	472922
50	23-24	Lessing	New York via Havre	7 Jul 1884	22 Jun 1884	1250-1264	472922
50	36-37	India	New York	15 Jul 1884	29 Jun 1884	1283-1295	472922
50	44-47	Bohemia	New York	17 Jul 1884	2 Jul 1884	1296-1322	472923
50	57-59	Wieland	New York	21 Jul 1884	9 Jul 1884	1350-1366	472923
50	59-61	Westphalia	New York via Havre	22 Jul 1884	6 Jul 1884	1323-1345	472923
50	75-76	Polaria	New York	28 Jul 1884	10 Jul 1884	1367-1375	472923
50	76-77	Rhaetia	New York via Havre	28 Jul 1884	14 Jul 1884	1376-1393	472923
50	88-90	Suevia	New York	1 Aug 1884	17 Jul 1884	1394-1412	472923
50	95-97	Rugia	New York	5 Aug 1884	23 Jul 1884	1423-1445	472923
50	100-101	Polynesia	New York	6 Aug 1884	20 Jul 1884	1415-1422	472923
50	110-112	Hammonia	New York	11 Aug 1884	27 Jul 1884	1446-1465	472923
50	117-118	California	New York	13 Aug 1884	30 Jul 1884	1466-1476	472923
50	158-160	Westphalia	New York	30 Aug 1884	17 Aug 1884	1549-1565	472923
50	160-161	Australia	New York	1 Sep 1884	14 Aug 1884	1538-1548	472923
50	171-172	Hungaria	New York	4 Sep 1884	20 Aug 1884	1570-1584	472923
50	182-184	Wieland	New York	8 Sep 1884	24 Aug 1884	1586-1605	472923
50	187-188	Rhaetia	New York	9 Sep 1884	27 Aug 1884	1606-1621	472923
50	200-201	India	New York	15 Sep 1884	27 Aug 1884	1622-1629	472923
50	201-203	Suevia	New York via Havre	15 Sep 1884	31 Aug 1884	1630-1646	472923
50	206-208	Frisia	New York	18 Sep 1884	4 Sep 1884	1647-1663	472923
50	215-216	Hammonia	New York via Havre	20 Sep 1884	7 Sep 1884	1669-1687	472923
50	222-223	Rugia	New York	22 Sep 1884	10 Sep 1884	1696-1709	472923
50	239-240	Polaria	New York	25 Sep 1884	7 Sep 1884	1688-1695	472923

Germans to America vol. and page nos.		Name of the Ship	Route and U.S. Port(s) of Arrival	Date of Arrival	Date of Departure	*HPL* Page numbers	FHL micro-film no.
50	244-246	Moravia	New York	30 Sep 1884	17 Sep 1884	1725-1735	472923
50	249-252	Lessing	New York	2 Oct 1884	14 Sep 1884	1709a-1722	472923
50	260-263	Gellert	New York via Havre	6 Oct 1884	21 Sep 1884	1747-1761	472923
50	273-274	Polynesia	New York	9 Oct 1884	20 Sep 1884	1739-1746	472923
50	285-287	Silesia	New York	11 Oct 1884	24 Sep 1884	1762-1775	472923
50	287-289	Westphalia	New York via Havre	11 Oct 1884	28 Sep 1884	1776-1791	472923
50	296-298	Bohemia	New York	15 Oct 1884	1 Oct 1884	1792-1806	472923
50	308-311	Wieland	New York	20 Oct 1884	5 Oct 1884	1825-1845	472923
50	311-313	California	New York	21 Oct 1884	4 Oct 1884	1809-1820	472923
50	314-317	Rhaetia	New York	22 Oct 1884	8 Oct 1884	1846-1861	472923
50	334-336	Suevia	New York via Havre	27 Oct 1884	12 Oct 1884	1864-1876	472923
50	337-339	Frisia	New York	28 Oct 1884	15 Oct 1884	1877-1891	472923
50	352-356	Hammonia	New York via Havre	1 Nov 1884	19 Oct 1884	1896-1916	472923
50	357-360	Rugia	New York	5 Nov 1884	22 Oct 1884	1929-1945	472923
50	364-366	Australia	New York	8 Nov 1884	19 Oct 1884	1917-1926	472923
50	378-382	Lessing	New York via Havre	10 Nov 1884	26 Oct 1884	1946-1968	472923
50	387-390	Moravia	New York	14 Nov 1884	30 Oct 1884	1970-1990	472923
50	403-406	Polaria	New York	21 Nov 1884	31 Oct / 1 Nov 1884	1991-2005	472923
50	406-409	Silesia	New York	21 Nov 1884	5 Nov 1884	2025-2034	472923
50	413-414	Westphalia	New York via Havre	22 Nov 1884	9 Nov 1884	2042-2051	472923
50	416-417	India	New York	28 Nov 1884	8 Nov 1884	2035-2041	472923
50	419-420	Wieland	New York	28 Nov 1884	12 Nov 1884	2052-2064	472923
51	1-3	Bohemia	New York	3 Dec 1884	19 Nov 1884	2065-2080	472923

Germans to America vol. and page nos.		Name of the Ship	Route and U.S. Port(s) of Arrival	Date of Arrival	Date of Departure	*HPL* Page numbers	FHL micro-film no.
51	9-10	Polynesia	New York	6 Dec 1884	20 Nov 1884	2084-2090	472923
51	12-13	Suevia	New York	9 Dec 1884	23 Nov 1884	2091-2099	472923
51	16	Rugia	New York	18 Dec 1884	3 Dec 1884	2111-2117	472923
51	18-19	California	New York	22 Dec 1884	4 Dec 1884	2118-2122	472923
51	21	Gellert	New York via Havre	23 Dec 1884	7 Dec 1884	2123-2129	472923
51	23-24	Moravia	New York	29 Dec 1884	12 Dec 1884	2130-2134	472923
51	26-27	Westphalia	New York	30 Dec 1884	17 Dec 1884	2135-2141	472923
51	32-33	Wieland	New York	5 Jan 1885	24 Dec 1884	2147-2152	472923
51	33-34	Australia	New York	10 Jan 1885	21 Dec 1884	2144-2146	472923
51	35	Bohemia	New York	16 Jan 1885	31 Dec 1884	2153-2158	472923
51	43	Polaria	New York	27 Jan 1885	1 Jan 1885	1-3	472924
51	53-54	Rhaetia	New York	14 Feb 1885	28 Jan 1885	34-42	472924
51	56	Polynesia	New York	17 Feb 1885	25 Jan 1885	30-33	472924
51	61-62	Gellert	New York via Havre	23 Feb 1885	8 Feb 1885	58-62	472924
51	63	Westphalia	New York	25 Feb 1885	11 Feb 1885	63-68	472924
51	73-74	Bohemia	New York	7 Mar 1885	18 Feb 1885	69-77	472924
51	80-81	Wieland	New York	9 Mar 1885	25 Feb 1885	98-106	472924
51	81-82	Suevia	New York via Havre	10 Mar 1885	22 Feb 1885	90-97	472924
51	82-83	Australia	New York	12 Mar 1885	19 Feb 1885	83-89	472924
51	97-99	Lessing	New York via Havre	21 Mar 1885	8 Mar 1885	131-142	472924
51	102-103	Frisia	New York	25 Mar 1885	11 Mar 1885	143-154	472924
51	103-104	Polaria	New York	25 Mar 1885	5 Mar 1885	122-130	472924
51	116-117	Hammonia	New York via Havre	30 Mar 1885	15 Mar 1885	165-169	472924
51	121-123	India	New York	1 Apr 1885	14 Mar 1885	155-164	472924

Germans to America vol. and page nos.		Name of the Ship	Route and U.S. Port(s) of Arrival	Date of Arrival	Date of Departure	*HPL* Page numbers	FHL micro-film no.
51	129-132	Moravia	New York	2 Apr 1885	19 Mar 1885	170-186	472924
51	152-153	Polynesia	New York	14 Apr 1885	26 Mar 1885	211-222	472924
51	154-158	Gellert	New York	15 Apr 1885	25 Mar 1885	187-210	472924
51	163-167	Bohemia	New York	18 Apr 1885	2 Apr 1885	237-256	472924
51	167-170	California	New York	18 Apr 1885	2 Apr 1885	257-272	472924
51	194-198	Rugia	New York	28 Apr 1885	15 Apr 1885	323-348	472924
51	221	Europa	New York	2 May 1885	missing	missing	-----
51	228-230	Australia	New York	5 May 1885	16 Apr 1885	349-366	472924
51	230-235	Wieland	New York	5 May 1885	22 Apr 1885	395-422	472924
51	245-250	Moravia	New York	12 May 1885	29 Apr 1885	423-462	472924
51	250-253	Rhaetia	New York	12 May 1885	19 Apr 1885	374-394	472924
51	263-267	Hammonia	New York via Havre	15 May 1885	3 May 1885	486a-509	472924
51	289-292	Polaria	New York	18 May 1885	30 Apr 1885	463-485	472924
51	292-295	Frisia	New York	19 May 1885	6 May 1885	512-535	472924
51	303-305	India	New York	22 May 1885	7 May 1885	536-548	472924
51	315-319	Gellert	New York via Havre	23 May 1885	10 May 1885	549-576	472924
51	320-323	Westphalia	New York	25 May 1885	13 May 1885	581-607a	472924
51	350-352	Polynesia	New York	4 Jun 1885	17 May 1885	636-657	472924
51	352-356	Bohemia	New York	5 Jun 1885	20 May 1885	664-695	472924
51	380-383	Wieland	New York	6 Jun 1885	24 May 1885	696-713	472924
51	386-389	Rugia	New York	11 Jun 1885	28 May 1885	714-732	472924
51	393	Annie	New York	14 Jun 1885	missing	missing	-----
51	393-394	California	New York	15 Jun 1885	28 May 1885	733-747a	472924
51	395-401	Rhaetia	New York	17 Jun 1885	3 Jun 1885	750-786	472924

Germans to America vol. and page nos.		Name of the Ship	Route and U.S. Port(s) of Arrival	Date of Arrival	Date of Departure	*HPL* Page numbers	FHL micro-film no.
51	412-415	Moravia	New York	23 Jun 1885	10 Jun 1885	791-824	472924
51	423-426	Frisia	New York	30 Jun 1885	17 Jun 1885	864-884	472924
52	10-11	Polaria	New York	8 Jul 1885	21 Jun 1885	888-897	472924
52	17-19	Westphalia	New York via Havre	11 Jul 1885	28 Jun 1885	921-934	472924
52	20-22	Lessing	New York	13 Jul 1885	1 Jul 1885	942-955	472925
52	22-23	India	New York	14 Jul 1885	28 Jun 1885	935-941	472924
52	32-34	Bohemia	New York	23 Jul 1885	8 Jul 1885	962-97[illegible]	472925
52	39-40	Wieland	New York	25 Jul 1885	12 Jul 1885	979-991	472925
52	43-44	Rugia	New York	28 Jul 1885	15 Jul 1885	992-1003	472925
52	44-47	California	New York	31 Jul 1885	16 Jul 1885	1004-1018	472925
52	52-53	Rhaetia	New York	5 Aug 1885	22 Jul 1885	1019-1030	472925
52	56-58	Hammonia	New York via Havre	7 Aug 1885	26 Jul 1885	1031-1046	472925
52	63-64	Suevia	New York	10 Aug 1885	29 Jul 1885	1047-1057	472925
52	72-73	Polynesia	New York	15 Aug 1885	30 Jul 1885	1058-1064	472925
52	74-76	Moravia	New York	18 Aug 1885	5 Aug 1885	1088-1105	472925
52	88	Australia	New York	26 Aug 1885	8 Aug 1885	1117-1122	472925
52	89-90	Frisia	New York	27 Aug 1885	12 Aug 1885	1123-1141	472925
52	94-97	Westphalia	New York via Havre	28 Aug 1885	16 Aug 1885	1149-1167	472925
52	102-103	Lessing	New York	31 Aug 1885	19 Aug 1885	1170-1186	472925
52	103-104	Polaria	New York	31 Aug 1885	15 Aug 1885	1144-1148	472925
52	111-112	India	New York	7 Sep 1885	22 Aug 1885	1187-1194	472925
52	112-114	Rugia	New York	7 Sep 1885	26 Aug 1885	1195-1213	472925
52	117	Astronom	New York	10 Sep 1885	missing	missing	-----
52	121-122	Wieland	New York	12 Sep 1885	30 Aug 1885	1214-1228	472925

Germans to America vol. and page nos.		Name of the Ship	Route and U.S. Port(s) of Arrival	Date of Arrival	Date of Departure	*HPL* Page numbers	FHL micro-film no.
52	124-126	Rhaetia	New York	15 Sep 1885	2 Sep 1885	1231-1241	472925
52	133-135	Hammonia	New York via Havre	19 Sep 1885	6 Sep 1885	1255-1271	472925
52	139-140	California	New York	21 Sep 1885	5 Sep 1885	1246-1254	472925
52	141-142	Suevia	New York via Havre	24 Sep 1885	9 Sep 1885	1272-1284	472925
52	151-152	Frisia	New York via Havre	28 Sep 1885	13 Sep 1885	1285-1293	472925
52	154-155	Moravia	New York	29 Sep 1885	16 Sep 1885	1294-1302	472925
52	163-164	Polynesia	New York	5 Oct 1885	19 Sep 1885	1310-1317	472925
52	164-166	Westphalia	New York	5 Oct 1885	23 Sep 1885	1318-1335	472925
52	171-172	Lessing	New York via Havre	10 Oct 1885	27 Sep 1885	1336-1345	472925
52	177-178	Bohemia	New York	15 Oct 1885	30 Sep 1885	1346-1353	472925
52	184-186	Wieland	New York	17 Oct 1885	4 Oct 1885	1365-1375	472925
52	190-191	Australia	New York	20 Oct 1885	3 Oct 1885	1357-1364	472925
52	191-193	Rugia	New York	20 Oct 1885	7 Oct 1885	1386-1392	472925
52	203-204	Polaria	New York	26 Oct 1885	10 Oct 1885	1393-1401	472925
52	205-208	Rhaetia	New York	27 Oct 1885	14 Oct 1885	1403-1423	472925
52	208-211	Hammonia	New York	30 Oct 1885	18 Oct 1885	1433-1451	472925
52	220-221	India	New York	4 Nov 1885	17 Oct 1885	1425-1432	472925
52	222-223	Suevia	New York	4 Nov 1885	21 Oct 1885	1456-1468	472925
52	230-233	Moravia	New York	12 Nov 1885	28 Oct 1885	1470-1489	472925
52	242-244	California	New York	16 Nov 1885	29 Oct 1885	1490-1505	472925
52	245-246	Gellert	New York via Havre	16 Nov 1885	1 Nov 1885	1505a-1511	472925
52	246-247	Lessing	New York	16 Nov 1885	4 Nov 1885	1514-1523	472925
52	254	Bohemia	New York	25 Nov 1885	11 Nov 1885	1526-1535	472925
52	257-258	Wieland	New York	27 Nov 1885	15 Nov 1885	1547-1554	472925

Germans to America vol. and page nos.		Name of the Ship	Route and U.S. Port(s) of Arrival	Date of Arrival	Date of Departure	*HPL* Page numbers	FHL micro-film no.
52	260-261	Polynesia	New York	30 Nov 1885	14 Nov 1885	1536-1546	472925
52	261-262	Rugia	New York	30 Nov 1885	18 Nov 1885	1555-1563	472925
52	271-272	Rhaetia	New York	14 Dec 1885	25 Nov 1885	1570-1583	472925
52	273	Suevia	New York	16 Dec 1885	2 Dec 1885	1592-1601	472925
52	275-276	Australia	New York	18 Dec 1885	28 Nov 1885	1586-1591	472925
52	277-278	Moravia	New York	23 Dec 1885	9 Dec 1885	1609-1616	472925
52	278	Polaria	New York	24 Dec 1885	5 Dec 1885	1602-1604	472925
52	281	Gellert	New York	29 Dec 1885	16 Dec 1885	1620-1627	472925
52	281-282	India	New York	31 Dec 1885	12 Dec 1885	1617-1619	472925
52	284	Bohemia	New York	5 Jan 1886	23 Dec 1885	1625a-1627a; 1628	472925
52	284-285	California	New York	5 Jan 1886	22 Dec 1885	1621a-1624a	472925
52	288	Lessing	New York	14 Jan 1886	31 Dec 1885	1629-1634	472925
52	292	Rugia	New York	19 Jan 1886	6 Jan 1886	1-6	472926
52	293-294	Rhaetia	New York	21 Jan 1886	13 Jan 1886	10-15	472926
52	296	Polynesia	New York	28 Jan 1886	9 Jan 1886	7-9	472926
52	299	Suevia	New York	2 Feb 1886	20 Jan 1886	16-23	472926
52	309	Australia	New York	22 Feb 1886	23 Jan 1886	24-26	472926
52	310	Kehrwieder	New York	23 Feb 1886	31 Jan 1886	32-35	472926
52	311-312	India	New York	25 Feb 1886	missing	missing	-----
52	315-316	Rugia	New York	4 Mar 1886	18 Feb 1886	70-79	472926
52	321-322	Polaria	New York	8 Mar 1886	13/14 Feb 1886	64-66	472926
52	326-328	Rhaetia	New York	19 Mar 1886	4 Mar 1886	104-118	472926
52	329-330	California	New York	22 Mar 1886	28 Feb 1886	93-103	472926

Germans to America vol. and page nos.		Name of the Ship	Route and U.S. Port(s) of Arrival	Date of Arrival	Date of Departure	*HPL* Page numbers	FHL micro-film no.
52	332-333	Westphalia	New York	22 Mar 1886	10 Mar 1886	129-140	472926
52	334-335	Polynesia	New York	24 Mar 1886	6 Mar 1886	121-128	472926
52	352-354	Moravia	New York	9 Apr 1886	24 Mar 1886	173-188	472926
52	362-363	India	New York	12 Apr 1886	22 Mar 1886	161-172	472926
52	363-364	Wieland	New York	12 Apr 1886	28 Mar 1886	189-201	472926
52	384-386	Lessing	New York	19 Apr 1886	7 Apr 1886	233-251	472926
52	386-390	Rugia	New York	19 Apr 1886	3 Apr 1886	202-229	472926
52	401-403	Hammonia	New York via Havre	23 Apr 1886	11 Apr 1886	268-280	472926
52	408-409	Bohemia	New York	27 Apr 1886	14 Apr 1886	281-288	472926
52	409-411	Polaria	New York	27 Apr 1886	10 Apr 1886	252-267	472926
53	2-3	Westphalia	New York via Havre	1 May 1886	18 Apr 1886	302-309	472926
53	3-5	California	New York	3 May 1886	17 Apr 1886	291-301	472926
53	9-10	Rhaetia	New York	3 May 1886	21 Apr 1886	314-321	472926
53	20-21	Gellert	New York	10 May 1886	28 Apr 1886	336-344	472926
53	21-22	Suevia	New York	10 May 1886	25 Apr 1886	330-334	472926
53	24-25	Sorrento	New York	11 May 1886	24 Apr 1886	322-329	472926
53	36-39	Wieland	New York	15 May 1886	3 May 1886	348-367	472926
53	41-43	Moravia	New York	18 May 1886	5 May 1886	393-409	472926
53	52-54	Australia	New York	20 May 1886	4 May 1886	368-382	472926
53	55	Nicosia	New York	20 May 1886	missing	missing	-----
53	59-61	Lessing	New York	24 May 1886	12 May 1886	431-450	472926
53	61-63	Rugia	New York	24 May 1886	9 May 1886	410-430	472926
53	86-88	Polynesia	New York	1 Jun 1886	15 May 1886	453-470	472926
53	94-96	Westphalia	New York via Havre	4 Jun 1886	23 May 1886	512-536	472926

Germans to America vol. and page nos.		Name of the Ship	Route and U.S. Port(s) of Arrival	Date of Arrival	Date of Departure	*HPL* Page numbers	FHL micro-film no.
53	104-105	Bohemia	New York	9 Jun 1886	26 May 1886	536a-554	472926
53	107-108	India	New York	11 Jun 1886	26 May 1886	556-568	472926
53	113-114	Rhaetia	New York	14 Jun 1886	30 May 1886	569-592	472926
53	116-117	Suevia	New York	17 Jun 1886	4 Jun 1886	607-619	472926
53	121-123	Gellert	New York	19 Jun 1886	6 Jun 1886	623-637	472926
53	124-125	Poland	New York	21 Jun 1886	missing	missing	-----
53	126-127	California	New York	23 Jun 1886	9 Jun 1886	638-648	472926
53	131-132	Lessing	New York via Havre	25 Jun 1886	13 Jun 1886	659-669	472926
53	140-141	Sorrento	New York	1 Jul 1886	16 Jun 1886	670-680	472926
53	141-143	Hammonia	New York via Havre	2 Jul 1886	20 Jun 1886	686-706	472926
53	156-157	Australia	New York	12 Jul 1886	23 Jun 1886	707-720	472926
53	158-159	Rugia	New York	12 Jul 1886	27 Jun 1886	721-741	472926
53	163-165	Wieland	New York	16 Jul 1886	4 Jul 1886	753-769	472927
53	166-167	Polynesia	New York	19 Jul 1886	30 Jun 1886	742-750	472926
53	168	Rhaetia	New York	20 Jul 1886	7 Jul 1886	772-784	472927
53	177-178	Gellert	New York via Havre	24 Jul 1886	11 Jul 1886	785-799	472927
53	187-189	Suevia	New York via Havre	2 Aug 1886	18 Jul 1886	814-834	472927
53	189-190	Taormina	New York	2 Aug 1886	14 Jul 1886	800-810	472927
53	194	Lessing	New York via Havre	7 Aug 1886	25 Jul 1886	847-862	472927
53	198-199	Amalfi	New York	10 Aug 1886	21 Jul 1886	835-836, 839-846	472927
53	203	California	New York	13 Aug 1886	28 Jul 1886	863-871	472927
53	204-205	Hammonia	New York via Havre	13 Aug 1886	1 Aug 1886	872-888	472927
53	216	Bohemia	New York	21 Aug 1886	5 Aug 1886	894-895	472927
53	218-219	Rugia	New York via Havre	23 Aug 1886	8 Aug 1886	904-915	472927

Germans to America vol. and page nos.		Name of the Ship	Route and U.S. Port(s) of Arrival	Date of Arrival	Date of Departure	*HPL* Page numbers	FHL micro-film no.
53	219-220	Polaria	New York	24 Aug 1886	4 Aug 1886	896-903	472927
53	226-228	Wieland	New York	28 Aug 1886	15 Aug 1886	926-941	472927
53	229-230	Sorrento	New York	30 Aug 1886	11 Aug 1886	916-925	472927
53	239-240	Australia	New York	4 Sep 1886	18 Aug 1886	944-953	472927
53	244-245	Gellert	New York via Havre	6 Sep 1886	22 Aug 1886	958-975	472927
53	246-247	Westphalia	New York	6 Sep 1886	25 Aug 1886	978-988	472927
53	254-255	Polynesia	New York	11 Sep 1886	26 Aug 1886	989-995	472927
53	255-256	Rhaetia	New York via Havre	13 Sep 1886	29 Aug 1886	996-1008	472927
53	261-262	Suevia	New York	15 Sep 1886	2 Sep 1886	1020-1029	472927
53	267	Marsala	New York	18 Sep 1886	1 Sep 1886	1012-1019	472927
53	276-277	Hammonia	New York via Havre	25 Sep 1886	12 Sep 1886	1055-1073	472927
53	280-281	Taormina	New York	25 Sep 1886	8 Sep 1886	1047-1054	472927
53	289-290	California	New York	30 Sep 1886	15 Sep 1886	1076-1086	472927
53	296-298	Rugia	New York	2 Oct 1886	19 Sep 1886	1092-1108	472927
53	304-305	Lessing	New York via Havre	5 Oct 1886	5 Sep 1886	1030-1043	472927
53	312-313	Amalfi	New York	9 Oct 1886	22 Sep 1886	1111-1117	472927
53	313-314	Wieland	New York	9 Oct 1886	26 Sep 1886	1120-1135	472927
53	317-318	Westphalia	New York	11 Oct 1886	30 Sep 1886	1140-1150	472927
53	329-330	Gellert	New York	16 Oct 1886	3 Oct 1886	1154-1166	472927
53	334-335	Polaria	New York	19 Oct 1886	29 Sep 1886	1136-1139	472927
53	335-336	Rhaetia	New York	19 Oct 1886	6 Oct 1886	1170-1180	472927
53	350-351	Suevia	New York	25 Oct 1886	10 Oct 1886	1181-1191	472927
53	359-361	Hammonia	New York via Havre	29 Oct 1886	17 Oct 1886	1203-1221	472927
53	376-377	Polynesia	New York	6 Nov 1886	20 Oct 1886	1232-1239	472927

Germans to America vol. and page nos.		Name of the Ship	Route and U.S. Port(s) of Arrival	Date of Arrival	Date of Departure	*HPL* Page numbers	FHL micro-film no.
53	380-382	Rugia	New York via Havre	8 Nov 1886	24 Oct 1886	1240-1255	472927
53	395-396	Wieland	New York	13 Nov 1886	31 Oct 1886	1268-1283	472927
53	397-398	Australia	New York	16 Nov 1886	27 Oct 1886	1258-1267	472927
53	404-405	Gellert	New York via Havre	22 Nov 1886	7 Nov 1886	1299-1318	472927
53	410	Marsala	New York	23 Nov 1886	3 Nov 1886	1288-1295	472927
53	421-422	Bohemia	New York via Havre	30 Nov 1886	14 Nov 1886	1331-1348	472927
53	422-423	Taormina	New York	30 Nov 1886	10 Nov 1886	1319-1326	472927
53	430-432	Rhaetia	New York via Havre	6 Dec 1886	21 Nov 1886	1364-1382	472927
53	435-436	Polaria	New York	7 Dec 1886	17 Nov 1886	1353-1360	472927
53	442	Suevia	New York	9 Dec 1886	missing	missing	-----
53	443-444	Amalfi	New York	13 Dec 1886	24 Nov 1886	1383-1387	472927
53	447-449	Rugia	New York	16 Dec 1886	29 Nov 1886	1392-1404	472927
53	451-452	California	New York	21 Dec 1886	1 Dec 1886	1405-1408	472927
53	452-453	Moravia	New York via Havre	22 Dec 1886	5 Dec 1886	1412-1419	472927
53	461-462	Sorrento	New York	27 Dec 1886	8 Dec 1886	1420-1422	472927
53	462-463	Wieland	New York	29 Dec 1886	12 Dec 1886	1425-1432	472927
53	464	Polynesia	New York	3 Jan 1887	15 Dec 1886	1433-1434	472927
54	1-2	Westphalia	New York via Havre	3 Jan 1887	19 Dec 1886	1435-1438a	472927
54	7	Marsala	New York	10 Jan 1887	22 Dec 1886	1442-1443	472927
54	7-8	Rhaetia	New York	13 Jan 1887	30 Dec 1886	1446-1450	472927
54	16-17	Suevia	New York	26 Jan 1887	9 Jan 1887	5-11b	472928
54	17	Australia	New York	27 Jan 1887	5 Jan 1887	2-4	472928
54	25	Wieland	New York via Havre	7 Feb 1887	23 Jan 1887	28-36	472928
54	28	Polaria	New York	12 Feb 1887	20 Jan 1887	25-27	472928

Germans to America vol. and page nos.		Name of the Ship	Route and U.S. Port(s) of Arrival	Date of Arrival	Date of Departure	*HPL* Page numbers	FHL micro-film no.
54	31	Rugia	New York	15 Feb 1887	30 Jan 1887	40-46	472928
54	32	Sorrento	New York	17 Feb 1887	27 Jan 1887	37-39	472928
54	35-36	Bohemia	New York via Havre	21 Feb 1887	6 Feb 1887	53-59	472928
54	36	Polynesia	New York	21 Feb 1887	3 Feb 1887	50-52	472928
54	41	Amalfi	New York	26 Feb 1887	9 Feb 1887	59a-59f	472928
54	51-52	California	New York	7 Mar 1887	17 Feb 1887	71-78	472928
54	66-67	Marsala	New York	14 Mar 1887	24 Feb 1887	91-96	472928
54	69-70	Moravia	New York via Havre	16 Mar 1887	1 Mar 1887	97-108	472928
54	81	Australia	New York	22 Mar 1887	4 Mar 1887	111-120	472928
54	84-85	Rugia	New York	22 Mar 1887	9 Mar 1887	135-145	472928
54	91-92	Lessing	New York via Havre	26 Mar 1887	13 Mar 1887	146-160a	472928
54	117-118	Wieland	New York	4 Apr 1887	20 Mar 1887	176-191	472928
54	122-123	Polaria	New York	6 Apr 1887	16 Mar 1887	163-175	472928
54	138-141	Suevia	New York	11 Apr 1887	29 Mar 1887	192-214	472928
54	159-162	Hammonia	New York	18 Apr 1887	6 Apr 1887	240-256	472928
54	164-165	Polynesia	New York	18 Apr 1887	31 Mar 1887	215-223	472928
54	165-167	Rhaetia	New York via Havre	18 Apr 1887	3 Apr 1887	226-239	472928
54	197-198	Amalfi	New York	27 Apr 1887	10 Apr 1887	261-168	472928
54	205-206	California	New York	29 Apr 1887	13 Apr 1887	269-278	472928
54	215-216	Rugia	New York	3 May 1887	21 Apr 1887	314a-322	472928
54	237-239	Lessing	New York via Havre	6 May 1887	24 Apr 1887	323-339	472928
54	240-242	Taormina	New York	6 May 1887	20 Apr 1887	300-314	472928
54	268-271	Wieland	New York	14 May 1887	1 May 1887	352-377	472928
54	271-272	Australia	New York	16 May 1887	27 Apr 1887	341-351	472928

Germans to America vol. and page nos.		Name of the Ship	Route and U.S. Port(s) of Arrival	Date of Arrival	Date of Departure	*HPL* Page numbers	FHL micro-film no.
54	289-290	Sorrento	New York	20 May 1887	4 May 1887	380-397	472928
54	296-298	Rhaetia	New York via Havre	23 May 1887	9 May 1887	398-426	472928
54	320-321	Marsala	New York	26 May 1887	11 May 1887	427-440	472928
54	322-324	Hammonia	New York	27 May 1887	15 May 1887	455-478	472928
54	332-333	Suevia	New York	31 May 1887	15 May 1887	441-454	472928
54	342-344	Gellert	New York via Havre	4 Jun 1887	22 May 1887	502-525	472928
54	353-354	Polynesia	New York	6 Jun 1887	18 May 1887	479-496	472928
54	362	Amalfi	New York	9 Jun 1887	25 May 1887	526-535	472928
54	365-367	Lessing	New York via Havre	10 Jun 1887	29 May 1887	536-557	472928
54	381-382	California	New York	16 Jun 1887	1 Jun 1887	558-566	472928
54	382-383	Marsala	New York	16 Jul 1887	29 Jun 1887	686-697	472928
54	386-387	Wieland	New York	17 Jun 1887	5 Jun 1887	569-587	472928
54	402-403	Taormina	New York	24 Jun 1887	8 Jun 1887	588-600	472928
54	407-408	Rugia	New York	25 Jun 1887	12 Jun 1887	603-622	472928
54	420-421	Polaria	New York	30 Jun 1887	15 Jun 1887	623-632	472928
55	3-4	Hammonia	New York via Havre	1 Jul 1887	19 Jun 1887	636-655	472928
55	12-13	Sorrento	New York	8 Jul 1887	22 Jun 1887	659-667	472928
55	14-15	City of Chester	New York via Havre	9 Jul 1887	missing	missing	-----
55	15-16	Bohemia	New York via Havre	12 Jul 1887	26 Jun 1887	668-685	472928
55	25-26	Rhaetia	New York via Havre	18 Jul 1887	3 Jul 1887	16-Jan	472929
55	29-30	Moravia	New York	21 Jul 1887	7 Jul 1887	19-30	472929
55	34-35	Gellert	New York via Havre	23 Jul 1887	10 Jul 1887	31-44	472929
55	42-43	Lessing	New York via Havre	29 Jul 1887	17 Jul 1887	58-73	472929
55	43-44	Amalfi	New York	30 Jul 1887	13 Jul 1887	47-57	472929

Germans to America vol. and page nos.		Name of the Ship	Route and U.S. Port(s) of Arrival	Date of Arrival	Date of Departure	*HPL* Page numbers	FHL micro-film no.
55	49-50	California	New York	5 Aug 1887	20 Jul 1887	74-83	472929
55	51-53	Rugia	New York	6 Aug 1887	24 Jul 1887	86-100	472929
55	64-66	Hammonia	New York via Havre	11 Aug 1887	31 Jul 1887	110-126	472929
55	69-70	Polynesia	New York	12 Aug 1887	27 Jul 1887	101-107	472929
55	74	Taormina	New York	18 Aug 1887	3 Aug 1887	127-133	472929
55	79	Wieland	New York via Havre	19 Aug 1887	7 Aug 1887	149-152	472929
55	88-89	Polaria	New York	27 Aug 1887	10 Aug 1887	153-162	472929
55	89-90	Bohemia	New York via Havre	29 Aug 1887	7 Aug 1887	138-148	472929
55	91-92	Rhaetia	New York via Havre	29 Aug 1887	14 Aug 1887	165-178	472929
55	99-101	Gellert	New York via Havre	5 Sep 1887	21 Aug 1887	191-206	472929
55	110-111	Sorrento	New York	7 Sep 1887	17 Aug 1887	179-186	472929
55	111	Suevia	New York	7 Sep 1887	25 Aug 1887	214-221	472929
55	118	Australia	New York	12 Sep 1887	24 Aug 1887	207-213	472929
55	127-128	Amalfi	New York	16 Sep 1887	31 Aug 1887	239-246	472929
55	129-130	Hammonia	New York via Havre	16 Sep 1887	4 Sep 1887	249-269	472929
55	138-139	Rugia	New York	20 Sep 1887	8 Sep 1887	279-287	472929
55	140	Marsala	New York	22 Sep 1887	7 Sep 1887	272-278	472929
55	146-147	Wieland	New York via Havre	23 Sep 1887	11 Sep 1887	288-300	472929
55	155-156	Polynesia	New York	29 Sep 1887	14 Sep 1887	304-312	472929
55	162-163	Rhaetia	New York via Havre	3 Oct 1887	18 Sep 1887	313-326	472929
55	169-170	Taormina	New York	6 Oct 1887	21 Sep 1887	333-340	472929
55	175	Gellert	New York via Havre	10 Oct 1887	27 Sep 1887	354-356	472929
55	175-176	Moravia	New York via Havre	10 Oct 1877	25 Sep 1887	341-353	472929
55	181-182	California	New York	13 Oct 1887	28 Sep 1887	359-369	472929

Germans to America vol. and page nos.		Name of the Ship	Route and U.S. Port(s) of Arrival	Date of Arrival	Date of Departure	*HPL* Page numbers	FHL micro-film no.
55	186-187	Suevia	New York via Havre	15 Oct 1887	2 Oct 1887	370-385	472929
55	187-188	Lessing	New York via Havre	17 Oct 1887	5 Oct 1887	389-400	472929
55	196-198	Gothia	New York via Stettin	18 Oct 1887	missing	missing	-----
55	199-200	Hammonia	New York via Havre	21 Oct 1887	9 Oct 1887	403-419	472929
55	210-211	Sorrento	New York	27 Oct 1887	12 Oct 1887	420-429	472929
55	215-216	Wieland	New York	28 Oct 1887	16 Oct 1887	432-443	472929
55	232-233	Rhaetia	New York via Havre	15 Nov 1887	30 Oct 1887	489-504	472929
55	238-239	Australia	New York	19 Nov 1887	27 Oct 1887	475-476	472929
55	239-240	Marsala	New York	19 Nov 1887	2 Nov 1887	507-514	472929
55	242-243	Moravia	New York via Havre	21 Nov 1887	6 Nov 1887	515-527	472929
55	248	Lessing	New York via Havre	25 Nov 1887	13 Nov 1887	540-549	472929
55	252	Polynesia	New York	26 Nov 1887	9 Nov 1887	528-535	472929
55	258-259	Amalfi	New York	2 Dec 1887	16 Nov 1887	550-558	472929
55	262-263	Suevia	New York via Havre	5 Dec 1887	20 Nov 1887	562-570	472929
55	263-264	California	New York	8 Dec 1887	23 Nov 1887	571-578	472929
55	269-270	Rugia	New York	12 Dec 1887	28 Nov 1887	583-591	472929
55	280-281	Bohemia	New York via Havre	22 Dec 1887	4 Dec 1887	600-609	472929
55	284	Taormina	New York	23 Dec 1887	30 Nov 1887	592-597	472929
55	287-288	Sorrento	New York	27 Dec 1887	7 Dec 1887	610-616	472929
55	288	Rhaetia	New York via Havre	29 Dec 1887	11 Dec 1887	619-625	472929
55	292-293	Polaria	New York	3 Jan 1888	14 Dec 1887	628-633	472929
55	294-295	Marsala	New York	10 Jan 1888	25 Dec 1887	642-649	472929
55	301-302	Rugia	New York	25 Jan 1888	8 Jan 1888	23-28	472930
55	305	Australia	New York	28 Jan 1888	4 Jan 1888	6-12	472930

Germans to America vol. and page nos.		Name of the Ship	Route and U.S. Port(s) of Arrival	Date of Arrival	Date of Departure	*HPL* Page numbers	FHL micro-film no.
55	307	Bohemia	New York via Havre	2 Feb 1888	17 Jan 1888	43-49	472930
55	308	Amalfi	New York	3 Feb 1888	11 Jan 1888	34-37	472930
55	308-309	California	New York	3 Feb 1888	18 Jan 1888	50-53	472930
55	311-312	Rhaetia	New York via Havre	6 Feb 1888	22 Jan 1888	57-61	472930
55	317-318	Moravia	New York via Havre	13 Feb 1888	29 Jan 1888	71-78	472930
55	318	Polynesia	New York	13 Feb 1888	25 Jan 1888	62-67	472930
55	320-321	Lessing	New York via Havre	18 Feb 1888	5 Feb 1888	92-101	472930
55	322	Taormina	New York	20 Feb 1888	1 Feb 1888	83-89	472930
55	328	Gellert	New York via Havre	25 Feb 1888	12 Feb 1888	113-121a	472930
55	329	Polaria	New York	27 Feb 1888	10 Feb 1888	105-111	472930
55	332-333	Rugia	New York via Havre	5 Mar 1888	19 Feb 1888	135-147	472930
55	333-334	Sorrento	New York	5 Mar 1888	15 Feb 1888	123-129	472930
55	343-345	Bohemia	New York via Havre	13 Mar 1888	26 Feb 1888	153-175	472930
55	347-348	Marsala	New York	15 Mar 1888	29 Feb 1888	177-187	472930
55	354-355	Rhaetia	New York via Havre	19 Mar 1888	4 Mar 1888	190-210	472930
55	365-366	Wieland	New York	26 Mar 1888	11 Mar 1888	232-257	472930
55	368-369	Australia	New York	28 Mar 1888	7 Mar 1888	214-228	472930
55	378-379	Moravia	New York via Havre	2 Apr 1888	18 Mar 1888	272-291	472930
55	389-390	California	New York	9 Apr 1888	21 Mar 1888	298-313	472930
55	390-393	Suevia	New York via Havre	9 Apr 1888	25 Mar 1888	315-336	472930
55	408-410	Rugia	New York via Havre	16 Apr 1888	1 Apr 1888	357-376	472930
55	416-417	Hammonia	New York	17 Apr 1888	5 Apr 1888	379-398	472930
55	429-431	Gellert	New York	26 Apr 1888	13 Apr 1888	463-491	472930
55	444-446	Taormina	New York	28 Apr 1888	11 Apr 1888	442-459	472930

Germans to America vol. and page nos.		Name of the Ship	Route and U.S. Port(s) of Arrival	Date of Arrival	Date of Departure	*HPL* Page numbers	FHL micro-film no.
55	446-449	Wieland	New York	28 Apr 1888	15 Apr 1888	492-517	472930
56	14-16	Lessing	New York	4 May 1888	22 Apr 1888	582-611	472930
56	16-18	Polaria	New York	4 May 1888	18 Apr 1888	521-546	472930
56	18-20	Rhaetia	New York via Havre	4 May 1888	20 Apr 1888	550-579	472930
56	43-50	Bohemia	New York via Havre	12 May 1888	8 Apr 1888	400-437	472930
56	50-53	Sorrento	New York	14 May 1888	25 Apr 1888	613-636	472930
56	53-55	Suevia	New York via Havre	14 May 1888	30 Apr 1888	656-683	472930
56	56	Hungaria	New York	15 May 1888	27 Apr 1888	639-655	472930
56	72-74	Marsala	New York	19 May 1888	2 May 1888	687-702	472931
56	74-77	Rugia	New York	19 May 1888	6 May 1888	706-744	472931
56	84-85	Australia	New York	22 May 1888	9 May 1888	748-767	472931
56	96	Moravia	New York	24 May 1888	11 May 1888	768-806	472931
56	103-104	Hammonia	New York via Havre	25 May 1888	13 May 1888	807-829	472931
56	120-123	Wieland	New York	31 May 1888	20 May 1888	852-880	472931
56	123-124	Amalfi	New York	1 Jun 1888	16 May 1888	835-846	472931
56	137-139	California	New York	8 Jun 1888	23 May 1888	882-913	472931
56	145-147	Gellert	New York via Havre	9 Jun 1888	27 May 1888	917-945	472931
56	158-159	Polynesia	New York	15 Jun 1888	30 May 1888	946-966	472931
56	162-164	Rhaetia	New York via Havre	18 Jun 1888	3 Jun 1888	970-1004	472931
56	176-178	Bohemia	New York via Havre	25 Jun 1888	10 Jun 1888	1028-1054	472931
56	180-181	Taormina	New York	25 Jun 1888	6 Jun 1888	1008-1026	472931
56	183-184	Rugia	New York	26 Jun 1888	13 Jun 1888	1056-1071	472931
56	189-191	Hammonia	New York via Havre	29 Jun 1888	17 Jun 1888	1085-1106	472931
56	194-195	Polaria	New York	2 Jul 1888	15 Jun 1888	1072-1081	472931

Germans to America vol. and page nos.		Name of the Ship	Route and U.S. Port(s) of Arrival	Date of Arrival	Date of Departure	*HPL* Page numbers	FHL micro-film no.
56	204-205	Sorrento	New York	7 Jul 1888	20 Jun 1888	1113-1124	472931
56	216-217	Wieland	New York	12 Jul 1888	1 Jul 1888	1151-1176	472932
56	229-231	Rhaetia	New York via Havre	23 Jul 1888	5/8 Jul 1888	1189-1196, 1201-1214	472932
56	231-232	Amalfi	New York	24 Jul 1888	5 Jul 1888	1180-1188	472932
56	238-239	Gellert	New York	25 Jul 1888	13 Jul 1888	1217-1231	472932
56	245-246	Suevia	New York via Havre	31 Jul 1888	15 Jul 1888	1232-1243	472932
56	254	Marsala	New York	4 Aug 1888	18 Jul 1888	1250-1259	472932
56	255-256	Rugia	New York via Havre	4 Aug 1888	22 Jul 1888	1265-1279	472932
56	262-264	Hammonia	New York via Havre	9 Aug 1888	29 Jul 1888	1296-1318	472932
56	268-269	Polynesia	New York	10 Aug 1888	25 Jul 1888	1282-1291	472932
56	275-276	Bohemia	New York	15 Aug 1888	1 Aug 1888	1322-1332	472932
56	278-279	Taormina	New York	17 Aug 1888	8 Aug 1888	1357-1366	472932
56	279-280	Wieland	New York via Havre	17 Aug 1888	5 Aug 1888	1337-1353	472932
56	296-298	Gellert	New York via Havre	28 Aug 1888	15 Aug 1888	1374-1400	472932
56	307-309	Suevia	New York via Havre	3 Sep 1888	19 Aug 1888	1413-1429	472932
56	309	Sorrento	New York	4 Sep 1888	17 Aug 1888	1404-1411	472932
56	320-321	Polaria	New York	8 Sep 1888	23 Aug 1888	1434-1444	472932
56	326-327	California	New York	13 Sep 1888	29 Aug 1888	1463-1470	472932
56	331-332	Hammonia	New York via Havre	14 Sep 1888	2 Sep 1888	1473-1489	472932
56	337-338	Rhaetia	New York via Havre	19 Sep 1888	5 Sep 1888	1494-1504	472932
56	344	Amalfi	New York	22 Sep 1888	6 Sep 1888	1505-1510	472932
56	357-358	Marsala	New York	1 Oct 1888	14 Sep 1888	1533-1540	472932
56	358-359	Moravia	New York via Havre	1 Oct 1888	16 Sep 1888	1542-1554	472932

Germans to America vol. and page nos.		Name of the Ship	Route and U.S. Port(s) of Arrival	Date of Arrival	Date of Departure	*HPL* Page numbers	FHL micro-film no.
56	365-367	Gellert	New York via Havre	6 Oct 1888	23 Sep 1888	1576-1591	472932
56	367-368	Polynesia	New York	6 Oct 1888	20 Sep 1888	1561-1570	472932
56	368-369	Bohemia	New York	9 Oct 1888	26 Sep 1888	1594-1601	472932
56	376-377	Suevia	New York via Havre	15 Oct 1888	30 Sep 1888	1609-1620	472932
56	380-381	Rugia	New York via Havre	16 Oct 1888	3 Oct 1888	1622-1629	472932
56	382-384	Hammonia	New York via Havre	19 Oct 1888	7 Oct 1888	1641-1659	472932
56	387	Taormina	New York	22 Oct 1888	4 Oct 1888	1630-1635	472932
56	394-396	Wieland	New York	26 Oct 1888	14 Oct 1888	1678-1695	472932
56	396-398	Polaria	New York	29 Oct 1888	14 Oct 1888	1667-1677	472932
56	407-408	Sorrento	New York	2 Nov 1888	17 Oct 1888	1697-1706	472932
56	413-414	Rhaetia	New York via Havre	5 Nov 1888	21 Oct 1888	1716-1730	472932
56	422-423	Gellert	New York	12 Nov 1888	30 Oct 1888	1753-1765	472932
56	444-445	Amalfi	New York	23 Nov 1888	2 Nov 1888	1767-1778	472932
56	447-448	Hammonia	New York	24 Nov 1888	12 Nov 1888	1814-1824	472932
56	451	Polynesia	New York	27 Nov 1888	9 Nov 1888	1803-1810	472932
57	4-5	Bohemia	New York via Havre	3 Dec 1888	11 Nov 1888	1812	472932
57	12-13	Rugia	New York	3 Dec 1888	16 Nov 1888	1827-1830	472932
57	14-15	Marsala	New York	6 Dec 1888	16 Nov 1888	1831-1839	472932
57	15-17	Wieland	New York	7 Dec 1888	25 Nov 1888	1857-1872	472932
57	21-22	Australia	New York	13 Dec 1888	22 Nov 1888	1848-1854	472932
57	29-30	Rhaetia	New York	18 Dec 1888	2 Dec 1888	1885-1891	472932
57	33	Polaria	New York	21 Dec 1888	30 Nov 1888	1877-1882	472932
57	36-38	Moravia	New York via Havre	25 Dec 1888	9 Dec 1888	1904-1915	472932
57	39	Taormina	New York	28 Dec 1888	7 Dec 1888	1896-1901	472932

Germans to America vol. and page nos.		Name of the Ship	Route and U.S. Port(s) of Arrival	Date of Arrival	Date of Departure	*HPL* Page numbers	FHL micro-film no.
57	43-44	Suevia	New York	1 Jan 1889	16 Dec 1888	1927-1932	472932
57	44	Sorrento	New York	3 Jan 1889	12 Dec 1888	1917-1920	472932
57	49	Rugia	New York	8 Jan 1889	24 Dec 1888	1941-1948	472932
57	58	Bohemia	New York	23 Jan 1889	6 Jan 1889	13-19	472933
57	60-61	Amalfi	New York	26 Jan 1889	2 Jan 1889	3-9	472933
57	63	Australia	New York	28 Jan 1889	9 Jan 1889	21-24	472933
57	65-66	Rhaetia	New York	28 Jan 1889	13 Jan 1889	26-31	472933
57	72-73	Moravia	New York via Havre	6 Feb 1889	22 Jan 1889	42-49	472933
57	73	Marsala	New York	8 Feb 1889	17 Jan 1889	37-39	472933
57	76	Suevia	New York via Havre	11 Feb 1889	27 Jan 1889	54-60	472933
57	81	Wieland	New York	16 Feb 1889	3 Feb 1889	70-76	472933
57	89-90	Gellert	New York via Havre	25 Feb 1889	10 Feb 1889	86-93	472933
57	92	Polaria	New York	25 Feb 1889	1 Feb 1889	64-68	472933
57	95	Taormina	New York	27 Feb 1889	6 Feb 1889	79-82	472933
57	102-104	Rhaetia	New York	4 Mar 1889	19 Feb 1889	108-121	472933
57	108	Sorrento	New York	6 Mar 1889	17 Feb 1889	99-105	472933
57	114-115	Rugia	New York via Havre	11 Mar 1889	24 Feb 1889	128-141	472933
57	117-118	California	New York	14 Mar 1889	27 Feb 1889	143-149	472933
57	126-127	Moravia	New York via Havre	19 Mar 1889	4 Mar 1889	154-165	472933
57	141-142	Polynesia	New York	25 Mar 1889	7 Mar 1889	171-179	472933
57	142-144	Bohemia	New York via Havre	26 Mar 1889	10 Mar 1889	180-195	472933
57	151-152	Marsala	New York	29 Mar 1889	13 Mar 1889	202-212	472933
57	154-155	Wieland	New York	29 Mar 1889	17 Mar 1889	218-234	472933
57	174	Gothia	Baltimore	5 Apr 1889	15 Mar 1889	213-214	472933

Germans to America vol. and page nos.		Name of the Ship	Route and U.S. Port(s) of Arrival	Date of Arrival	Date of Departure	*HPL* Page numbers	FHL micro-film no.
57	179-182	Gellert	New York via Havre	6 Apr 1889	24 Mar 1889	251-267	472933
57	179	Amalfi	New York	8 Apr 1889	21 Mar 1889	236-249	472933
57	198-200	Hammonia	New York	15 Apr 1889	3 Apr 1889	327-344	472933
57	204-206	Polaria	New York	15 Apr 1889	28 Mar 1889	272-292	472933
57	207-208	Suevia	New York	15 Apr 1889	31 Mar 1889	295-312a	472933
57	223-224	Taormina	New York	20 Apr 1889	4 Apr 1889	315-324	472933
57	234-236	Rhaetia	New York via Havre	22 Apr 1889	7 Apr 1889	347-363	472933
57	252-254	California	New York	26 Apr 1889	11 Apr 1889	366-382	472933
57	261-263	Rugia	New York via Havre	29 Apr 1889	14 Apr 1889	387-401	472933
57	268-269	Hungaria	Baltimore	3 May 1889	15 Apr 1889	402-407	472933
57	272-273	Sorrento	New York	6 May 1889	17 Apr 1889	408-416	472933
57	273-275	Wieland	New York via Havre	6 May 1889	21 Apr 1889	423-432	472933
57	279-280	Bohemia	New York	9 May 1889	25 Apr 1889	435-441	472933
57	293-295	Gellert	New York via Havre	11 May 1889	28 Apr 1889	446-463	472933
57	322-324	Marsala	New York	20 May 1889	2 May 1889	468-482	472933
57	325-327	Suevia	New York via Havre	20 May 1889	5 May 1889	487-509	472933
57	327-329	Victoria	New York	20 May 1889	9 May 1889	511-532	472933
57	333-334	Moravia	New York	23 May 1889	10 May 1889	533-552	472933
57	342-344	Hammonia	New York via Southampton	24 May 1889	12 May 1889	558-578	472933
57	366-368	Gothia	Baltimore	1 Jun 1889	15 May 1889	579-587	472933
57	370-372	Rhaetia	New York	1 Jun 1889	18 May 1889	608-628	472933
57	372-373	Amalfi	New York	3 Jun 1889	15 May 1889	588-601	472933
57	379-381	Rugia	New York	4 Jun 1889	22 May 1889	630-645	472933
57	277-279	Wieland	New York via Havre	8 Jun 1889	26 May 1889	649-668	472933

Germans to America vol. and page nos.		Name of the Ship	Route and U.S. Port(s) of Arrival	Date of Arrival	Date of Departure	*HPL* Page numbers	FHL micro-film no.
57	408-409	Gellert	New York via Havre	15 Jun 1889	2 Jun 1889	689-703	472933
57	414-415	Taormina	New York	17 Jun 1889	29 May 1889	670-679	472933
57	433	Hungaria	New York	26 Jun 1889	8 Jun 1889	716-719	472933
57	440	Sorrento	New York	29 Jun 1889	12 Jun 1889	722-726	472933
58	14-15	Rhaetia	New York via St. Thomas	8 Jul 1889	23 Jun 1889	781-791	472933
58	20	Marsala	New York	11 Jul 1889	26 Jun 1889	793a-800	472933
58	27	Gothia	Baltimore	16 Jul 1889	1 Jul 1889	818-821	472934
58	32-33	California	New York	19 Jul 1889	4 Jul 1889	822-828	472934
58	35-36	Wieland	New York via Havre	19 Jul 1889	7 Jul 1889	833-845	472934
58	36-37	Augusta Victoria	New York via Southampton	20 Jul 1889	11 Jul 1889	852-866	472934
58	41	Gellert	New York via Havre	26 Jul 1889	14 Jul 1889	871-879	472934
58	45	Amalfi	New York	27 Jul 1889	10 Jul 1889	847-851	472934
58	45-46	Columbia	New York via Southampton	27 Jul 1889	18 Jul 1889	882-895	472934
58	59-60	Rugia	New York via Havre	5 Aug 1889	21 Jul 1889	901-910	472934
58	75-76	Hammonia	New York via Southampton	9 Aug 1889	28 Jul 1889	922-935	472934
58	77	Hungaria	Baltimore	10 Aug 1889	23 Jul 1889	912-914	472934
58	77	Taormina	New York	10 Aug 1889	24 Jul 1889	916-919	472934
58	80	Bohemia	New York	15 Aug 1889	31 Jul 1889	938-943	472934
58	81-83	Augusta Victoria	New York via Southampton	17 Aug 1889	8 Aug 1889	959-981	472934
58	87	Rhaetia	New York via Havre	19 Aug 1889	4 Aug 1889	948-956	472934
58	100	Suevia	New York via Havre	26 Aug 1889	11 Aug 1889	984-991	472934
58	106-108	Columbia	New York via Southampton	30 Aug 1889	22 Aug 1889	1034-1053	472934
58	120-121	Gellert	New York via Havre	6 Sep 1889	25 Aug 1889	1055-1071	472934
58	121-122	Marsala	New York	6 Sep 1889	21 Aug 1889	1028-1033	472934

Germans to America vol. and page nos.		Name of the Ship	Route and U.S. Port(s) of Arrival	Date of Arrival	Date of Departure	*HPL* Page numbers	FHL micro-film no.
58	125-126	California	New York	11 Sep 1889	28 Aug 1889	1077-1082	472934
58	128-129	Hammonia	New York via Southampton	12 Sep 1889	1 Sep 1889	1087-1104	472934
58	135-137	Augusta Victoria	New York via Southampton	14 Sep 1889	5 Sep 1889	1106-1133	472934
58	147-148	Rugia	New York via Havre	21 Sep 1889	8 Sep 1889	1144-1155	472934
58	148	Sorrento	New York	23 Sep 1889	5 Sep 1889	1134-1139	472934
58	163	Rhaetia	New York	27 Sep 1889	14 Sep 1889	1179-1187	472934
58	164	Bohemia	New York	28 Sep 1889	13 Sep 1889	1168-1178	472934
58	164-166	Columbia	New York via Southampton	28 Sep 1889	19 Sep 1889	1198-1218	472934
58	166-167	Hungaria	Baltimore	28 Sep 1889	11 Sep 1889	1156-1161	472934
58	182	Wieland	New York via Havre	5 Oct 1889	22 Sep 1889	1231-1241	472934
58	186-188	Augusta Victoria	New York	12 Oct 1889	3 Oct 1889	1284-1311	472934
58	190	Gellert	New York via Havre	14 Oct 1889	29 Sep 1889	1266-1274	472934
58	203-205	Hammonia	New York via Southampton	19 Oct 1889	6/8 Oct 1889	1320-1338	472934
58	209-210	Taormina	New York	22 Oct 1889	3 Oct 1889	1277-1283	472934
58	210-212	Moravia	New York	23 Oct 1889	9 Oct 1889	1341-1350	472934
58	216-217	Columbia	New York via Southampton	26 Oct 1889	17 Oct 1889	1367-1386	472934
58	224-225	Rugia	New York	28 Oct 1889	13 Oct 1889	1358-1365	472934
58	234-235	Marsala	New York	2 Nov 1889	17 Oct 1889	1392-1397	472934
58	235-236	Rhaetia	New York via Havre	2 Nov 1889	20 Oct 1889	1407-1415	472934
58	236-237	California	Baltimore	4 Nov 1889	19 Oct 1889	1401-1405	472934
58	242-243	Suevia	New York	8 Nov 1889	25 Oct 1889	1420-1429	472934
58	253-254	Gellert	New York via Havre	16 Nov 1889	3 Nov 1889	1486-1496	472934
58	254-255	Gothia	Baltimore	16 Nov 1889	Missing	Missing	Missing
58	262	Bohemia	New York	22 Nov 1889	6 Nov 1889	1500-1510	472934

Germans to America vol. and page nos.		Name of the Ship	Route and U.S. Port(s) of Arrival	Date of Arrival	Date of Departure	*HPL* Page numbers	FHL micro-film no.
58	262-264	Hammonia	New York via Southampton	22 Nov 1889	10 Nov 1889	1515-1531	472934
58	286-287	Rhaetia	New York	10 Dec 1889	24 Nov 1889	1569-1574	472934
58	287	Gothia	Baltimore	11 Dec 1889	23 Nov 1889	1566-1569	472934
58	292	Taormina	New York	17 Dec 1889	27 Nov 1889	1577-1580	472934
58	298	Dania	New York via Havre	31 Dec 1889	15 Dec 1889	1615-1618	472934
58	300-301	Marsala	New York	2 Jan 1890	8 Dec 1889	1608-1611	472934
58	304	Bohemia	New York	7 Jan 1890	19 Dec 1889	1622-1625	472934
58	309	Scandia	New York	14 Jan 1890	31 Dec 1889	1642-1647	472934
58	310	Rugia	New York via Havre	15 Jan 1890	24 Dec 1889	1630-1633	472934
58	300-301	Marsala	New York	2 Jan 1890	8 Dec 1889	1608-1611	472934
58	304	Bohemia	New York	7 Jan 1890	19 Dec 1889	1622-1625	472934
58	309	Scandia	New York	14 Jan 1890	31 Dec 1889	1642-1647	472934
58	310	Rugia	New York via Havre	15 Jan 1890	24 Dec 1889	1630-1633	472934
58	313	Moravia	New York	21 Jan 1890	8 Jan 1890	10-11	472935
58	317-318	Marsala	New York	28 Jan 1890	Missing	Missing	Missing
58	318	Russia	New York via Havre	28 Jan 1890	12 Jan 1890	16-19	472935
58	326-327	Dania	New York via Havre	10 Feb 1890	26 Jan 1890	39-44	472935
58	328	Amalfi	New York	13 Feb 1980	15 Jan 1890	24-25	472935
58	333-334	Bohemia	New York via Havre	20 Feb 1890	2 Feb 1890	55-60	472935
58	339-340	Rugia	New York	26 Feb 1890	10 Feb 1890	65-72	472935
58	361-362	Italia	New York	25 Mar 1890	6 Mar 1890	134-141	472935
58	362-364	Russia	New York via Havre	25 Mar 1890	9 Mar 1890	147-160	472935
58	371-372	California	New York	1 Apr 1890	13 Mar 1890	165-171a	472935
58	405	Amalfi	New York	14 Apr 1890	19 Mar 1890	191-196	472935

Germans to America vol. and page nos.		Name of the Ship	Route and U.S. Port(s) of Arrival	Date of Arrival	Date of Departure	*HPL* Page numbers	FHL micro-film no.
58	406-407	Taormina	New York	15 Apr 1890	27 Mar 1890	222-229	472935
58	415-417	Bohemia	New York	18 Apr 1890	2 Apr 1890	245-250	472935
58	417-420	Columbia	New York via Southampton	19 Apr 1890	10 Apr 1890	263-274	472935
58	438-442	Augusta Victoria	New York via Southampton	26 Apr 1890	17 Apr 1890	295-308	472935
59	12-14	Moravia	New York	5 May 1890	18 Apr 1890	310-319	472935
59	15-16	Wieland	New York	5 May 1890	20 Apr 1890	326-335	472935
59	31-32	Russia	New York	9 May 1890	26 Apr 1890	345-354	472935
59	37-38	Rugia	New York via Havre	12 May 1890	27 Apr 1890	356-365	472935
59	38-39	Sorrento	New York	12 May 1890	23 Apr 1890	337-342	472935
59	44-45	California	New York	16 May 1890	30 Apr 1890	368-375	472935
59	50-53	Columbia	New York via Southampton	17 May 1890	8 May 1890	404-417	472935
59	53-55	Gellert	New York via Havre	17 May 1890	4 May 1890	393-402	472935
59	55-56	Italia	New York	19 May 1890	3 May 1890	381-390	472935
59	70-72	Dania	New York	22 May 1890	10 May 1890	419-434	472935
59	86-87	Dania	Baltimore	26 May 1890	10 May 1890	419-434	472935
59	98-100	Normannia	New York via Southampton	31 May 1890	22 May 1890	491-504	472935
59	103	Bohemia	New York	2 Jun 1890	18 May 1890	469-480	472935
59	111-112	Wieland	New York	6 Jun 1890	25 May 1890	511-518	472935
59	115	Taormina	New York	9 Jun 1890	23 May 1890	505-508	472935
59	115-116	Scandia	New York	10 Jun 1890	30 May 1890	523-528	472935
59	123-125	Columbia	New York via Southampton	13 Jun 1890	5 Jun 1890	546-557	472935
59	131-132	Rugia	New York via Havre	16 Jun 1890	1 Jun 1890	534-541	472935
59	140-142	Augusta Victoria	New York via Southampton	21 Jun 1890	12 Jun 1890	578-590	472935
59	147	Marsala	New York	23 Jun 1890	4 Jun 1890	544-545	472935

Germans to America vol. and page nos.		Name of the Ship	Route and U.S. Port(s) of Arrival	Date of Arrival	Date of Departure	*HPL* Page numbers	FHL micro-film no.
59	167-169	Columbia	New York via Southampton	11 Jul 1890	3 Jul 1980	661-672	475678
59	169	Dania	Baltimore	11 Jul 1890	26 Jun 1890	637-644	472935
59	173-174	Wieland	New York via Havre	12 Jul 1890	29 Jun 1890	649-656	472935
59	184-186	Augusta Victoria	New York via Southampton	19 Jul 1890	10 Jul 1890	683-694	475678
59	186	Scandia	New York via Havre	19 Jul 1890	6 Jul 1890	674-681	475678
59	197-199	Normannia	New York via Southampton	26 Jul 1890	17 Jul 1890	711-722	475678
59	199-200	Rugia	New York	26 Jul 1890	13 Jul 1890	697-704	475678
59	210	Gellert	New York via Havre	2 Aug 1890	20 Jul 1890	728-734	475678
59	211	Amalfi	New York	4 Aug 1890	18 Jul 1890	723-724	475678
59	218	Russia	Baltimore	8 Aug 1890	23 Jul 1890	738-745	475678
59	223-224	Suevia	New York via Havre	11 Aug 1890	27 Jul 1890	748-753	475678
59	229-231	Augusta Victoria	New York via Southampton	16 Aug 1890	7 Aug 1890	790-803	475678
59	232-233	Rhaetia	New York via Havre	18 Aug 1890	3 Aug 1890	780-787	475678
59	233	Taormina	New York	18 Aug 1890	1 Aug 1890	776-777	475678
59	239-241	Normannia	New York	22 Aug 1890	14 Aug 1890	821-834	475678
59	243	Dania	New York	23 Aug 1890	9 Aug 1890	806-811	475678
59	244-245	Wieland	New York via Havre	23 Aug 1890	10 Aug 1890	812-817	475678
59	255	Marsala	New York	1 Sep 1890	15 Aug 1890	837-837a	475678
59	264-266	Columbia	New York via Southampton	5 Sep 1890	28 Aug 1890	878-891	475678
59	269-270	Slavonia	New York	6 Sep 1890	21 Aug 1890	851-858	475678
59	278	Slavonia	Balitmore	10 Sep 1890	21 Aug 1890	851-858	475678
59	283-285	Augusta Victoria	New York via Southampton	13 Sep 1890	4 Sep 1890	913-928	475678
59	285-286	Suevia	New York via Havre	13 Sep 1890	31 Aug 1890	899-910	475678
59	289	Sorrento	New York	15 Sep 1890	29 Aug 1890	892-894	475678

Germans to America vol. and page nos.		Name of the Ship	Route and U.S. Port(s) of Arrival	Date of Arrival	Date of Departure	*HPL* Page numbers	FHL micro-film no.
59	302-303	Rhaetia	New York via Havre	22 Sep 1890	7 Sep 1890	938-943	475678
59	303-305	Normannia	New York	23 Sep 1890	11 Sep 1890	946-959	475678
59	321-323	Columbia	New York	3 Oct 1890	25 Sep 1890	995-1008	475678
59	328-329	Rugia	New York via Havre	6 Oct 1890	21 Sep 1890	985-990	475678
59	339-342	Augusta Victoria	New York via Southampton	11 Oct 1890	2 Oct 1890	1033-1046	475679
59	342-343	Gellert	New York via Havre	11 Oct 1890	28 Sep 1890	1018-1025	475678
59	345	Scandia	New York	11 Oct 1890	27 Sep 1890	1014-1017	475678
59	348	Taormina	New York	13 Oct 1890	26 Sep 1890	1012-1013	475678
59	353-355	Normannia	New York	17 Oct 1890	9 Oct 1890	1061-1074	475679
59	360-361	Suevia	New York via Havre	20 Oct 1890	5 Oct 1890	1047-1054	475679
59	365-366	Rhaetia	New York via Havre	27 Oct 1890	12 Oct 1890	1081-1086	475679
59	378-381	Augusta Victoria	New York via Southampton	8 Nov 1890	30 Oct 1890	1146-1161	475679
59	389-390	Russia	New York via Havre	11 Nov 1890	26 Oct 1890	1134-1143	475679
59	390	Sorrento	New York	12 Nov 1890	24 Oct 1890	1130-1133	475679
59	404-406	Rugia	New York via Havre	22 Nov 1890	2 Nov 1890	1167-1179	475679
59	406-407	Gellert	New York via Havre	24 Nov 1890	9 Nov 1890	1204-1213	475679
60	3-5	Suevia	New York via Havre	1 Dec 1890	16 Nov 1890	1227-1238	475679
60	13-14	Rhaetia	New York via Havre	8 Dec 1890	23 Nov 1890	1250-1261	475679
60	23-24	Dania	New York via Havre	16 Dec 1890	30 Nov 1890	1277-1286	475679
60	26-27	Taormina	New York	16 Dec 1890	19 Nov 1890	1243-1248	475679
60	33	Russia	New York via Havre	23 Dec 1890	7 Dec 1890	1297-1304	475679
60	35-36	Slavonia	New York	26 Dec 1890	3 Dec 1890	1290-1293	475679
60	39	Bohemia	New York via Havre	2 Jan 1891	14 Dec 1890	1314-1321	475679
60	42	Scandia	New York via Havre	5 Jan 1891	21 Dec 1891	1333-1338	475679

Germans to America vol. and page nos.		Name of the Ship	Route and U.S. Port(s) of Arrival	Date of Arrival	Date of Departure	*HPL* Page numbers	FHL micro-film no.
60	42-43	Sorrento	New York	6 Jan 1891	19 Dec 1891	1329-1332	475679
60	48-49	Rhaetia	New York via Havre	20 Jan 1891	4 Jan 1891	2-7	475680
60	60	Rugia	New York via Havre	2 Feb 1891	11 Jan 1891	21-26	475680
60	65-67	Moravia	New York	9 Feb 1891	18 Jan 1891	35-44	475680
60	70-71	Russia	New York via Havre	11 Feb 1891	25 Jan 1891	47-54	475680
60	78	Scandia	New York via Havre	16 Feb 1891	1 Feb 1891	63-68	475680
60	84	Bohemia	New York	24 Feb 1891	6 Feb 1891	73-78	475680
60	85	Suevia	New York via Havre	24 Feb 1891	8 Feb 1891	81-86	475680
60	94	Taormina	New York	2 Mar 1891	29 Jan 1891	59-60	475680
60	101-102	Slavonia	New York	6 Mar 1891	18 Feb 1891	108-112	475680
60	105	Slavonia	Baltimore	10 Mar 1891	18 Feb 1891	108-112	475680
60	118-120	Rugia	New York via Havre	16 Mar 1891	1 Mar 1891	140-155	475680
60	133-135	Russia	New York via Havre	23 Mar 1891	8 Mar 1891	177-188	475680
60	147-149	Gellert	New York via Havre	28 Mar 1891	15 Mar 1891	207-220	475680
60	168-170	Dania	New York via Havre	6 Apr 1891	22 Mar 1891	239-250	475680
60	196-198	Rhaetia	New York via Havre	13 Apr 1891	29 Mar 1891	266-277	475680
60	230-236	Suevia	New York via Havre	22 Apr 1891	5 Apr 1891	309-320	475680
60	236-237	Taormina	New York	22 Apr 1891	4 Apr 1891	301-308	475680
60	251-253	Wieland	New York	22 Apr 1891	10 Apr 1891	336-349	475680
60	260-264	Augusta Victoria	New York via Southampton	27 Apr 1891	17 Apr 1891	390-405	475680
60	275-278	Slavonia	Baltimore via New York	28 Apr 1891	11 Apr 1891	351-360	475680
60	318	Columbia	New York via Southampton	9 May 1891	1 May 1891	467-480	475681
60	323-325	Scandia	New York via Havre	11 May 1891	25 Apr 1891	449-452	475681
60	331-332	Scandia	Balitmore	14 May 1981	25 Apr 1891	449-452	475681

Germans to America vol. and page nos.		Name of the Ship	Route and U.S. Port(s) of Arrival	Date of Arrival	Date of Departure	*HPL* Page numbers	FHL micro-film no.
60	332-334	Dania	New York via Havre	15 May 1891	3 May 1891	484-495	475681
60	337-339	Furst Bismark	New York via Southampton	16 May 1891	8 May 1891	505-520	475681
60	355-356	Amalfi	New York	22 May 1891	6 May 1891	502-503	475681
60	356	Augusta Victoria	New York via Southampton	23 May 1891	15 May 1891	548-562	475681
61	1-2	Suevia	New York via Havre	1 Jun 1891	17 May 1891	564-574	475681
61	17-19	Wieland	New York via Havre	5 Jun 1891	24 May 1891	601-612	475681
61	19-20	Columbia	New York via Southampton	6 Jun 1891	19 May 1891	636-649	475681
61	21-22	Taormina	New York	6 Jun 1891	20 May 1891	575-578	475681
61	26-27	Moravia	New York	9 Jun 1891	27 May 1891	618-627	475681
61	40	Rugia	New York via Havre	13 Jun 1891	31 May 1891	652-665	475681
61	56-57	Marsala	New York	20 Jun 1891	5 Jun 1891	676-679	475681
61	58-59	Gellert	New York via Havre	20 Jun 1891	7 Jun 1891	708-719	475681
61	61-63	Augusta Victoria	New York via Southampton	22 Jun 1891	9 Jun 1891	735-748	475681
61	69	Russia	New York	24 Jun 1891	9 Jun 1891	720-727	475681
61	73-74	Slavonia	Baltimore via New York	25 Jun 1891	6 Jun 1891	698-707	475681
61	74-75	Dania	New York via Havre	26 Jun 1891	14 Jun 1891	751-758	475681
61	76-78	Normannia	New York via Southampton	27 Jun 1891	19 Jun 1891	767-782	475681
61	90-92	Columbia	New York via Southampton	6 Jul 1891	26 Jun 1891	813-826	475681
61	93-95	Rhaetia	New York via Havre	6 Jul 1891	21 Jun 1891	785-800	475681
61	101-102	Scandia	New York	10 Jul 1891	27 Jun 1891	834-845	475681
61	104-106	Furst Bismark	New York via Southampton	11 Jul 1891	3 Jul 1891	859-874	475681
61	116	Suevia	New York via Havre	15 Jul 1891	1 Jul 1891	850-855	475681
61	119	Slavonia	New York	17 Jul 1891	Missing	Missing	Missing
61	119-120	Wieland	New York via Havre	18 Jul 1891	5 Jul 1891	877-884	475681

Germans to America vol. and page nos.		Name of the Ship	Route and U.S. Port(s) of Arrival	Date of Arrival	Date of Departure	*HPL* Page numbers	FHL micro-film no.
61	121-122	Augusta Victoria	New York via Southampton	20 Jul 1891	10 Jul 1891	899-912	475681
61	129	Bohemia	New York	23 Jul 1891	8 Jul 1891	889-894	475681
61	132-133	Normannia	New York	25 Jul 1891	17 Jul 1891	939-952	475681
61	135-136	Gellert	New York	27 Jul 1891	14 Jul 1891	917-926	475681
61	149	Amalfi	New York	31 Jul 1891	15 Jul 1891	928-935	475681
61	150-152	Columbia	New York via Southampton	1 Aug 1891	24 Jul 1891	977-989	475681
61	161-163	Furst Bismark	New York via Southampton	8 Aug 1891	31 Jul 1891	1022-1039	475681
61	163-164	Dania	New York via Havre	8 Aug 1891	26 Jul 1891	922-1001	475681
61	172	Taormina	New York	14 Aug 1891	29 Jul 1891	1005-1010	475681
61	175-176	Rugia	New York via Havre	15 Aug 1891	2 Aug 1891	1046-1053	475682
61	176-178	Augusta Victoria	New York via Southampton	17 Aug 1891	7 Aug 1891	1069-1083	475682
61	182	Slavonia	Baltimore	19 Aug 1891	1 Aug 1891	1040-1045	475682
61	190	Marsala	New York	21 Aug 1891	5 Aug 1891	1058-1065	475682
61	193-194	Normannia	New York	24 Aug 1891	14 Aug 1891	1116-1129	475682
61	206-207	Scandia	New York	27 Aug 1891	15 Aug 1891	1132-1137	475682
61	207-208	Suevia	New York via Havre	27 Aug 1891	9 Aug 1891	1086-1097	475682
61	208-209	California	New York	28 Aug 1891	12 Aug 1891	1100-1107	475682
61	209-210	Columbia	New York via Southampton	29 Aug 1891	21 Aug 1891	1160-1173	475682
61	212-213	Wieland	New York via Havre	31 Aug 1891	16 Aug 1891	1142-1149	475682
61	230-233	Furst Bismark	New York via Southampton	7 Sep 1891	28 Aug 1891	1196-1210	475682
61	237-238	Rhaetia	New York via Havre	8 Sep 1891	23 Aug 1891	1175-1184	475682
61	244	Bohemia	New York	12 Sep 1891	26 Aug 1891	1188-1193	475682
61	246-248	Augusta Victoria	New York via Southampton	14 Sep 1891	4 Sep 1891	1250-1264	475682
61	248-249	Gothia	New York	14 Sep 1891	29 Aug 1891	1211-1220	475682

Germans to America vol. and page nos.		Name of the Ship	Route and U.S. Port(s) of Arrival	Date of Arrival	Date of Departure	*HPL* Page numbers	FHL micro-film no.
61	249-250	Gellert	New York	14 Sep 1891	30 Aug 1891	1223-1234	475682
61	253	Moravia	New York	15 Sep 1891	2 Sep 1891	1237-1244	475682
61	263-264	Dania	New York via Havre	18 Sep 1891	6 Sep 1891	1272-1283	475682
61	267-268	Normannia	New York via Southampton	21 Sep 1891	11 Sep 1891	1293-1307	475682
61	285-286	Amalfi	New York	26 Sep 1891	9 Sep 1891	1288-1291	475682
61	286-288	Columbia	New York via Southampton	26 Sep 1891	18 Sep 1891	1341-1354	475682
61	288-289	Russia	New York	28 Sep 1891	12 Sep 1891	1314-1325	475682
61	291-292	Rugia	New York via Havre	28 Sep 1891	13 Sep 1891	1308-1313	475682
61	298-299	Russia	Balitimore	1 Oct 1891	12 Sep 1891	1314-1325	475682
61	303	Virginia	New York	1 Oct 1891	16 Sep 1891	1328-1335	475682
61	310-313	Furst Bismark	New York via Southampton	5 Oct 1891	25 Sep 1891	1387-1402	475682
61	315-317	Suevia	New York via Havre	6 Oct 1891	20 Sep 1891	1356-1369	475682
61	330-331	Augusta Victoria	New York via Southampton	12 Oct 1891	2 Oct 1891	1424-1439	475683
61	331-332	Taormina	New York	12 Oct 1891	23 Sep 1891	1375-1378	475682
61	332-333	Wieland	New York via Havre	12 Oct 1891	27 Sep 1891	1405-1412	475682
61	334-335	Slavonia	New York	13 Oct 1891	26 Sep 1891	1381-1386	475682
61	342	California	New York	16 Oct 1891	30 Sep 1891	1415-1418	475682
61	354-355	Rhaetia	New York via Havre	20 Oct 1891	4 Oct 1891	1440-1449	475683
61	363-364	Scandia	New York	23 Oct 1891	10 Oct 1891	1478-1484	475683
61	364-366	Columbia	New York via Southampton	26 Oct 1891	16 Oct 1891	1495-1508	475683
61	366-367	Marsala	New York	26 Oct 1891	7 Oct 1891	1456-1457	475683
61	380-381	Venetia	New York via Havre	29 Oct 1891	12 Oct 1891	1485-1488	475683
61	385-388	Furst Bismark	New York via Southampton	31 Oct 1891	23 Oct 1891	1541-1556	475683
61	388-390	Dania	New York via Havre	31 Oct 1891	18 Oct 1891	1512-1521	475683

Germans to America vol. and page nos.		Name of the Ship	Route and U.S. Port(s) of Arrival	Date of Arrival	Date of Departure	*HPL* Page numbers	FHL micro-film no.
62	11-14	Augusta Victoria	New York via Southampton	9 Nov 1891	30 Oct 1891	1582-1593	475683
62	14	Gothia	New York	9 Nov 1891	24 Oct 1891	1557-1562	475683
62	14-15	Sorrento	New York	9 Nov 1891	22 Oct 1891	1537-1540	475683
62	18-19	Rugia	New York via Havre	9 Nov 1891	25 Oct 1891	1563-1568	475683
62	22-23	Moravia	New York	12 Nov 1891	29 Oct 1891	1570-1575	475683
62	26-29	Normannia	New York via Southampton	16 Nov 1891	6 Nov 1891	1616-1631	475683
62	32	Russia	New York via Havre	18 Nov 1891	2 Nov 1891	1598-1605	475683
62	43-44	Amalfi	New York	24 Nov 1891	5 Nov 1891	1609-1610	475683
62	56-58	Rhaetia	New York	8 Dec 1891	24 Nov 1891	1707-1720	475683
62	68-69	Dania	New York via Havre	15 Dec 1891	29 Nov 1891	1725-1736	475683
62	70	Bohemia	New York	21 Dec 1891	2 Dec 1891	1740-1743	475683
62	74-75	Rugia	New York	22 Dec 1891	6 Dec 1891	1752-1759	475683
62	75-76	Havel	New York via Southampton	24 Dec 1891	Missing	Missing	Missing
62	77-78	Venetia	New York	24 Dec 1891	5 Dec 1891	1749-1750	475683
62	79-80	Moravia	New York	28 Dec 1891	11 Dec 1891	1765-1774	475683
62	81-82	Russia	New York via Havre	31 Dec 1891	13 Dec 1891	1779-1786	475683
62	86-87	Suevia	New York	4 Jan 1892	20 Dec 1891	1799-1804	475683
62	87	Sorrento	New York	5 Jan 1892	17 Dec 1891	1792-1795	475683
62	89-90	California	New York	9 Jan 1892	23 Dec 1891	1808-1811	475683
62	91	Scandia	New York via Havre	12 Jan 1892	29 Dec 1891	1813-1820	475683
62	93	Amalfi	New York	16 Jan 1892	31 Dec 1891	1822-1825	475683
62	96	Steinhoeft	New York via Havre	19 Jan 1892	13 Dec 1891	1778	475683
62	100	Rhaetia	New York via Havre	21 Jan 1892	3 Jan 1892	5-10	475684
62	100-101	Dania	New York via Havre	23 Jan 1892	10 Jan 1892	21-28	475684

Germans to America vol. and page nos.		Name of the Ship	Route and U.S. Port(s) of Arrival	Date of Arrival	Date of Departure	*HPL* Page numbers	FHL micro-film no.
62	106-107	Rugia	New York via Havre	2 Feb 1892	17 Jan 1892	40-47	475684
62	107	Taormina	New York	3 Feb 1892	13 Jan 1892	34-37	475684
62	113	Bohemia	New York	9 Feb 1892	20 Jan 1892	50-55	475684
62	115	Slavonia	New York	12 Feb 1892	21 Jan 1892	57-58	475684
62	116-117	Russia	New York	15 Feb 1892	26 Jan 1892	63-72	475684
62	121-122	Suevia	New York	16 Feb 1892	31 Jan 1892	82-89	475684
62	128	Marsala	New York	19 Feb 1892	29 Jan 1892	74-77	475684
62	129-130	Moravia	New York	20 Feb 1892	3 Feb 1892	93-98	475684
62	130-131	Scandia	New York	22 Feb 1892	7 Feb 1892	104-113	475684
62	138	Sorrento	New York	26 Feb 1892	10 Feb 1892	118-122	475684
62	140-142	Rhaetia	New York	29 Feb 1892	15 Feb 1892	129-140	475684
62	150	California	New York	5 Mar 1892	17 Feb 1892	142-149	475684
62	151-152	Dania	New York	7 Mar 1892	23 Feb 1892	159-172	475684
62	163	Amalfi	New York	14 Mar 1892	25 Feb 1892	173-178	475684
62	171	Rugia	New York	17 Mar 1892	2 Mar 1892	196-205	475684
62	172-173	Wieland	New York via Havre	21 Mar 1892	6 Mar 1892	213-226	475684
62	187-188	Suevia	New York via Havre	28 Mar 1892	13 Mar 1892	259-270	475684
62	188-189	Taormina	New York	28 Mar 1892	10 Mar 1892	243-250	475684
62	199-200	Moravia	New York	30 Mar 1892	17 Mar 1892	285-300	475684
62	202-203	Bohemia	New York	31 Mar 1892	15 Mar 1892	271-282	475684
62	204-206	Scandia	New York via Havre	2 Apr 1892	20 Mar 1892	304-323	475684
62	219-220	Marsala	New York	9 Apr 1892	23 Mar 1892	329-340	475684
62	221-223	Rhaetia	New York	11 Apr 1892	27 Mar 1892	356-375	475684
62	223-225	Venetia	New York via Havre	11 Apr 1892	26 Mar 1892	348-355	475684

Germans to America vol. and page nos.		Name of the Ship	Route and U.S. Port(s) of Arrival	Date of Arrival	Date of Departure	*HPL* Page numbers	FHL micro-film no.
62	239-242	Dania	New York via Havre	16 Apr 1892	3 Apr 1892	407-422	475684
62	242-247	Normannia	New York	18 Apr 1892	8 Apr 1892	436-451	475684
62	247	California	New York	18 Apr 1892	2 Apr 1892	393-406	475684
62	266-268	Gothia	New York	22 Apr 1892	6 Apr 1892	424-433	475684
62	269-272	Columbia	New York via Southampton	25 Apr 1892	15 Apr 1892	473-486	475684
62	283	Sorrento	New York	29 Apr 1892	13 Apr 1892	456-457	475684
62	284-287	Rugia	New York	2 May 1892	17 Apr 1892	458-471b	475684
62	287-288	Pickhuben	New York	2 May 1892	17 Apr 1892	490-497	475684
62	302-303	Wieland	New York via Havre	7 May 1892	24 Apr 1892	528-537	475684
62	303-304	Rhaetia	New York via Havre	8 May 1892 (sic)	8 May 1892	632-641	475684
62	305-307	Augusta Victoria	New York via Southampton	9 May 1892	29 Apr 1892	551-564	475684
62	321-325	Normannia	New York	14 May 1892	6 May 1892	595-610	475685
62	325-327	Suevia	New York via Havre	16 May 1892	1 May 1892	570-581	475685
62	340-342	Scandia	Baltimore	20 May 1892	7 May 1892	612-631	475685
62	345-347	Columbia	New York via Southampton	23 May 1892	13 May 1892	663-676	475685
62	348	Taormina	New York	23 May 1892	4 May 1892	586-591	475685
62	348-349	Rhaetia	New York via Havre	23 May 1892	8 May 1892	632-641	475685
62	357	Russia	New York	24 May 1892	27 Apr 1892	539-548	475685
62	362-363	Moravia	New York	26 May 1892	11 May 1892	646-657	475685
62	367-368	Dania	New York via Havre	30 May 1892	15 May 1892	680-695	475685
62	375-378	Furst Bismark	New York	31 May 1892	20 May 1892	714-729	475685
63	7-8	Gellert	New York	3 Jun 1892	22 May 1892	740-755	475685
63	9	Marsala	New York	4 Jun 1892	18 May 1892	698-705	475685

Germans to America vol. and page nos.		Name of the Ship	Route and U.S. Port(s) of Arrival	Date of Arrival	Date of Departure	*HPL* Page numbers	FHL micro-film no.
63	10-12	Augusta Victoria	New York via Southampton	4 Jun 1892	27 May 1892	774-787	475685
63	17-18	Venetia	New York via Havre	6 Jun 1892	21 May 1892	732-739	475685
63	29-31	Bohemia	New York	10 Jun 1892	25 May 1892	757-772	475685
63	34-35	Rugia	New York via Havre	13 Jun 1892	29 May 1892	792-805	475685
63	35-37	Normannia	New York	13 Jun 1892	3 Jun 1892	822-837	475685
63	44	Wieland	New York via Havre	18 Jun 1892	5 Jun 1892	844-849	475685
63	44-46	Columbia	New York via Southampton	18 Jun 1892	10 Jun 1892	856-867	475685
63	49-50	Sorrento	New York	20 Jun 1892	1 Jun 1892	812-815	475685
63	60	Virginia	New York	24 Jun 1892	9 Jun 1892	850-853	475685
63	60-61	Suevia	New York	25 Jun 1892	12 Jun 1892	874-881	475685
63	62-64	Furst Bismark	New York	25 Jun 1892	17 Jun 1892	893-908	475685
63	73-74	Amalfi	New York	2 Jul 1892	15 Jun 1892	884-889	475685
63	74-75	Russia	New York	2 Jul 1892	18 Jun 1892	910-923	475685
63	77-78	Augusta Victoria	New York via Southampton	5 Jul 1892	24 Jun 1892	948-961	475685
63	78-79	Rhaetia	New York via Havre	5 Jul 1892	19 Jun 1892	924-929	475685
63	85-86	Moravia	New York	7 Jul 1892	22 Jun 1892	934-943	475685
63	88	Dania	New York via Havre	9 Jul 1892	26 Jun 1892	963-972	475685
63	89-90	Normannia	New York via Southampton	9 Jul 1892	1 Jul 1892	987-1000	475686
63	98	Scandia	New York	18 Jul 1892	3 Jul 1892	1004-1015	475686
63	99	Gellert	New York via Havre	18 Jul 1892	3 Jul 1892	1016-1019	475686
63	102	Taormina	New York	19 Jul 1892	29 Jun 1892	976-979	475685
63	106	Bohemia	New York	22 Jul 1892	7 Jul 1892	1021-1026	475686
63	107-109	Furst Bismark	New York via Southampton	23 Jul 1892	15 Jul 1892	1070-1083	475686
63	112	Rugia	New York via Havre	25 Jul 1892	10 Jul 1892	1042-1051	475686

Germans to America vol. and page nos.		Name of the Ship	Route and U.S. Port(s) of Arrival	Date of Arrival	Date of Departure	*HPL* Page numbers	FHL micro-film no.
63	120-122	Augusta Victoria	New York via Southampton	30 Jul 1892	22 Jul 1892	1120-1131	475686
63	122-123	Polynesia	New York	30 Jul 1892	13 Jul 1892	1060-1067	475686
63	123	Venetia	New York	30 Jul 1892	16 Jul 1892	1086-1095	475686
63	123-124	Wieland	New York via Havre	30 Jul 1892	17 Jul 1892	1096-1101	475686
63	134	Virginia	New York	3 Aug 1892	20 Jul 1892	1103-1110	475686
63	138-140	Normannia	New York	6 Aug 1892	29 Jul 1892	1150-1161	475686
63	140-141	Suevia	New York via Havre	6 Aug 1892	24 Jul 1892	1133-1140	475686
63	152-153	Marsala	New York	12 Aug 1892	27 Jul 1892	1143-1148	475686
63	153-154	Columbia	New York via Southampton	13 Aug 1892	5 Aug 1892	1196-1207	475686
63	154-155	Rhaetia	New York via Havre	13 Aug 1892	31 Jul 1892	1175-1180	475686
63	158	California	New York	15 Aug 1892	30 Jul 1892	1165-1174	475686
63	168-169	Slavonia	New York	19 Aug 1892	3 Aug 1892	1185-1192	475686
63	169-171	Furst Bismark	New York via Southampton	20 Aug 1892	12 Aug 1892	1237-1250	475686
63	171-172	Dania	New York via Havre	20 Aug 1892	7 Aug 1892	1217-1222	475686
63	187-188	Gellert	New York via Havre	27 Aug 1892	14 Aug 1892	1263-1272	475686
63	191-193	Augusta Victoria	New York via Southampton	29 Aug 1892	19 Aug 1892	1288-1301	475686
63	193-194	Russia	New York	29 Aug 1892	13 Aug 1892	1251-1162	475686
63	194-195	Sorrento	New York	29 Aug 1892	10 Aug 1892	1224-1229	475686
63	211	Scandia	New York	9 Sep 1892	27 Aug 1892	1341-1356	475686
63	223	Wieland	New York	19 Sep 1892	28 Aug 1892	1357-1358	475686
63	226-228	Normannia	New York via Southampton	22 Sep 1892	26 Aug 1892	1327-1340	475686
63	228	Moravia	New York	22 Sep 1892	17 Aug 1892	1276-1283	475686
63	228-229	Rugia	New York via Havre	22 Sep 1892	21 Aug 1892	1309-1316	475686
63	234	Rhaetia	New York	29 Sep 1892	11 Sep 1892	1381-1382	475686

Germans to America vol. and page nos.		Name of the Ship	Route and U.S. Port(s) of Arrival	Date of Arrival	Date of Departure	*HPL* Page numbers	FHL micro-film no.
63	238	Dania	New York	4 Oct 1892	18 Sep 1892	1387-1388	475686
63	241-242	Bohemia	New York	8 Oct 1892	1 Sep 1892	1361-1370	475686
63	262	Russia	New York	31 Oct 1892	16 Oct 1892	1403-1404	472936
63	267-268	Suevia	New York	7 Nov 1892	23 Oct 1892	1407-1410	472936
63	278-279	Dania	New York	18 Nov 1892	6 Nov 1892	1419-1422	472936
63	294-296	Rhaetia	New York	28 Nov 1892	13 Nov 1892	1434-1439	472936
63	309	Sorrento	New York	30 Nov 1892	12 Nov 1892	1432-1433	472936
63	315-318	Scandia	New York	5 Dec 1892	20 Nov 1892	1446-1455	472936
63	322-323	Marsala	New York	6 Dec 1892	19 Nov 1892	1442-1445	472936
63	328-329	Russia	New York	12 Dec 1892	27 Nov 1892	1468-1473	472936
63	330	Bohemia	New York	13 Dec 1892	25 Nov 1892	1466-1467	472936
63	346	Taormina	New York	19 Dec 1892	3 Dec 1892	1484-1485	472936
63	348	Suevia	New York via Havre	20 Dec 1892	4 Dec 1892	1486-1491	472936
63	349-350	Columbia	New York	20 Dec 1892	11 Dec 1892	1503-1508	472936
63	355	Moravia	New York	29 Dec 1892	11 Dec 1892	1499-1502	472936
64	1	Dania	New York	2 Jan 1893	18 Dec 1892	1521-1526	472936
64	14-15	Amalfi	New York	5 Jan 1893	16 Dec 1892	1516-1519	472936
64	15	Stubbenhuk	New York via Havre	5 Jan 1893	18 Dec 1892	1527-1528	472936
64	20	Cheruskia	New York	10 Jan 1893	24 Dec 1892	1533-1534	472936
64	28-30	Scandia	New York via Havre	14 Jan 1893	31 Dec 1892	1543-1550	472936
64	32	Sorrento	New York	23 Jan 1893	31 Dec 1892	1551-1556	472936
64	1	Dania	New York	2 Jan 1893	18 Dec 1892	1521-1526	472936
64	14-15	Amalfi	New York	5 Jan 1893	16 Dec 1892	1516-1519	472936

Germans to America vol. and page nos.		Name of the Ship	Route and U.S. Port(s) of Arrival	Date of Arrival	Date of Departure	*HPL* Page numbers	FHL micro-film no.
64	15	Stubbenhuk	New York via Havre	5 Jan 1893	18 Dec 1892	1527-1528	472936
64	20	Cheruskia	New York	10 Jan 1893	24 Dec 1892	1533-1534	472936
64	28-30	Scandia	New York via Havre	14 Jan 1893	31Dec 1892	1542-1550	472936
64	32	Sorrento	New York	3 Jan 1893	31Dec 1892	1551-1556	472936
64	35-36	Fürst Bismarck	New York via Southampton	30 Jan 1893	20 Jan 1893	15-18	472937
64	41	Bohemia	New York via Havre	8 Feb 1893	18 Jan 1893	12-13	472937
64	42	Dania	New York	13 Feb 1893	29 Jan 1893	31-34	472937
64	46	Slavonia	New York	18 Feb 1893	29 Jan 1893	35	472937
64	53	Augusta Victoria	New York	27 Feb 1893	16 Feb 1893	54-57	472937
64	54-55	Moravia	New York	27 Feb 1893	6 Feb 1893	43-44	472937
64	56	Scandia	New York	28 Feb 1893	12 Feb 1893	50-53	472937
64	57-58	Suevia	New York	3 Mar 1893	22 Jan 1893	20-23	472937
64	61-62	Rugia	New York	7 Mar 1893	20 Feb 1893	64-71	472937
64	70-71	Russia	New York via Havre	13 Mar 1893	26 Feb 1893	85-92	472937
64	85	Amalfi	New York	20 Mar 1893	2 Mar 1893	94-95	472937
64	85-87	Rhaetia	New York	20 Mar 1893	5 Mar 1893	98-111	472937
64	95-98	Dania	New York via Havre	25 Mar 1893	12 Mar 1893	129-146	472937
64	98-99	Essen	New York	25 Mar 1893	8 Mar 1893	114-117	472937
64	99-101	Normannia	New York via Southampton	25 Mar 1893	16 Mar 1893	159-166	472937
64	113-114	Sorrento	New York	1 Apr 1893	15 Mar 1893	147-156	472937
64	121-124	Gellert	New York	4 Apr 1893	19 Mar 1893	169-184	472937

Germans to America vol. and page nos.		Name of the Ship	Route and U.S. Port(s) of Arrival	Date of Arrival	Date of Departure	*HPL* Page numbers	FHL micro-film no.
64	133-136	Columbia	New York	10 Apr 1893	30 Mar 1893	227-236	472937
64	139-140	Moravia	New York	10 Apr 1893	24 Mar 1893	189-202	472937
64	141-144	Scandia	New York via Havre	10 Apr 1893	26 Mar 1893	211-224	472937
64	152-154	Augusta Victoria	New York via Southampton	15 Apr 1893	6 Apr 1893	253-262	472937
64	155	Markomannia	New York	15 Apr 1893	30 Mar 1893	237-238	472937
64	155-156	Rugia	New York via Havre	17 Apr 1893	2 Apr 1893	239-248	472937
64	166	Taormina	New York	24 Apr 1893	6 Apr 1893	263-268	472937
64	180-185	Fürst Bismarck	New York via Southampton	28 Apr 1893	20 Apr 1893	340-355	472937
64	191-192	California	New York	29 Apr 1893	12 Apr 1893	290-299	472937
64	237-240	Normannia	New York via Southampton	19 May 1893	11 May 1893	480-489	472937
64	247	Amalfi	New York	22 May 1893	4 May 1893	437-442	472937
64	258-261	Fürst Bismarck	New York via Southampton	26 May 1893	18 May 1893	524-533	472937
64	262-263	Rugia	New York via Havre	29 May 1893	14 May 1893	502-515	472937
64	273-275	Columbia	New York via Southampton	1 Jun 1893	25 May 1893	555-562	472937
64	277-278	Wieland	New York via Havre	3 Jun 1893	21 May 1893	540-551	472937
64	295	Sorrento	New York	8 Jun 1893	17 May 1893	518-521	472937
64	297-300	Augusta Victoria	New York via Southampton	10 Jun 1893	1 Jun 1893	594-601	472937
64	300-301	Suevia	New York	10 Jun 1893	28 May 1893	572-581	472937
64	309-310	Gellert	New York	17 Jun 1893	4 Jun 1893	606-615	472937
64	310	Taormina	New York	17 Jun 1893	31 May 1893	590-593	472937
64	320-322	Fürst Bismarck	New York via Southampton	23 Jun 1893	15 Jun 1893	669-678	472937

Germans to America vol. and page nos.		Name of the Ship	Route and U.S. Port(s) of Arrival	Date of Arrival	Date of Departure	*HPL* Page numbers	FHL micro-film no.
64	324	Steinhoeft	New York	23 Jun 1893	8 Jun 1893	629-632	472937
64	332-334	Columbia	New York via Southampton	30 Jun 1893	22 Jun 193	710-717	472937
64	334-335	Rhaetia	New York	1 Jul 1893	18 Jun 1893	692-699	472937
64	341-342	Augusta Victoria	New York via Southampton	7 Jul 1893	29 Jun 1893	736-743	472937
64	342-343	Chemnitz	New York	8 Jul 1893	22 Jun 1893	706-709	472937
64	343	Rugia	New York	8 Jul 1893	25 Jun 1893	723-728	472937
64	354-356	Normannia	New York via Southampton	14 Jul 1893	6 Jul 1893	767-774	472938
64	356	Amalfi	New York	15 Jul 1893	28 Jun 1893	729-730	472937
64	360-361	Moravia	New York	18 Jul 1893	6 Jul 1893	761-764	472938
64	366-369	Fürst Bismarck	New York	21 Jul 1893	13 Jul 1893	792-799	472938
64	369	Suevia	New York	22 Jul 1893	9 Jul 1893	779-782	472938
64	379-381	Columbia	New York via Southampton	28 Jul 1893	20 Jul 1893	820-827	472938
64	381	Gellert	New York	29 Jul 1893	16 Jul 1893	810-815	472938
64	381-382	Sorrento	New York	29 Jul 1893	12 Jul 1893	788-789	472938
65	7-8	Dania	New York	3 Aug 1893	23 Jul 1893	838-841	472938
65	9-11	Augusta Victoria	New York via Southampton	4 Aug 1893	27 Jul 1893	849-856	472938
65	11	Solingen	New York	4 Aug 1893	20 Jul 1893	818-819	472938
65	20-21	Normannia	New York via Southampton	11 Aug 1893	3 Aug 1893	880-887	472938
65	22	Taormina	New York	12 Aug 1893	26 Jul 1893	846-847	472938
65	27-28	Gothia	New York	17 Aug 1893	3 Aug 1893	878-879	472938
65	30-33	Fürst Bismarck	New York via Southampton	18 Aug 1893	10 Aug 1893	900-911	472938

Germans to America vol. and page nos.		Name of the Ship	Route and U.S. Port(s) of Arrival	Date of Arrival	Date of Departure	*HPL* Page numbers	FHL micro-film no.
65	33-34	Rugia	New York	19 Aug 1893	6 Aug 1893	890-895	472938
65	46-47	Columbia	New York via Southampton	25 Aug 1893	17 Aug 1893	933-940	472938
65	47-48	Marsala	New York	26 Aug 1893	9 Aug 1893	898-899	472938
65	49	Wieland	New York	26 Aug 1893	13 Aug 1893	924-927	472938
65	49	Essen	New York	28 Aug 1893	10 Aug 1893	912-913	472938
65	53	Moravia	New York	29 Aug 1893	16 Aug 1893	931-932	472938
65	61-62	Augusta Victoria	New York via Southampton	1 Sep 1893	24 Aug 1893	958-967	472938
65	63	Suevia	New York	2 Sep 1893	20 Aug 1893	946-951	472938
65	74-75	Gellert	New York	8 Sep 1893	27 Aug 1893	978-983	472938
65	75-77	Normannia	New York via Southampton	8 Sep 1893	31 Aug 1893	989-996	472938
65	77-78	Amalfi	New York	9 Sep 1893	23 Aug 1893	956-957	472938
65	89	Dania	New York	14 Sep 1893	3 Sep 1893	1001-1004	472938
65	90-91	Fürst Bismarck	New York via Southampton	15 Sep 1893	7 Sep 1893	1014-1023	472938
65	92	Hungaria	New York	15 Sep 1893	30 Aug 1893	985-986	472938
65	103-105	Columbia	New York via Southampton	22 Sep 1893	14 Sep 1893	1036-1044	472938
65	107	Sorrento	New York	23 Sep 1893	7 Sep 1893	1010-1011	472938
65	107-108	Rhaetia	New York	23 Sep 1893	10 Sep 1893	1027-1030	472938
65	117-118	Gothia	New York	23 Sep 1893	14 Sep 1893	1045-1046	472938
65	120-121	Rugia	New York	2 Oct 1893	17 Sep 1893	1054-1059	472938
65	136-137	Moravia	New York	12 Oct 1893	29 Sep 1893	1088-1091	472938
65	137-139	Russia	New York	13 Oct 1893	24 Sep 1893	1077-1084	472938

Germans to America vol. and page nos.		Name of the Ship	Route and U.S. Port(s) of Arrival	Date of Arrival	Date of Departure	*HPL* Page numbers	FHL micro-film no.
65	140-142	Fürst Bismarck	New York	14 Oct 1893	missing	missing	-----
65	142-143	Suevia	New York	14 Oct 1893	1 Oct 1893	1102-1105	472938
65	150-151	Dania	New York	20 Oct 1893	9 Oct 1893	1118-1121	472938
65	151	Marsala	New York	21 Oct 1893	6 Oct 1893	1109-1110	472938
65	160-162	Columbia	New York	27 Oct 1893	missing	missing	-----
65	162-164	Gellert	New York	27 Oct 1893	15 Oct 1893	1135-1140	472938
65	166	Amalfi	New York	30 Oct 1894	14 Oct 1893	1127-1128	472938
65	169	Hungaria	New York	4 Nov 1893	18 Oct 1893	1141-1142	472938
65	172-173	Rhaetia	New York	6 Nov 1893	22 Oct 1893	1157-1162	472938
65	175-177	Fürst Bismarck	New York via Southampton	10 Nov 1893	2 Nov 1893	1186-1193	472938
65	179	Gothia	New York	11 Nov 1893	26 Oct 1893	1165-1166	472938
65	179-180	Rugia	New York	11 Nov 1893	29 Oct 1893	1173-1176	472938
65	191	Russia	New York	20 Nov 1893	7 Nov 1893	1202-1205	472938
65	191-192	Sorrento	New York	20 Nov 1893	2 Nov 1893	1184-1185	472938
65	197-198	Columbia	New York via Southampton	25 Nov 1893	16 Nov 1893	1232-1239	472938
65	198-199	Moravia	New York via Havre	25 Nov 1893	10 Nov 1893	1210-1213	472938
65	201	Dania	New York via Havre	28 Nov 1893	13 Nov 1893	1215-1218	472938
65	205	Suevia	New York via Havre	4 Dec 1893	19 Nov 1893	1241-1244	472938
65	205-206	Taormina	New York	4 Dec 1893	16 Nov 1893	1227-1228	472938
65	213-214	Normannia	New York via Southampton	8 Dec 1893	30 Nov 1893	1268-1273	472938
65	214-215	Scandia	New York via Havre	9 Dec 1893	26 Nov 1893	1257-1262	472938

Germans to America vol. and page nos.		Name of the Ship	Route and U.S. Port(s) of Arrival	Date of Arrival	Date of Departure	*HPL* Page numbers	FHL micro-film no.
65	219-220	Rhaetia	New York via Havre	20 Dec 1893	3 Dec 1893	1279-1282	472938
65	220	Marsala	New York	21 Dec 1893	29 Nov 1893	1264-1265	472938
65	224	Gothia	New York	29 Dec 1893	7 Dec 1893	1287-1288	472938
65	225	Rugia	New York via Havre	30 Dec 1893	10 Dec 1893	1292-1295	472938
65	228-229	Russia	New York via Havre	3 Jan 1894	17 Dec 1893	1308-1309	472938
65	229	Amalfi	New York	4 Jan 1894	13 Dec 1893	1298-1299	472938
65	231-232	Wieland	New York	15 Jan 1894	31 Dec 1893	1324-1325	472938
65	233	Sorrento	New York	18 Jan 1894	29 Dec 1893	1318-1319	472938
65	233-234	Dania	New York via Havre	20 Jan 1894	7 Jan 1894	7-10	472939
65	236-247	Fürst Bismarck	New York	27 Jan 1894	18 Jan 1894	26-31	472939
65	237-238	Scandia	New York via Havre	29 Jan 1894	14 Jan 1894	22-23	472939
65	240-241	Taormina	New York	5 Feb 1894	12 Jan 1894	18-19	472939
65	244-245	Rugia	New York via Havre	14 Feb 1894	28 Jan 1894	49-50	472939
65	245	Marsala	New York	16 Feb 1894	26 Jan 1894	46-47	472939
65	248	Augusta Victoria	New York via Southampton	20 Feb 1894	10 Feb 1894	70-73	472939
65	253	Moravia	New York via Havre	28 Feb 1894	11 Feb 1894	74-75	472939
65	256	Dania	New York via Havre	5 Mar 1894	18 Feb 1894	83-86	472939
65	257-258	Amalfi	New York	6 Mar 1894	15 Feb 1894	79-80	472939
65	259	Suevia	New York	10 Mar 1894	21 Feb 1894	92-95	472939
65	268-269	Rhaetia	New York via Havre	20 Mar 1894	4 Mar 1894	115-118	472939
65	269	Sorrento	New York	20 Mar 1894	28 Feb 1894	105-106	472939

Germans to America vol. and page nos.		Name of the Ship	Route and U.S. Port(s) of Arrival	Date of Arrival	Date of Departure	*HPL* Page numbers	FHL micro-film no.
65	269-270	Scandia	New York via Havre	21 Mar 1894	25 Feb 1894	98-101	472939
65	276-277	Gellert	New York via Havre	26 Mar 1894	11 Mar 1894	131-136	472939
65	280	Bohemia	New York	29 Mar 1894	8 Mar 1894	124-127	472939
65	284-285	Russia	New York via Havre	3 Apr 1894	18 Mar 1894	153-158	472939
65	287	Essen	New York	5 Apr 1894	6 Mar 1894	120-121	472939
65	289	Taormina	New York	6 Apr 1894	14 Mar 1894	138-141	472939
65	293-294	Moravia	New York via Havre	10 Apr 1894	25 Mar 1894	167-172	472939
65	296-298	Dania	New York via Havre	14 Apr 1894	4 Apr 1894	186-193	472939
65	303	Stubbenhuk	New York	19 Apr 1894	5 Apr 1894	198-203	472939
65	306-307	Rhaetia	New York	23 Apr 1894	10 Apr 1894	206-213	472939
65	313-315	Augusta Victoria	New York via Havre and Southampton	28 Apr 1894	19 Apr 1894	238-247	472939
65	317	Scandia	New York via Havre	30 Apr 1894	15 Apr 1894	225-232	472939
65	322-324	Normannia	New York via Southampton	4 May 1894	26 Apr 1894	265-270	472939
65	324-325	Amalfi	New York	7 May 1894	18 Apr 1894	234-237	472939
65	327-328	Bohemia	New York via Havre	8 May 1894	22 Apr 1894	256-259	472939
65	332-333	Fürst Bismarck	New York via Southampton	11 May 1894	3 May 1894	284-289	472939
65	336-337	Russia	New York via Havre	15 May 1894	29 Apr 1894	271-274	472939
65	341-342	Columbia	New York via Southampton	19 May 1894	10 May 1894	308-313	472939
65	342-343	Sorrento	New York	21 May 1894	3 May 1894	281-282	472939
65	345	Moravia	New York via Havre	21 May 1894	6 May 1894	298-301	472939
65	347	Dania	New York via Havre	25 May 1894	13 May 1894	318-321	472939

Germans to America vol. and page nos.		Name of the Ship	Route and U.S. Port(s) of Arrival	Date of Arrival	Date of Departure	*HPL* Page numbers	FHL micro-film no.
65	348-349	Augusta Victoria	New York via Southampton	26 May 1894	17 May 1894	324-327	472939
65	350	Grimm	New York	28 May 1894	9 May 1894	304-305	472939
65	356-357	Normannia	New York and Southampton	1 Jun 1894	24 May 1894	347-350	472939
65	357	Taormina	New York	4 Jun 1894	17 May 1894	328-331	472939
65	359	Rhaetia	New York via Havre	4 Jun 1894	20 May 1894	336-339	472939
65	363-364	Fürst Bismarck	New York via Southampton	8 Jun 1894	31 May 1894	369-374	472939
65	364-365	Scandia	New York via Havre	9 Jun 1894	27 May 1894	357-360	472939
65	369-370	Columbia	New York via Southampton	15 Jun 1894	7 Jun 1894	394-399	472939
65	371-372	Marsala	New York	16 Jun 1894	30 May 1894	363-366	472939
65	374	Rugia	New York via Havre	18 Jun 1894	3 Jun 1894	381-384	472939
65	377	Augusta Victoria	New York via Southampton	23 Jun 1894	14 Jun 1894	414-417	472939
65	381	Russia	New York via Havre	26 Jun 1894	10 Jun 1894	401-404	472939
65	385	Normannia	New York via Southampton	29 Jun 1894	21 Jun 1894	431-434	472939
65	385-386	Amalfi	New York	30 Jun 1894	13 Jun 1894	410-413	472939
66	2-3	Moravia	New York via Havre	2 Jul 1894	17 Jun 1894	425-426	472939
66	5-6	Fürst Bismarck	New York via Southampton	6 Jul 1894	28 Jun 1894	456-461	472939
66	8	Prussia	New York via Havre	9 Jul 1894	24 Jun 1894	440-443	472939
66	15	Rhaetia	New York	16 Jul 1894	1 Jul 1894	465-468	472940
66	15-16	Sorrento	New York	16 Jul 1894	27 Jun 1894	450-453	472939
66	19	California	New York	20 Jul 1894	4 Jul 1894	473-476	472940
66	19	Scandia	New York via Havre	21 Jul 1894	8 Jul 1894	488-489	472940

Germans to America vol. and page nos.		Name of the Ship	Route and U.S. Port(s) of Arrival	Date of Arrival	Date of Departure	*HPL* Page numbers	FHL micro-film no.
66	24	Persia	New York	27 Jul 1894	15 Jul 1894	502-505	472940
66	24-25	Normannia	New York via Southampton	27 Jul 1894	19 Jul 1894	512-517	472940
66	26	Taormina	New York	28 Jul 1894	10 Jul 1894	493-494	472940
66	30-31	Fürst Bismarck	New York	3 Aug 1894	26Jul 1894	532-539	472940
66	32	Polaria	New York	4 Aug 1894	18 Jul 1894	509-510	472940
66	36	Marsala	New York	10 Aug 1894	25 Jul 1894	527-528	472940
66	36-37	Columbia	New York via Southampton	10 Aug 1894	5 Jul 1894	479-484	472940
66	38-39	Rugia	New York via Havre	13 Aug 1894	29 Jul 1894	542-545	472940
66	43	Bohemia	New York	16 Aug 1894	1 Aug 1894	547-548	472940
66	44-45	Augusta Victoria	New York via Southampton	17 Aug 1894	9 Aug 1894	570-577	472940
66	45-46	Prussia	New York via Havre	18 Aug 1894	5 Aug 1894	562-563	472940
66	49-50	Normannia	New York via Southampton	24 Aug 1894	16 Aug 1894	600-605	472940
66	50	Amalfi	New York	25 Aug 1894	8 Aug 1894	567-568	472940
66	52-53	Rhaetia	New York via Havre	27 Aug 1894	12 Aug 1894	585-588	472940
66	55	Moravia	New York	29 Aug 1894	15 Aug 1894	598-599	472940
66	56-57	Fürst Bismarck	New York via Southampton	31 Aug 1894	23 Aug 1894	619-628	472940
66	57	Scandia	New York via Havre	1 Sep 1894	19 Aug 1894	608-609	472940
66	64-65	Sorrento	New York	7 Sep 1894	22 Aug 1894	615-616	472940
66	65-66	Persia	New York via Havre	8 Sep 1894	26 Aug 1894	631-634	472940
66	66	Wieland	New York	10 Sep 1894	29 Aug 1894	636-639	472940
66	71-72	Augusta Victoria	New York via Southampton	15 Sep 1894	6 Sep 1894	668-675	472940

Germans to America vol. and page nos.		Name of the Ship	Route and U.S. Port(s) of Arrival	Date of Arrival	Date of Departure	*HPL* Page numbers	FHL micro-film no.
66	73	Russia	New York via Havre	17 Sep 1894	2 Sep 1894	654-657	472940
66	79	Dania	New York via Havre	21 Sep 1894	9 Sep 1894	679-682	472940
66	79-80	Normannia	New York via Southampton	21 Sep 1894	13 Sep 1894	692-701	472940
66	81-82	Taormina	New York	22 Sep 1894	5 Sep 1894	663-664	472940
66	89-90	Fürst Bismarck	New York via Southampton	28 Sep 1894	20 Sep 1894	717-726	472940
66	91	Prussia	New York via Havre	29 Sep 1894	16 Sep 1894	705-708	472940
66	99-100	Augusta Victoria	New York	13 Oct 1894	4 Oct 1894	768-775	472940
66	104	Amalfi	New York	19 Oct 1894	3 Oct 1894	760-761	472940
66	108	Persia	New York via Havre	22 Oct 1894	7 Oct 1894	778-781	472940
66	113-115	Fürst Bismarck	New York via Southampton	26 Oct 1894	18 Oct 1894	807-816	472940
66	116	Moravia	New York via Havre	29 Oct 1894	14 Oct 1894	796-799	472940
66	123	Sorrento	New York	3 Nov 1894	17 Oct 1894	804-805	472940
66	124-125	Columbia	New York via Southampton	3 Nov 1894	25 Oct 1894	832-839	472940
66	126	Dania	New York via Havre	5 Nov 1894	21 Oct 1894	825-828	472940
66	131	Prussia	New York	12 Nov 1894	28 Oct 1894	848-849	472940
66	133	Suevia	New York via Havre	13 Nov 1894	26 Oct 1894	843-844	472940
66	139-140	Rhaetia	New York	22 Nov 1894	4 Nov 1894	860-863	472940
66	142	Scandia	New York via Havre	26 Nov 1894	11 Nov 1894	876-879	472940
66	147	Taormina	New York	1 Dec 1894	31 Oct 1894	852-853	472940
66	147-148	Persia	New York	3 Dec 1894	18 Nov 1894	895-902	472940
66	148-149	Polaria	New York	3 Dec 1894	7 Nov 1894	866-867	472940

Germans to America vol. and page nos.		Name of the Ship	Route and U.S. Port(s) of Arrival	Date of Arrival	Date of Departure	*HPL* Page numbers	FHL micro-film no.
66	154	Amalfi	New York	10 Dec 1894	22 Nov 1894	904-907	472940
66	155-156	Moravia	New York via Havre	11 Dec 1894	25 Nov 1894	912-915	472940
66	157	Patria	New York	17 Dec 1894	2 Dec 1894	927-932	472940
66	158	Marsala	New York	17 Dec 1894	28 Nov 1894	919-922	472940
66	162-163	Dania	New York	24 Dec 1894	9 Dec 1894	945-950	472940
66	164	Hispania	New York via Havre	28 Dec 1894	9 Dec 1894	943-944	472940
66	165	Prussia	New York	31 Dec 1894	16 Dec 1894	968-971	472940
66	167	Scandia	New York	4 Jan 1895	23 Dec 1894	980-983	472940
66	172	Augusta Victoria	New York via Drogheda	17 Jan 1895	8 Jan 1895	15-18	472941
66	173	Slavonia	New York via Havre	17 Jan 1895	31 Dec 1894	987-990	472940
66	176	Persia	New York	24 Jan 1895	6 Jan 1895	10-13	472941
66	178	Amalfi	New York	28 Jan 1895	9 Jan 1895	19-20	472941
66	179	Phoenicia	New York via Havre	29 Jan 1895	13 Jan 1895	26-27	472941
66	181-182	Patria	New York	4 Feb 1895	20 Jan 1895	37-40	472941
66	184	Dania	New York via Havre	12 Feb 1895	27 Jan 1895	51-53	472941
66	187	Scandia	New York	18 Feb 1895	3 Feb 1895	63-67	472941
66	191-192	Marsala	New York	25 Feb 1895	7 Feb 1895	74-75	472941
66	192	Prussia	New York via Havre	25 Feb 1895	10 Feb 1895	79-82	472941
66	195-196	Russia	New York via Havre	4 Mar 1895	17 Feb 1895	90-95	472941
66	199-200	Persia	New York via Havre	12 Mar 1895	24 Feb 1895	100-107	472941
66	202	Phoenicia	New York	18 Mar 1895	3 Mar 1895	117-124	472941

Germans to America vol. and page nos.		Name of the Ship	Route and U.S. Port(s) of Arrival	Date of Arrival	Date of Departure	*HPL* Page numbers	FHL micro-film no.
66	209	Amalfi	New York	25 Mar 1895	7 Mar 1895	126-128	472941
66	214	Dania	New York	1 Apr 1895	17 Mar 1895	146-155	472941
66	221-222	Scandia	New York via Havre	8 Apr 1895	24 Mar 1895	169-174	472941
66	223	Taormina	New York	11 Apr 1895	22 Mar 1895	162-167	472941
66	227-228	Russia	New York	15 Apr 1895	31 Mar 1895	181-190	472941
66	232	Phoenicia	New York	27 Apr 1895	14 Apr 1895	231-233	472941
66	236-237	Persia	New York	3 May 1895	21 Apr 1895	246-250	472941
66	237	Albano	New York	3 May 1895	18 Apr 1895	241	472941
66	237-238	Columbia	New York via Southampton	4 May 1895	25 Apr 1895	255-260	472941
66	242	Palatia	New York	11 May 1895	28 Apr 1895	268-277	472941
66	243-244	Markomannia	New York via Havre	13 May 1895	23 Apr 1895	253-254	472941
66	249	Amalfi	New York via Havre	20 May 1895	1 May 1895	281-287	472941
66	251-251	Fürst Bismarck	New York via Southampton	24 May 1895	16 May 1895	363-368	472941
66	252	Columbia	New York via Drogheda	1 Jun 1895	23 May 1895	388-391	472941
66	252-254	Prussia	New York	1 Jun 1895	19 May 1895	369-374	472941
66	255	Taormina	New York via Havre	3 Jun 1895	15 May 1895	353-358	472941
66	257	Augusta Victoria	New York via Southampton	4 Jun 1895	28 May 1895	405-408	472941
66	258	California	New York via Havre	8 Jun 1895	21 May 1895	376-383	472941
66	262	Phoenicia	New York	10 Jun 1895	26 May 1895	397-401	472941
66	267-268	Normannia	New York via Southampton	14 Jun 1895	6 Jun 1895	437-440	472941
66	268	Persia	New York	14 Jun 1895	2 Jun 1895	428-431	472941

Germans to America vol. and page nos.		Name of the Ship	Route and U.S. Port(s) of Arrival	Date of Arrival	Date of Departure	*HPL* Page numbers	FHL micro-film no.
66	269	Marsala	New York	15 Jun 1895	29 May 1895	416-423	472941
66	272-273	Fürst Bismarck	New York	21 Jun 1895	13 Jun 1895	463-468	472941
66	273	Palatia	New York	22 Jun 1895	9 Jun 1895	442-445	472941
66	276	Polaria	New York via Havre	25 Jun 1895	6 Jun 1895	433-436	472941
66	279	Albano	New York via Havre	28 Jun 1895	12 Jun 1895	452-457	472941
66	280	Dania	New York	29 Jun 1895	16 Jun 1895	474-479	472941
66	285	Prussia	New York	12 Jul 1895	30 Jun 1895	517-520	472941
66	285-286	Normannia	New York	12 Jul 1895	4 Jul 1895	536-540	472942
66	286	Amalfi	New York via Havre	15 Jul 1895	26 Jun 1895	503-506	472941
66	290	Phoenicia	New York	19 Jul 1895	7 Jul 1895	543-547	472942
66	290-291	Fürst Bismarck	New York via Southampton	19 Jul 1895	11 Jul 1895	556-561	472942
66	292	Italia	New York via Havre	20 Jul 1895	3 Jul 1895	525-529	472942
66	296-297	Persia	New York	26 Jul 1895	14 Jul 1895	569-576	472942
66	297	Taormina	New York via Havre	27 Jul 1895	10 Jul 1895	553-554	472942
66	303-304	Palatia	New York	1 Aug 1895	21 Jul 1895	582-590	472942
66	304	Augusta Victoria	New York via Southampton	3 Aug 1895	25 Jul 1895	601-608	472942
66	308-309	Normannia	New York via Southampton	9 Aug 1895	1 Aug 1895	626-631	472942
66	310	Dania	New York	9 Aug 1895	28 Jul 1895	612-619	472942
66	310	Marsala	New York	12 Aug 1895	24 Jul 1895	596-597	472942
66	315-316	Patria	New York	15 Aug 1895	4 Aug 1895	635-640	472942
66	317-318	Fürst Bismarck	New York via Southampton	16 Aug 1895	8 Aug 1895	648-655	472942

Germans to America vol. and page nos.		Name of the Ship	Route and U.S. Port(s) of Arrival	Date of Arrival	Date of Departure	*HPL* Page numbers	FHL micro-film no.
66	318	Bohemia	New York via Havre	16 Aug 1895	31 Jul 1895	621-623	472942
66	323	Prussia	New York	22 Aug 1895	11 Aug 1895	662-669	472942
66	323-324	Albano	New York	22 Aug 1895	7 Aug 1895	644-646	472942
66	325	Columbia	New York via Southampton	24 Aug 1895	15 Aug 1895	683-690	472942
66	330-331	Phoenicia	New York	30 Aug 1895	18 Aug 1895	695-704	472942
66	331-332	Augusta Victoria	New York via Southampton	31 Aug 1895	22 Aug 1895	714-723	472942
66	342-343	Normannia	New York	7 Sep 1895	29 Aug 1895	748-759	472942
66	343-344	Persia	New York	7 Sep 1895	25 Aug 1895	731-742	472942
66	351	Dania	New York	20 Sep 1895	8 Sep 1895	802-813	472942
66	352	Columbia	New York via Southampton	20 Sep 1895	12 Sep 1895	819-826	472942
66	354-355	Taormina	New York	23 Sep 1895	5 Sep 1895	779-781	472942
66	359-360	Patria	New York	27 Sep 1895	15 Sep 1895	832-841	472942
66	360-361	Augusta Victoria	New York via Southampton	28 Sep 1895	19 Sep 1895	850-857	472942
66	370-371	Prussia	New York	4 Oct 1895	22 Sep 1895	862-871	472942
66	371-372	Normannia	New York	4 Oct 1895	26 Sep 1895	878-886	472942
66	373	Persia	New York	6 Oct 1895	missing	missing	-----
66	375	Marsala	New York	7 Oct 1895	18 Sep 1895	847-848	472942
66	378	Phoenicia	New York	12 Oct 1895	29 Sep 1895	894-901	472942
66	379-380	Fürst Bismarck	New York	12 Oct 1895	3 Oct 1895	907-916	472942
66	381	Bohemia	New York	12 Oct 1895	25 Sep 1895	874-876	472942
66	386	Albano	New York via Havre	19 Oct 1895	3 Oct 1895	905-906	472942

Germans to America vol. and page nos.		Name of the Ship	Route and U.S. Port(s) of Arrival	Date of Arrival	Date of Departure	*HPL* Page numbers	FHL micro-film no.
66	390-391	Palatia	New York	24 Oct 1895	13 Oct 1895	949-956	472942
66	393-395	August Victoria	New York	26 Oct 1895	17 Oct 1895	969-978	472942
66	395	Moravia	New York via Havre	28 Oct 1895	10 Oct 1895	937-940	472942
66	399	Dania	New York	31 Oct 1895	20 Oct 1895	983-992	472942
67	1	Amalfi	New York via Havre	2 Nov 1895	17 Oct 1895	965-967	472942
67	6	Patria	New York	9 Nov 1895	27 Oct 1895	1007-1016	472942
67	6-7	Columbia	New York via Southampton	9 Nov 1895	31 Oct 1895	1025-1031	472942
67	8	Sicilia	New York via Havre	11 Nov 1895	24 Oct 1895	1000-1005	472942
67	12-13	Prussia	New York	18 Nov 1895	3 Nov 1895	1038-1047	472942
67	14	Taormina	New York	21 Nov 1895	31 Oct 1895	1021-1024	472942
67	16	Phoenicia	New York	25 Nov 1895	10 Nov 1895	1056-1064	472942
67	19	Persia	New York	30 Nov 1895	18 Nov 1895	1084-1095	472942
67	20-21	Marsala	New York	2 Dec 1895	14 Nov 1895	1075-1077	472942
67	22	Virginia	New York via Havre	4 Dec 1895	20 Nov 1895	1097	472942
67	24	Palatia	New York	11 Dec 1895	25 Nov 1895	1112-1117	472942
67	26	Albano	New York via Havre	16 Dec 1895	27 Nov 1895	1120-1123	472942
67	26	Scotia	New York	16 Dec 1895	23 Nov 1895	1108-1111	472942
67	28-29	Moravia	New York	20 Dec 1895	1 Dec 1895	1132-1137	472942
67	29	Normannia	New York via Southampton	21 Dec 1895	12 Dec 1895	1162-1167	472942
67	31	Patria	New York	26 Dec 1895	missing	missing	-----
67	32	Christiania	New York via Havre	28 Dec 1895	missing	missing	-----

Germans to America vol. and page nos.		Name of the Ship	Route and U.S. Port(s) of Arrival	Date of Arrival	Date of Departure	*HPL* Page numbers	FHL micro-film no.
67	33	Prussia	New York	30 Dec 1895	15 Dec 1895	1177-1182	472942
67	34	Amalfi	New York	31 Dec 1895	12 Dec 1895	1168-1170	472942
67	35	Persia	New York	13 Jan 1896	31 Dec 1895	1207-1211	472942
67	36	Taormine	New York via Havre	15 Jan 1896	28 Dec 1895	1203-1204	472942
67	39	Fürst Bismarck	New York via Southampton	23 Jan 1896	14 Jan 1896	33-36	472943
67	40	Italia	New York	24 Jan 1896	8 Jan 1896	14-17	472943
67	41	Marsala	New York via Havre	27 Jan 1896	8 Jan 1896	12-13	472943
67	44	Moravia	New York	4 Feb 1896	19 Jan 1896	46-49	472943
67	45-46	Patria	New York	10 Feb 1896	26 Jan 1896	60-63	472943
67	48	Albano	New York via Havre	14 Feb 1896	25 Jan 1896	56-58	472943
67	49	Prussia	New York	17 Feb 1896	2 Feb 1896	71-76	472943
67	53	Phoenicia	New York	24 Feb 1896	9 Feb 1896	91-96	472943
67	54	Christiania	New York via Havre	25 Feb 1896	5 Feb 1896	81-83	472943
67	56-57	Persia	New York	29 Feb 1896	16 Feb 1896	108-113	472943
67	59	Amalfi	New York via Havre	3 Mar 1896	12 Feb 1896	100-102	472943
67	62-63	Italia	New York	9 Mar 1896	23 Feb 1896	125-129	472943
67	63	California	New York via Havre	9 Mar 1896	19 Feb 1896	117-120	472943
67	66-67	Palatia	New York	16 Mar 1896	1 Mar 1896	140-150	472943
67	69	Taormina	New York via Havre	18 Mar 1896	26 Feb 1896	132-134	472943
67	73-74	Moravia	New York	24 Mar 1896	8 Mar 1896	159-170	472943
67	78-79	Patria	New York	31 Mar 1896	15 Mar 1896	181-196	472943

Germans to America vol. and page nos.		Name of the Ship	Route and U.S. Port(s) of Arrival	Date of Arrival	Date of Departure	*HPL* Page numbers	FHL micro-film no.
67	80	Scotia	New York via Havre	2 Apr 1896	12 Mar 1896	174-177	472943
67	84-85	Prussia	New York	8 Apr 1896	25 Mar 1896	206-220	472943
67	86-87	Phoenicia	New York	11 Apr 1896	29 Mar 1896	232-239	472943
67	87-88	Albano	New York via Havre	13 Apr 1896	26 Mar 1896	223-225	472943
67	94	Persia	New York	17 Apr 1896	5 Apr 1896	250-253	472943
67	94-95	Augusta Victoria	New York via Southampton	18 Apr 1896	9 Apr 1896	256-262	472943
67	96	Georgia	New York via Havre	18 Apr 1896	1 Apr 1896	240-242	472943
67	103	Palatia	New York	27 Apr 1896	12 Apr 1896	274-281	472943
67	109-110	Columbia	New York	1 May 1896	23 Apr 1896	320-325	472943
67	111-112	Scandia	New York	1 May 1896	19 Apr 1896	293-300, List 45 301-302	472943
67	112	Amalfi	New York via Havre	2 May 1896	15 Apr 1896	285-288	472943
67	115-116	Patria	New York	8 May 1896	26 Apr 1896	326-339	472943
67	116-117	Normannia	New York via Southampton	9 May 1896	30 Apr 1896	353-356	472943
67	121	Sorrento	New York via Havre	11 May 1896	22 Apr 1896	308-313	472943
67	124-125	Augusta Victoria	New York via Southampton	16 May 1896	7 May 1896	382-387	472943
67	125-127	Prussia	New York	18 May 1896	5 May 1896	360-371	472943
67	128	Taormina	New York via Havre	18 May 1896	30 Apr 1896	349-352	472943
67	133	Fürst Bismarck	New York via Southampton	22 May 1896	14 May 1896	410-417	472943
67	135-136	Marsala	New York via Havre	25 May 1896	8 May 1896	372-376	472943
67	136-137	Phoenicia	New York	25 May 1896	10 May 1896	395-404	472943
67	141-142	Persia	New York	29 May 1896	17 May 1896	423-434	472943

Germans to America vol. and page nos.		Name of the Ship	Route and U.S. Port(s) of Arrival	Date of Arrival	Date of Departure	*HPL* Page numbers	FHL micro-film no.
67	143-144	Columbia	New York	29 May 1896	21 May 1896	444-447	472943
67	147-148	Scandia	New York	5 Jun 1896	24 May 1896	451-456	472943
67	148	Normannia	New York	5 Jun 1896	28 May 1896	463-468	472943
67	149	Bohemia	New York via Havre	5 Jun 1896	21 May 1896	440-443	472943
67	154	Albano	New York via Havre	10 Jun 1896	27 May 1896	458-460	472943
67	155-156	Augusta Victoria	New York via Cuxhaven	13 Jun 1896	4 Jun 1896	489-494	472943
67	156-157	Palatia	New York	13 Jun 1896	31 May 1896	471-481	472943
67	161	Patria	New York	19 Jun 1896	7 Jun 1896	502-511	472943
67	162-163	Fürst Bismarck	New York via Southampton	19 Jun 1896	11 Jun 1896	521-526	472943
67	163	Hispania	New York via Havre	20 Jun 1896	3 Jun 1896	487-488	472943
67	167-168	Columbia	New York	26 Jun 1896	18 Jun 1896	553-558	472943
67	168	Prussia	New York	27 Jun 1896	14 Jun 1896	533-542	472943
67	169	Sorrento	New York via Havre	29 Jun 1896	10 Jun 1896	516-518	472943
67	173	Phoenicia	New York	6 Jul 1896	21 Jun 1896	560-566	472943
67	174	Normannia	New York	6 Jul 1896	25 Jun 1896	577-582	472943
67	177-178	Augusta Victoria	New York via Southampton	11 Jul 1896	2 Jul 1896	603-608	472944
67	178-179	Persia	New York	11 Jul 1896	28 Jun 1896	586-593	472943
67	180-181	Fürst Bismarck	New York via Southampton	17 Jul 1896	9 Jul 1896	626-633	472944
67	182	Scotia	New York	20 Jul 1896	1 Jul 1896	594-596	472944
67	182-183	Scandia	New York	20 Jul 1896	5 Jul 1896	613-619	472944
67	186-187	Palatia	New York	25 Jul 1896	12 Jul 1896	639-646	472944

Germans to America vol. and page nos.		Name of the Ship	Route and U.S. Port(s) of Arrival	Date of Arrival	Date of Departure	*HPL* Page numbers	FHL micro-film no.
67	187	Marsala	New York via Havre	25 Jul 1896	8 Jul 1896	623-624	472944
67	189	Bohemia	New York via Havre	31 Jul 1896	15 Jul 1896	651-653	472944
67	193	Albano	New York via Havre	7 Aug 1896	22 Jul 1896	675-676	472944
67	194	Augusta Victoria	New York via Southampton	7 Aug 1896	30 Jul 1896	701-708	472944
67	195	Prussia	New York	8 Aug 1896	26 Jul 1896	688-695	472944
67	197	Hispania	New York via Havre	14 Aug 1896	29 Jul 1896	699-700	472944
67	197-198	Fürst Bismarck	New York	14 Aug 1896	6 Aug 1896	735-741	472944
67	198	Phoenicia	New York	14 Aug 1896	2 Aug 1896	716-725	472944
67	202	Persia	New York	21 Aug 1896	9 Aug 1896	746-753	472944
67	203	Columbia	New York via Southampton	21 Aug 1896	13 Aug 1896	764-771	472944
67	207-208	Normannia	New York	28 Aug 1896	20 Aug 1896	791-802	472944
67	208-209	Scandia	New York	28 Aug 1896	16 Aug 1896	774-781	472944
67	214-215	Augusta Victoria	New York via Southampton	4 Sep 1896	27 Aug 1896	827-836	472944
67	216	Russia	New York	7 Sep 1896	24 Aug 1896	820-823	472944
67	216	Palatia	New York	7 Sep 1896	23 Aug 1896	808-819	472944
67	220	Fürst Bismarck	New York via Southampton	11 Sep 196	3 Sep 1896	868-878	472944
67	220-221	Patria	New York	11 Sep 1896	30 Aug 1896	848-857	472944
67	227-228	Columbia	New York via Southampton	18 Sep 1896	10 Sep 1896	897-903	472944
67	228	Prussia	New York	19 Sep 1896	6 Sep 1896	884-891	472944
67	233-234	Normannia	New York	25 Sep 1896	17 Sep 1896	925-933	472944
67	234	Bohemia	New York via Havre	26 Sep 1896	9 Sep 1896	893-894	472944

Germans to America vol. and page nos.		Name of the Ship	Route and U.S. Port(s) of Arrival	Date of Arrival	Date of Departure	*HPL* Page numbers	FHL micro-film no.
67	234-235	Phoenicia	New York	28 Sep 1896	15 Sep 1896	913-918	472944
67	240	Persia	New York	2 Oct 1896	20 Sep 1896	936-941	472944
67	241-242	Augusta Victoria	New York	3 Oct 1896	24 Sep 1896	948-957	472944
67	242	Albano	New York via Havre	5 Oct 1896	16 Sep 1896	919-920	472944
67	248-249	Fürst Bismarck	New York via Southampton	9 Oct 1896	1 Oct 1896	981-987	472945
67	249	Scandia	New York	9 Oct 1896	27 Sep 1896	966-971	472944
67	253-254	Columbia	New York	16 Oct 1896	8 Oct 1896	1004-1010	472945
67	254-255	Palatia	New York	16 Oct 196	4 Oct 1896	993-998	472945
67	257	Sorrento	New York via Havre	19 Oct 1896	30 Sep 1896	973-974	472945
67	260	California	New York	23 Oct 1896	7 Oct 1896	1002-1003	472945
67	260-261	Patria	New York	23 Oct 1896	11 Oct 1896	1021-1028	472945
67	261-262	Normannia	New York	24 Oct 1896	16 Oct 1896	1042-1049	472945
67	268-269	Prussia	New York	30 Oct 1896	18 Oct 1896	1052-1059	472945
67	269-270	Augusta Victoria	New York	31 Oct 1896	22 Oct 1896	1063-1070	472945
67	274-275	Phoenicia	New York	7 Nov 1896	25 Oct 1896	1076-1083	472945
67	275-276	Fürst Bismarck	New York via Southampton	7 Nov 1896	29 Oct 1896	1095-1102	472945
67	280	Persia	New York	14 Nov 1896	1 Nov 1896	1104-1109	472945
67	282	Marsala	New York via Havre	14 Nov 1896	28 Oct 1896	1089-1091	472945
67	284-285	Normannia	New York, Cuxhaven, Cherbourg, Southampton	21 Nov 1896	12 Nov 1896	1137-1142	472945
67	286	Bohemia	New York via Havre	25 Nov 1896	4 Nov 1896	1115-1116	472945
67	288	Albano	New York	30 Nov 1896	11 Nov 1896	1126-1127	472945

Germans to America vol. and page nos.		Name of the Ship	Route and U.S. Port(s) of Arrival	Date of Arrival	Date of Departure	*HPL* Page numbers	FHL micro-film no.
67	288	Armenia	New York	30 Nov 1896	11 Nov 1896	1128-1131	472945
67	288-289	Palatia	New York	1 Dec 1896	15 Nov 1896	1144-1149	472945
67	294	California	New York via Havre	11 Dec 1896	21 Nov 1896	1164-1165	472945
67	299	Prussia	New York	28 Dec 1896	13 Dec 1896	1200-1205	472945
67	301-302	Phoenicia	New York	6 Jan 1897	21 Dec 1896	1214-1217	472945
67	302	Sicilia	New York	6 Jan 1897	18 Dec 1896	1211	472945
67	304	Persia	New York	12 Jan 1897	29 Dec 1896	1226-1228	472945
67	305	Taormina	New York via Havre	16 Jan 1897	23 Dec 1896	1220	472945
67	307	Andalusia	New York	23 Jan 1897	6 Jan 1897	6-7	472946
67	307-308	Fürst Bismarck	New York via Cuxhaven, Cherbourg, Southampton	25 Jan 1897	16 Jan 1897	22-25	472946
67	311	Marsala	New York	1 Feb 1897	7 Jan 1897	11	472946
67	312	Armenia	New York	2 Feb 1897	15 Jan 1897	19-20	472946
67	314	Albano	New York via Havre	9 Feb 1897	20 Jan 1897	31-32	472946
67	316	Palatia	New York	11 Feb 1897	28 Jan 1897	40-43	472946
67	318-319	Patria	New York	19 Feb 1897	1 Feb 1897	50-53	472946
67	322-323	Phoenicia	New York	1 Mar 1897	14 Feb 1897	79-82	472946
67	323	Italia	New York	1 Mar 1897	5 Feb 1897	60-61	472946
67	323	Sorrento	New York via Havre	6 Mar 1897	10 Feb 1897	70	472946
67	325	Persia	New York	9 Mar 1897	21 Feb 1897	91-94	472946
67	329	Andalusia	New York	22 Mar 1897	27 Feb 18897	103-106	472946
67	330-331	Palatia	New York	25 Mar 1897	10 May 1897	120-125	472946

Germans to America vol. and page nos.		Name of the Ship	Route and U.S. Port(s) of Arrival	Date of Arrival	Date of Departure	*HPL* Page numbers	FHL micro-film no.
67	335-336	Pennsylvania	New York	5 Apr 1897	21 Mar 1897	140-153	472946
67	343-344	Patria	New York	14 Apr 1897	28 Mar 1897	170-176	472946
67	345	Marsala	New York via Havre	16 Apr 1897	26 Mar 1897	163-165	472946
67	346-347	Phoenicia	New York	19 Apr 1897	3 Apr 1897	189-194	472946
67	348	Albano	New York via Havre	21 Apr 1897	31 Mar 1897	179-180	472946
67	350-351	Normannia	New York via Cherbourg and Southhampton	24 Apr 1897	15 Apr 1897	223-228	472946
67	351-352	Persia	New York	24 Apr 1897	10 Apr 1897	210-217	472946
67	361-362	Columbia	New York via Southampton	8 May 1897	29 Apr 1897	261-268	472946
67	373-374	Pennsylvania	New York	20 May 1897	8 May 1897	279-288	472946
67	375-376	Fürst Bismarck	New York via Southampton	22 May 1897	13 May 1897	321-331	472946
67	381-382	Normannia	New York	29 May 1897	20 May 1897	352-357	472946
67	384	Pisa	New York	1 Jun 1897	19 May 1897	343-345	472946
67	386-387	Patria	New York	4 Jun 1897	22 May 1897	359-366	472946
67	387	Columbia	New York	5 Jun 1897	27 May 1897	372-376	472946
67	391	Persia	New York	11 Jun 1897	29 May 1897	381-386	472946
67	391	Adria	New York via Havre	12 Jun 1897	26 May 1897	370-371	472946
67	391-392	Augusta Victoria	New York via Cherbourg and Southampton	12 Jun 1897	3 Jun 1897	395-398	472946

CPSIA information can be obtained at www.ICGtesting.com
Printed in the USA
BVOW04s0813011015

420549BV00001B/1/P

9 780788 436505